Better Homes and Gardens®

1986 BEST-RECIPES YEARBOOK

Better Homes and Gardens.

Editorial Director DORIS M. EBY
Editor DAVID JORDAN
Managing Editor KATE GREER   Art Director ROBERT C. FURSTENAU

Food and Nutrition Editor NANCY BYAL
Department Head—Cook Books SHARYL HEIKEN
Senior Food Editor—Magazine JOY TAYLOR
Senior Food Editor—Special Interest Publicatons JOANNE JOHNSON
Recipe Development Editor MARION VIALL
Associate Department Heads JANET FIGG   SANDRA GRANSETH
ROSEMARY HUTCHINSON   ELIZABETH WOOLEVER
Senior Food Editors BARBARA ATKINS   LYNN HOPPE   JULIA MALLOY
MARCIA STANLEY   PAT TEBERG   JOYCE TROLLOPE
Associate Food Editors MOLLY CULBERTSON   LINDA HENRY   DIANA McMILLEN   MARY JO PLUTT
MAUREEN POWERS   LOIS WHITE   TERRI WOLF   LINDA WOODRUM   DIANE YANNEY

Editorial Marketing Services Director MARGARET McMAHON

Copy Chief—Magazine ELIZABETH HAHN BROOKS
Makeup Editor LINDA R. THOMAS
Associate Makeup Editors KATHRYN DAVIDSON   JUDY HUNSICKER

Managing Art Director GERALD PREATOR
Associate Art Directors KRISTIN FRANTZ   BRADFORD W. S. HONG
Assistant Art Director ALISANN DIXON   *Senior Graphic Designer* JERRY RANK
Graphic Designers BARTON WELCH   CATHERINE SPARKS   KEVIN S. LUDGATE

New York—Shopping Editor ANN LIVELY

Executive Director Editorial Services DUANE L. GREGG
Director, Editorial Planning DAVID R. HAUPERT
Director, Editorial Research C. RAY DEATON   *Research Assistant* DAVID S. JOHNSON
Administrative Editor ROSE ANDERSON   *Art Business Office Manager* DIANE BOYLE
Test Kitchen Director SHARON STILWELL   *Photo Studio Manager* DON WIPPERMAN

Books *Editor* GERALD KNOX   *Managing Editor* DAVID A. KIRCHNER
Art Director ERNEST SHELTON
Associate Art Directors: LINDA FORD VERMIE   NEOMA ALT WEST   RANDALL YONTZ
Copy and Production Editors: JAMES D. BLUME   MARSHA JAHNS
ROSANNE WEBER MATTSON   MARY HELEN SCHILTZ
Assistant Art Directors: LYNDA HAUPERT   HARIJS PRIEKULIS   TOM WEGNER
Senior Graphic Designers: JACK MURPHY   STAN SAMS   DARLA WHIPPLE-FRAIN
Graphic Designers: MIKE BURNS   SALLY COOPER   BRIAN WIGNALL   KIM ZARLEY

PUBLISHING GROUP PRESIDENT **JACK D. REHM**
Publishing Group Senior Vice Presidents
JAMES A. AUTRY General Manager, Magazines
FRED STINES General Manager, Books and Newspapers
Publishing Group Vice President DORIS M. EBY Editorial Director

Vice President–Publisher, Better Homes and Gardens J. WESLEY SILK
Publishing Services Director TERRY UNSWORTH
Advertising Sales Director LENNOX E. H. STUART
Associate Publisher/Development DEL RUSHER

CORPORATE OFFICERS **Chairman of the Board E. T. MEREDITH III**
President ROBERT A. BURNETT
Group Presidents JACK D. REHM, Publishing
W. C. McREYNOLDS, Broadcasting   ALLEN L. SABBAG, Real Estate
Vice Presidents DONALD L. ARNOLD, Corporate Relations
THOMAS G. FISHER, General Counsel and Assistant Secretary
NEIL KUEHNL, Product Development   HERB SCHULTE, Corporate Planning
WILLIAM H. STRAW, Finance   GERALD D. THORNTON, Administrative Services
Secretary BETTY CAMPBELL MADDEN   Treasurer MICHAEL A. SELL
Corporate Controller LARRY D. HARTSOOK

Our seal assures you that every recipe in the *1986 Best-Recipes Yearbook* has been tested in the Better Homes and Gardens® Test Kitchen. This means that each recipe is practical and reliable, and meets our high standards of taste appeal.

CONTENTS

Every month, *Better Homes and Gardens*® magazine offers ideas and recipes that keep pace with your family. We cover areas of food that concern you most—nutritious eating, quick-and-easy cooking, and creative, affordable entertaining. And so you won't have to clip and store all that timely information, we've compiled it into a book. In this, our fourth annual recipe yearbook, you'll rediscover the recipes we published for you in 1985.

JANUARY

Hearty Bare-Bone Soups

Picked to the bone, your holiday turkey or ham is ready—for soup making. Beans, other vegetables, and Italian seasonings complete the turkey soup. Southern favorites such as okra and shrimp flavor the ham-bone base. These easy, no-watch soups are festive enough for a party and sure to be a hit for a family meal.

JAMBALAYA HAM SOUP

1 1¼- to 1½-pound meaty ham bone
1 slice onion
1 cup celery leaves
2 to 3 parsley sprigs
¼ teaspoon ground red pepper
1 cup sliced celery
½ cup chopped onion
1 small clove garlic, minced
2 tablespoons butter
1 8-ounce can tomato sauce
¼ cup catsup
¼ cup long grain rice
1 10-ounce package frozen cut okra
1 4½-ounce can shrimp

Combine ham bone, onion slice, celery leaves, parsley sprigs, red pepper, 5 cups *water*, and ¼ teaspoon *black pepper*. Bring to boiling; reduce heat. Cover; simmer 30 to 45 minutes. Remove bone. Cool and cut off meat; chop. Discard bone. Strain broth. Cook sliced celery, onion, and garlic in butter till tender. Stir in broth, ham, tomato sauce, catsup, and *uncooked* rice. Bring to boiling; reduce heat. Cover; simmer 15 minutes. Add okra and *drained* shrimp. Return to boiling; reduce heat. Cover; simmer 5 minutes. Garnish with cooked crawfish and mustard greens. Serves 6.

Per serving: 241 cal., 15 g pro., 19 g carbo., 12 g fat, 75 mg chol., 739 mg sodium. USRDA: 19% vit. A, 25% vit. C, 14% iron.

MINESTRONE-STYLE TURKEY SOUP

1 meaty turkey carcass, cut apart
1 tablespoon instant chicken bouillon granules
1 bay leaf
2 cups shredded cabbage
1 14½-ounce can stewed tomatoes, cut up
1 15-ounce can great northern beans, drained
1 15-ounce can garbanzo beans, drained
1 large onion, chopped
1 clove garlic, minced
¼ cup snipped parsley
1 teaspoon dried basil, crushed

Combine turkey, bouillon granules, bay leaf, and 7 cups *water*. Bring to boiling; reduce heat. Cover; simmer 1 hour. Remove turkey carcass. When cool, remove meat from bones and chop. Discard bones. Strain broth. Return broth and chopped turkey to Dutch oven. Stir in cabbage, *undrained* tomatoes, beans, onion, garlic, parsley, basil, and ⅛ teaspoon *pepper*. Bring to boiling; reduce heat. Cover and simmer for 25 to 30 minutes. Serves 6.

Per serving: 287 cal., 25 g pro., 35 g carbo., 5 g fat, 43 mg chol., 413 mg sodium. USRDA: 16% vit. A, 45% vit. C, 26% iron.

Photograph: Ron Crofoot
Food stylist: Judy Tills

By Diana McMillen

Good-For-You
MAIN DISHES
that taste great!

Knowing what foods are best for your family is only half the challenge—serving food they'll enjoy is the real test. Eating right doesn't require hocus-pocus diet plans; the best advice is still moderation. Monitor meals for calories, fat, sugar, salt, and added fiber—but don't cut imagination!

These tasty main dishes illustrate exciting ways to serve your family nutritious foods they'll love.

By Diana McMillen

Upside-Down Pizza

There's more than one way to bake a pizza. This one's upside down! The bonus—the generous crock is filled with plenty of thick, rich filling. We've reduced the fat (and therefore the calories) in a typical pizza topping by substituting turkey and low-fat cheese.

Per serving: 437 cal., 40 g pro., 38 g carbo., 15 g fat, 79 mg chol., 682 mg sodium. USRDA: 36% vit. A, 113% vit. C, 19% thiamine, 28% riboflavin, 37% niacin, 49% calcium, 24% iron, 61% phosphorus.

Super Salad Bowl

▶ What you see here is no ordinary chef's salad. This leafy lettuce bowl packs a fresh and satisfying winter meal wallop. A mound of yogurt-sauced wheat berries and salmon is the center attraction in this mini smorgasbord of nutritious ingredients.

Per serving: 387 cal., 24 g pro., 47 g carbo., 12 g fat, 26 mg chol., 142 mg sodium. USRDA: 97% vit. A, 62% vit. C, 22% thiamine, 28% riboflavin, 36% niacin, 30% calcium, 37% iron, 50% phosphorus.

Photographs: Ron Crofoot; small photograph above: Perry Struse. Food stylist: Judy Tills

Good-For-You

Macaroni Cloud in a Mug

◄ Kids can dig into dinner from their favorite cup. This new version of macaroni and cheese adds eggs for puffy texture and more complete protein. Calories, fat, and sodium are lower, too.

Per serving: 288 cal., 14 g pro., 19 g carbo., 18 g fat, 173 mg chol., 330 mg sodium. USRDA: 21% vit. A, 15% vit. C, 8% thiamine, 22% riboflavin, 5% niacin, 31% calcium, 7% iron.

Pork in Squash Boats

► Not all spaghetti comes from a box. This golden vegetable variety, spaghetti squash, is cooked and served in its own shell. (The baked squash turns into spaghetti threads when raked with the tines of a fork.) Combine the vitamin-packed vegetable with today's leaner-than-ever pork and you have a nutritious, tasty main dish.

Per serving: 560 cal., 24 g pro., 40 g carbo., 34 g fat, 70 mg chol., 422 mg sodium. USRDA: 127% vit. A, 110% vit. C, 72% thiamine, 27% riboflavin, 34% niacin, 9% calcium, 31% iron, 34% phosphorus.

Chicken 'n Chips

◄ Here's a totally new Mexican dish! Chunks of chicken breast are coated with a chili powder seasoning; the golden orange chips are made from sweet potatoes (rich in vitamin C). Both are baked instead of fried, trimming fat and calories. Dunk them in a creamy Neufchâtel dip with chili peppers.

Per serving: 280 cal., 30 g pro., 19 g carbo., 9 g fat, 75 mg chol., 204 mg sodium. USRDA: 63% vit. A, 22% vit. C, 7% thiamine, 17% riboflavin, 60% niacin, 8% calcium, 9% iron, 31% phosphorus.

UPSIDE-DOWN PIZZA

To prevent sticking, grease rims and the insides of baking dishes—

- 2 tablespoons cracked wheat
- 1 16-ounce package whole wheat bread mix
- 1 7½-ounce can tomatoes, cut up
- 1 small green pepper, chopped
- ½ of a 6-ounce can tomato paste (⅓ cup)
- 1 teaspoon fennel seed, crushed
- ½ teaspoon dried oregano, crushed
- ½ teaspoon dried basil, crushed
- ¼ teaspoon pepper
- 1½ cups chopped cooked turkey *or* chicken
- 1 6-ounce can sliced mushrooms, drained
- ¼ cup grated Parmesan cheese (optional)
- 1 cup shredded low-fat mozzarella cheese (4 ounces)

Milk
Fresh oregano sprigs (optional)
Ripe olives (optional)

In a small mixing bowl combine cracked wheat and enough boiling water to cover. Let stand 5 minutes; drain. Prepare the bread mix according to package directions, *except* stir in the softened cracked wheat. Let dough rest according to package directions.

Meanwhile, in a medium saucepan combine the *undrained* tomatoes, green pepper, tomato paste, fennel, oregano, basil, and pepper. Bring to boiling, then reduce heat. Cover and simmer for 10 minutes. Stir in turkey or chicken and sliced mushrooms.

Spray nonstick vegetable spray coating inside and on the outer rims of four 10- to 12-ounce ovenproof baking dishes with handles. (Or, grease dishes and sprinkle Parmesan cheese over bottoms of dishes.) Divide mozzarella cheese evenly among the dishes. Spoon turkey mixture into baking dishes.

Divide dough in half. Use *half* of the dough to prepare dinner rolls or a loaf of bread, following package directions. Divide the remaining dough into 4 portions. On a lightly floured surface roll each portion to extend ¾ inch beyond the edge of baking dishes.

Place the dough atop each dish, overlapping rim. Brush dough with milk. Bake in a 375° oven about 15 minutes or till light brown. To serve, loosen crust and invert onto serving plate. Garnish with fresh oregano and olives. Makes 4 servings.

Per serving: 437 cal., 40 g pro., 38 g carbo., 15 g fat, 79 mg chol., 682 mg sodium. USRDA: 36% vit. A, 113% vit. C, 19% thiamine, 28% riboflavin, 37% niacin, 49% calcium, 24% iron, 61% phosphorus.

SUPER SALAD BOWL

Wheat berries add fiber and flavor to this main-dish salad. Look for the berries, also called unpolished whole wheat kernels, in the cereal section of your supermarket or in health food stores—

- 1 cup water
- ½ cup wheat berries
- ⅔ cup plain yogurt
- ½ teaspoon dried dillweed

Several dashes bottled hot pepper sauce
- 1 3¾-ounce can salmon, drained, skin and bones removed, and flaked
- ¼ cup sliced celery
- 2 tablespoons sliced almonds
- 2 small heads Bibb *or* butterhead lettuce
- ½ cup finely shredded carrot
- 6 radishes, finely shredded

Crinkle-cut carrot and celery sticks (optional)
Sesame breadsticks (optional)
Lemon peel flowers (optional)
Carrot tops (optional)

In a small saucepan combine the water and wheat berries. Bring to boiling; reduce heat. Cover and simmer wheat berries for 1 hour. Remove saucepan from heat. Drain and cool.

For dressing: in a small mixing bowl combine plain yogurt, dillweed, and bottled hot pepper sauce. In a medium mixing bowl stir together the wheat berries, flaked salmon, sliced celery, and sliced almonds.

Divide the yogurt mixture in half. Add *half* of the dressing to the wheat berry mixture; toss gently till just mixed. Cover and chill. Chill the remaining yogurt dressing separately till serving time.

To serve, remove centers from the small heads of lettuce, leaving outer leaves intact to form a bowl. Reserve centers of the lettuce for another use. On 2 individual salad plates place the hollowed lettuce bowls. Arrange the shredded carrot, shredded radishes, and the chilled wheat berry mixture in the lettuce bowls. Arrange the carrot sticks, celery sticks, and breadsticks around each filled lettuce bowl. Garnish with lemon peel flowers and carrot tops. Serve with the remaining dressing. Makes 2 main-dish servings.

Per serving: 387 cal., 24 g pro., 47 g carbo., 12 g fat, 26 mg chol., 142 mg sodium. USRDA: 97% vit. A, 62% vit. C, 22% thiamine, 28% riboflavin, 36% niacin, 30% calcium, 37% iron, 50% phosphorus.

MACARONI CLOUD IN A MUG

Bake this kid-appealing recipe in an ovenproof coffee mug. The baking time is based on using a 10-ounce mug, so you'll need to adjust the baking time if you use a different size—

> 2 ounces elbow macaroni (½ cup)
> 2 tablespoons finely chopped green pepper
> 1 tablespoon finely chopped onion
> 2 tablespoons butter *or* margarine
> 4 teaspoons cornstarch
> Several dashes bottled hot pepper sauce
> Dash pepper
> 1 cup skim milk
> 1 cup shredded cheddar cheese (4 ounces)
> 1 cup frozen corn, thawed
> 2 egg yolks
> 2 egg whites
> ⅛ teaspoon cream of tartar

In a small saucepan cook macaroni, uncovered, in boiling salted water about 8 minutes or just till tender. Drain in a colander. Rinse with cold water; drain again. Set aside.

In the same saucepan cook green pepper and onion in butter or margarine till tender but not brown. Stir in cornstarch, hot pepper sauce, and pepper. Add milk all at once. Cook and stir till the mixture is thickened and bubbly. Cook and stir for 2 minutes more. Reduce heat to low. Add the shredded cheese and corn; stir till cheese is melted. Remove from heat.

In a medium mixing bowl beat the egg yolks slightly. Gradually add the hot cheese mixture, stirring constantly. Fold the cooked macaroni into the cheese-yolk mixture. Cool slightly.

Wash the beaters thoroughly. In a small mixer bowl beat the egg whites and cream of tartar with an electric mixer on medium speed till stiff peaks form (tips stand straight). Gradually fold the beaten egg whites into the cheese-macaroni mixture.

Fill four 10-ounce ovenproof mugs with *one-fourth* of the egg mixture, leaving ¾-inch headspace. Place on a baking sheet. Bake in a 350° oven for 25 to 30 minutes or till tops are golden brown. Makes 4 main-dish servings.

Per serving: 288 cal., 14 g pro., 19 g carbo., 18 g fat, 173 mg chol., 330 mg sodium. USRDA: 21% vit. A, 15% vit. C, 8% thiamine, 22% riboflavin, 5% niacin, 31% calcium, 7% iron.

PORK IN SQUASH BOATS

This tasty meal borrows flavor from the dried fruit. For fast cooking, micro-cook the spaghetti squash—

> ½ pound boneless lean pork, cut into 1-inch cubes
> 1½ teaspoons cooking oil
> 1 small tomato, peeled, seeded, and cut up
> 1 small onion, cut into wedges
> ¼ cup water
> ¼ cup dry red wine
> 2 tablespoons raisins
> 2 tablespoons snipped dried apricots *or* raisins
> 1 small clove garlic, minced
> ¼ teaspoon dried thyme, crushed
> ¼ teaspoon dried tarragon, crushed
> ¼ teaspoon salt
> Dash pepper
> ½ cup green *or* red sweet pepper cut into strips
> 2 tablespoons sliced pitted ripe olives
> 1 small spaghetti squash (about 2 pounds)
> Passion fruit wedges (optional)
> Fresh thyme sprigs (optional)

In a medium saucepan brown pork in hot oil. Add tomato, onion, water, red wine, raisins, apricots, garlic, thyme, tarragon, salt, and pepper. Bring to boiling; reduce heat. Cover and simmer for 1 hour. Add green pepper strips and olive slices. Cover and simmer for 5 minutes more.

Meanwhile, halve squash lengthwise; remove seeds. Place the squash halves, cut side down, in a shallow baking pan. Cover with foil. Bake in a 375° oven about 1 hour or till tender.

Invert cooked squash halves onto a serving platter; fluff with a fork. Spoon hot pork mixture into squash shells. Garnish with passion fruit wedges and fresh thyme. Makes 2 servings.

Microwave directions: Prepare the pork-fruit mixture as above. Meanwhile, halve the squash lengthwise; remove seeds. Place the squash halves, cut side down, in a 12x7½x2-inch nonmetal baking dish. Micro-cook, covered, on 100% power (HIGH) for 10 to 14 minutes or till tender. Let stand, covered, for 10 minutes.

Invert squash halves onto a serving platter; fluff with a fork. Serve as above. Makes 2 servings.

Per serving: 560 cal., 24 g pro., 40 g carbo., 34 g fat, 70 mg chol., 422 mg sodium. USRDA: 127% vit. A, 110% vit. C, 72% thiamine, 27% riboflavin, 34% niacin, 9% calcium, 31% iron, 34% phosphorus.

CHICKEN 'N' CHIPS

Combine yogurt with Neufchâtel cheese to make a creamy dipping sauce that's low in calories—

    2 tablespoons cornmeal
    ½ teaspoon chili powder
    ⅛ teaspoon salt
    ⅛ teaspoon pepper
    ⅛ teaspoon ground red pepper
    2 whole medium chicken breasts, skinned, boned, and cut into bite-size pieces (1-inch cubes)
    1 large sweet potato, very thinly sliced crosswise
    ½ cup plain yogurt
    2 ounces Neufchâtel cheese
    2 tablespoons skim milk
    2 tablespoons chopped green chili peppers
Shredded romaine (optional)
Green Chili Flower (optional)

In a small mixing bowl combine the cornmeal, chili powder, salt, pepper, and red pepper. Toss chicken pieces in cornmeal mixture to coat. Place in a single layer on a shallow baking pan.

On another baking pan arrange sweet potato slices. Bake sweet potato in a 350° oven about 20 minutes and chicken pieces about 12 minutes or till done, turning the potato and chicken pieces once.

To make dipping sauce: In a small mixer bowl combine the yogurt, Neufchâtel cheese, and skim milk; beat with an electric mixer till smooth. Stir in chopped green chili peppers.

To serve, arrange the chicken and sweet potatoes atop romaine. Serve with the dipping sauce garnished with Green Chili Flower. Makes 4 servings.

Green Chili Flower: Cut lengthwise slashes in 1 fresh *green chili pepper* from the tip to, but not through, the stem. Place in ice water about 15 minutes to curl slashes.

Per serving: 280 cal., 30 g pro., 19 g carbo., 9 g fat, 75 mg chol., 204 mg sodium. USRDA: 63% vit. A, 22% vit. C, 7% thiamine, 17% riboflavin, 60% niacin, 8% calcium, 9% iron, and 31% phosphorus.

MIGHTY MUFFINS

With bran for fiber and raisins for iron, these muffins are strong on nutrition—

    1½ cups whole bran cereal
    1 cup skim milk
    1 beaten egg
    ⅓ cup molasses
    ¼ cup butter *or* margarine, melted
    ½ cup all-purpose flour
    ½ cup whole wheat flour
    2 tablespoons toasted wheat germ
    2 teaspoons baking powder
    ½ teaspoon baking soda
    ½ cup raisins
    ½ cup chopped nuts

In a small mixing bowl combine bran and milk; let stand for 3 minutes. Stir in egg, molasses, and butter or margarine; set aside.

In a medium mixing bowl combine all-purpose flour, whole wheat flour, wheat germ, baking powder, and baking soda. Make a well in the center. Add bran mixture; stir till moistened. Fold in raisins and nuts.

Grease muffin cups or line with paper bake cups; fill two-thirds full. Bake in a 400° oven for 20 to 25 minutes or till muffins are done. Cool. Cover and chill to store. Makes 12.

Per muffin: 159 cal., 5 g pro., 21 g carbo., 8 g fat, 33 mg chol., 227 mg sodium. USRDA: 11% vit. A, 10% vit. C, 9% iron.

WAKE-UP SHAKE

A shake for breakfast or after a workout is way to gulp down good nutrition—

    ¾ cup skim milk
    ½ cup strawberry yogurt, chilled
    1 ripe medium banana, peeled, halved, wrapped, and frozen
    ¼ cup orange juice, chilled

In a blender container combine milk, yogurt, banana, and orange juice. Cover and blend till smooth. Serve in tall glasses. Makes 2 (8-ounce) servings.

Per serving: 127 cal., 6 g pro., 24 g carbo., 1 g fat, 6 mg chol., 78 mg sodium, 37% USRDA of vit. C.

GRAIN AND FRUIT CEREAL

Create your own quick and easy cereal mix with cornmeal, bulgur, dried fruits, almonds, and cinnamon. Look for bulgur (precooked cracked wheat) at your local supermarket or a nearby health food store—

    1 cup cornmeal
    ⅔ cup bulgur
    1 6-ounce package chopped mixed dried fruits
    ½ cup slivered almonds, toasted
    ½ teaspoon ground cinnamon

In a mixing bowl stir together cornmeal, bulgur, mixed dried fruits, toasted almonds, and cinnamon. Place the mixture in an airtight storage container. Cover and store at room temperature. Makes about 2½ cups.

For one serving: In a small saucepan bring 1 cup *water* and a dash *salt* to boiling. Slowly stir in ⅓ cup of the cereal mixture. Simmer the cereal mixture, uncovered, for 10 to 15 minutes or to desired consistency. If desired, serve with sugar and milk.

For 2 servings: Prepare as above, *except* use *2 cups* water, ⅛ *teaspoon* salt, and ⅔ *cup* of the cereal mixture.

For 4 servings: Prepare as above, *except* use *4 cups* water, ¼ *teaspoon* salt, and 1⅓ *cups* of the cereal mixture.

Per serving: 156 cal., 4 g pro., 27 g carbo., 4 g fat, 00 mg chol., 33 mg sodium, 10% USRDA of vit. A.

February 1985 • $1.50

Better Homes and Gardens.

FRESH OUTLOOKS FOR YOUR WINDOWS
Fabrics Are Back More Beautiful Than Ever!

Sweetheart Desserts For Those You Love

REMODELING:
Turning Cramped Rooms Into Wide-Open Spaces

FAMILY FITNESS RESORTS: HAVE FUN, SHAPE UP!

CRAFTS:
Create Muslin Masterpieces In A Weekend!

DREAM KITCHEN:
Packed With Bright Ideas and High-Tech Wonders!

PARENTING:
How To Make Stepchildren Part Of The Family

DESSERTS FOR
SWEETHEARTS

By Joy Taylor

Lace valentines and homemade sweets won hearts in our grandparents' day. Come February 14 (or any other special day), follow the enchanting tradition and share one of these delicious delights with your loved ones. They'll be smitten!

PETAL TARTS

- 1 **package piecrust mix (for 2-crust pie)**
- 3 **tablespoons sugar**
- ⅓ **cup chocolate-flavored syrup**
- 1 **20-ounce can calorie-reduced cherry pie filling**
- 2 **tablespoons burgundy**
- ½ **cup dairy sour cream**
- 1 **recipe Hearts**

Combine crust mix and *2 tablespoons* sugar; add syrup and mix well. On floured surface, roll dough to ⅛-inch thickness. Cut into forty-eight 2-inch circles, rerolling the trimmings as necessary. Place a dough circle in bottom of eight ungreased 6-ounce custard cups. Overlap 5 circles around sides of cups; press to seal. Bake in 350° oven 20 minutes. Cool slightly. Remove from cups. Cool thoroughly. Combine pie filling and burgundy; spoon into cups. Chill. To serve, combine sour cream and remaining sugar; spoon over filling. Top each with a Heart. Makes 8.

Hearts: Melt ⅓ cup *semisweet chocolate pieces* with 1 teaspoon *butter* or *margarine;* spread ⅛ inch thick on waxed-paper-lined baking sheet. Chill 10 minutes. Press small heart cutter into chocolate. Chill till firm. Lift out cutouts. Cover; chill. Remelt trimmings; drizzle over hearts. Rechill till needed.

Photograph: William K. Sladcik
Food stylist: Fran Paulson

LEMON TORTE

    4 egg whites
    1 teaspoon vanilla
    ½ teaspoon cream of tartar
    ¼ teaspoon almond extract
    ¾ cup sugar
    2 tablespoons sliced almonds
    ⅔ cup sugar
    1 teaspoon unflavored gelatin
    6 beaten egg yolks
    ½ teaspoon finely shredded
       lemon peel
    ⅓ cup lemon juice
    2 tablespoons butter or
       margarine
    ¾ cup whipping cream
    1 recipe Raspberry Sauce

Line two or three baking sheets
with brown paper; draw three 7-inch
circles and grease lightly. In a large
mixer bowl beat egg whites, vanilla,
cream of tartar, and extract with an
electric mixer on medium speed to
soft peaks. Gradually add the ¾ cup
sugar, beating to stiff peaks. Spoon
one-third of the mixture into a pastry
bag fitted with a star tip. Pipe a
lattice design within one of the
circles; pipe a border around the
lattice. Sprinkle almonds over lattice.
Spread remaining egg white mixture
over remaining circles. Bake in 300°
oven 45 minutes. Turn off oven; let
meringues dry in oven 3 hours or
overnight (do not open oven door).

In saucepan combine ⅔ cup sugar
and gelatin. Add yolks, lemon peel
and juice, butter, and ⅓ cup *water*.
Cook and stir till bubbly; cook 2
minutes more. Remove from heat.
Cover surface with waxed paper; cool.
Chill till mixture mounds slightly
when spooned. Beat cream to soft
peaks; fold into lemon mixture. Place
one solid meringue on platter; spread
half of the lemon mixture over it.
Top with second solid meringue, then
remaining lemon mixture. Top with
lattice meringue. Cover loosely; chill 6
hours or overnight. Serve with
Raspberry Sauce: In saucepan
combine one 10-ounce package *frozen
raspberries*, thawed, 2 tablespoons
sugar, and 1 tablespoon *cornstarch*.
Cook till bubbly; cook 2 minutes
more. Press through a fine sieve;
discard seeds. Cover sauce; chill.
Makes 10 servings.

The World's Easiest and Tastiest MAIN DISHES

By Joy Taylor

Busy people in Peking, Paris, and beyond are just like you! On hectic days, they too rely on timesaving recipes to feed their families, and you'll find some of the world's best-tasting examples right here. One taste of these internationally acclaimed main dishes and you'll agree that the formula for fuss-free cooking is the same in every language—fresh foods, simple seasonings, and basic techniques. Your family will exclaim, "Trés bien!"

45 MINUTES FROM START TO FINISH

Arrive home at 6 and sit down to a home-cooked dinner before 7. It's easy to do when your menu includes one of these time-shaving, mouth-watering specialties from Spain, France, or Greece.

AIOLI PLATTER
◀ This meal shows off the love of the French for garlic and unassuming sauces. In minutes, three garlic cloves flavor the classic aioli (ay-O-lee) sauce that crowns vegetables, fish, and eggs.

EGGS SOFRITO
▶ Cooks worldwide recognize the quick-to-fix virtue of eggs. Spaniards poach them in sofrito, a spicy tomato sauce, with sassy results. Serve the meal from the skillet and include a traditional accompaniment, corn bread.

REDDENED VEAL
▶ Enjoy great Greek food in your own kitchen. Here, veal is seasoned with tomatoes and mint, capped with feta cheese, and served with orzo—a pastalike grain found by the rice in supermarkets.

The World's Easiest
FIX-AND-FORGET

No need to hover over the pot when you put these dishes on the stove or in the oven. During the after-work, after-school rush, a self-simmering dinner from Italy, Hungary, or China frees you for an hour or more. The aromas will beckon you back when dinner's ready.

Choose heavy saucepans and skillets for walk-away-from-the-stove meals. Utensils made from cast iron and stainless steel withstand high temperatures, preventing the food from scorching. These reliable utensils also ensure proper doneness of the food at the expected time.

LAMB FRICASSEE
◄ The name "fricassee" sounds exotic, but the preparation and cleanup are far from it. Meat and vegetables (in this case lamb chops, pearl onions, and whole mushrooms) oven-braise in a skillet that's reused for making the egg-yolk-thickened lemon glaze. Top it all off with crumbled bacon.

Cook a pot of linguine, toss together a salad, and uncork a bottle of wine to complete the meal in true Italian style.

BEEF GOULASH
◄ Goulash, a mainstay of Hungarian cooking, is renowned worldwide. It's not surprising—making Goulash is nearly effortless! For this sauerkraut stew, stove-top simmering produces succulent flavor that's hard to beat. Beer and caraway season the broth.

ORIENTAL HENS
◄ Chinese cooks steam more than just vegetables; meat, poultry, and fish benefit from the same preparation. For this Far East main-dish favorite, stir together some hoisin sauce and five-spice powder to glaze the Cornish hens.

The World's Easiest
COOK-AT-THE-TABLE

**Cooks from east to west have taken themselves and the
kettle out of the kitchen. They've discovered the benefits of
tabletop cooking: pleasing food, mealtime fun, and—just as
important—simplicity for everyone. Venture out of your
kitchen and enjoy these dishes right at the dinner table.**

Set a pretty, yet functional, dinner table when you cook atop it with friends and family. Center the activity around a table that's small enough for everyone to participate. Choose wash-and-wear linens that can stand up to any drips and drops. And avoid centerpieces or glassware that might interfere with the group cooking.

SHABU-SHABU
▶ Japanese cooks perfected tabletop cooking centuries ago. And one of their best-kept secrets is Shabu-Shabu (SHAH-boo).

For this colorful meal, diners swirl paper-thin beef strips, vegetables, and tofu through hot broth using tongs or chopsticks. Then, each dunks the just-cooked pieces in a soy-lemon or sesame dipping sauce and catches any drips over a bowl of hot cooked rice. To conclude the meal, serve bowls of the richly flavored hot broth from the electric wok or hot pot.

Photographs: William K. Sladcik
Food stylist: Fran Paulson

FRIED CHEESE
▶ One bite, and you'll understand why croquettes are so popular throughout Belgium. The cheese-and-shrimp squares can be mixed and shaped ahead, then stored in the freezer. To serve, bring a saucepan and hot plate, small deep-fryer, or electric fondue pot to the table so everyone can cook the morsels, and enjoy them hot. Serve with Spinach Mayonnaise.

AIOLI PLATTER

Aioli sauce is a classic French sauce that is really just a highly garlic-seasoned mayonnaise. The name originates from ail, *the French word for garlic—*

- 4 **eggs**
- ¾ **cup water**
- 2 **large carrots, peeled and quartered**
- 1 **9-ounce package frozen artichoke hearts**
- 2 **4- to 6-ounce fresh halibut steaks**
- ½ **cup dry white wine**
- 1 **egg**
- 2 **tablespoons lemon juice**
- 3 **or 4 cloves garlic, chopped**
- ¼ **teaspoon salt**
- ½ **cup salad oil**
- ½ **cup olive oil**
- **Romaine leaves**
- 1 **cup fresh whole mushrooms**
- 1 **cup cherry tomatoes, halved**
- **Pitted ripe olives (optional)**
- **Snipped chives (optional)**

Place the 4 eggs in a large saucepan; add enough water to cover the eggs. Bring to boiling over high heat. Reduce heat so water is just below simmering. Cover and cook the eggs for 15 to 20 minutes. Pour off the water; add cold water and ice cubes to cool the eggs.

Meanwhile, in a 3-quart saucepan bring the ¾ cup water to boiling. Add carrots. Cover and cook for 8 minutes. Add artichokes; cover and cook for 7 to 8 minutes more or till the vegetables are tender. Drain well; keep warm.

In a small skillet cover halibut with wine. Bring to boiling; reduce heat. Cover and simmer for 5 to 8 minutes or till the fish flakes easily with a fork. Drain well; keep warm.

For aioli sauce, in a blender container or a food processor bowl combine one egg, lemon juice, garlic, and salt. Cover and blend for 5 seconds. With the blender running, *gradually* add salad oil. (When necessary, stop blender and scrape sides.) With the blender running, slowly add olive oil, blending to a mayonnaiselike consistency.

To serve, peel and slice the hard-cooked eggs. On a romaine-lined serving platter, arrange the eggs, carrots, artichoke hearts, halibut, mushrooms, tomatoes, and olives. Spoon the aioli sauce in the center. Sprinkle chives over sauce. Pass the remaining sauce. Makes 4 servings.

Microwave directions: Conventionally cook eggs, carrots, and artichoke hearts as directed; prepare sauce as directed. Meanwhile, arrange halibut steaks in a 12x7½x2-inch nonmetal baking dish; pour wine over fish. Cover with vented clear plastic wrap. Micro-cook, on 70% power (MEDIUM-HIGH) for 7 to 8 minutes or till the fish flakes easily with a fork, giving the dish a half-turn after 3 minutes. Drain well. Serve as directed.

Per serving: 749 cal., 23 g pro., 14 g carbo., 67 g fat, 353 mg chol., 294 mg sodium. USRDA: 112% vit. A, 39% vit. C, 14% thiamine, 26% riboflavin, 34% niacin, 16% iron, 34% phosphorus.

EGGS SOFRITO

Use purchased garlic puree and frozen chopped onion to save time when making this simple skillet dinner—

- 1 **16-ounce can tomatoes, cut up**
- 1 **medium onion, chopped (½ cup)**
- 2 **cloves garlic, minced**
- 1 **bay leaf**
- ⅛ **teaspoon pepper**
- 1 **cup frozen peas**
- 4 **eggs**
- 1 **cup sliced smoked sausage or fully cooked ham cut into bite-size strips**
- 1 **2-ounce jar sliced pimiento, drained**

In a 10-inch skillet combine *undrained* tomatoes, onion, garlic, bay leaf, and pepper. Bring to boiling; reduce heat. Simmer, uncovered, for 8 to 10 minutes or till most of the liquid is evaporated and onion is tender. Discard bay leaf. Stir peas into tomato mixture.

Break the eggs into tomato mixture, being careful not to break yolks. Arrange the sliced smoked sausage or ham strips around eggs in the skillet. Sprinkle pimiento over all. Bring to boiling; reduce heat. Cover and simmer over low heat for 10 to 12 minutes or till the eggs are of desired doneness. Serve from the skillet. Makes 4 servings.

Per serving: 274 cal., 17 g pro., 14 g carbo., 17 g fat, 271 mg chol., 610 mg sodium. USRDA: 44% vit. A., 70% vit. C., 23% thiamine, 18% riboflavin, 16% niacin, 21% iron, 25% phosphorus.

REDDENED VEAL

For a pantry-shelf substitute, use hot cooked macaroni instead of the orzo—

- 1 **pound boneless veal or lamb leg round steak**
- 4 **green onions, sliced**
- 2 **tablespoons cooking oil**
- 1 **7½-ounce can tomatoes, cut up**
- ½ **of a 6-ounce can tomato paste (⅓ cup)**
- 2 **tablespoons dry white wine**
- 2 **teaspoons dried mint, crushed**
- 1 **teaspoon sugar**
- 1 **small zucchini, sliced**
- ⅔ **cup orzo (4 ounces)**
- ¼ **cup crumbled feta cheese**

Cut the veal or lamb into ¾-inch cubes. In a 10-inch skillet cook the meat and green onions in hot oil till meat is brown and green onions are tender. Add the *undrained* tomatoes, tomato paste, wine, mint, and sugar. Bring to boiling; reduce heat. Cover and simmer for 12 to 15 minutes or till the meat is nearly tender. Add the zucchini. Simmer gently, uncovered, about 5 minutes more or till zucchini is tender.

Meanwhile, cook the orzo in a large amount of lightly salted boiling water for 5 to 8 minutes or till tender; drain well. To serve, sprinkle the feta cheese over meat mixture and serve with hot orzo. Makes 4 servings.

Microwave directions: In a 1½-quart nonmetal casserole stir together meat, green onions, *undrained* tomatoes, tomato paste, wine, mint, and sugar. Micro-cook, covered, on 100% power (HIGH) for 5 to 6 minutes or till mixture is boiling; stir. Micro-cook, covered, on 50% power (MEDIUM) for 10 to 12 minutes more or till the meat is nearly tender. Stir in zucchini slices. Micro-cook, covered, on 50% power (MEDIUM) about 4 minutes or till the zucchini is tender.

Per serving: 422 cal., 29 g pro., 32 g carbo., 19 g fat, 87 mg chol., 240 mg sodium. USRDA: 27% vit. A, 52% vit. C, 34% thiamine, 28% riboflavin, 53% niacin, 30% iron, 34% phosphorus.

LAMB FRICASSEE

A fricassee is a meat or poultry dish in which the meat is first browned, then cooked in a liquid or sauce. Stew is the term most often used to describe this cooking process—

- 2 slices bacon
- 2 lamb leg sirloin chops, cut 1 inch thick
- ⅓ cup water
- ⅓ cup dry white wine
- 10 whole fresh mushrooms
- 10 whole tiny boiling onions
- 1 teaspoon instant chicken bouillon granules
- ¼ teaspoon ground nutmeg
- 1 egg yolk
- 1 tablespoon lemon juice
- Hot cooked linguine *or* fettuccine
- Butter *or* margarine
- Grated Parmesan cheese

In a 10-inch ovenproof skillet cook the bacon till crisp. Drain bacon on paper towels; crumble and set aside. Reserve *1 tablespoon* of the drippings in skillet.

Brown chops on both sides in reserved drippings. Add the water, wine, mushrooms, onions, bouillon granules, and nutmeg to skillet. Cover and bake in a 325° oven about 1 hour or till meat is tender. Transfer meat and vegetables to a warm serving platter, reserving pan juices; keep warm.

For sauce: skim fat from the pan juices. Stir together egg yolk and lemon juice. Stir ¼ *cup* of the hot pan juices into yolk mixture. Return to skillet and cook over medium heat till sauce is slightly thickened.

Combine hot pasta, butter or margarine, and Parmesan cheese, then toss gently to coat. Arrange chops, vegetables, and pasta on the platter; spoon sauce over and top with bacon pieces. Makes 2 servings.

Per serving: 754 cal., 36 g pro., 33 g carbo., 50 g fat, 283 mg chol., 588 mg sodium. USRDA: 15% vit. A, 41% vit. C, 32% thiamine, 51% riboflavin, 55% niacin, 23% calcium, 24% iron, 53% phosphorus.

ORIENTAL HENS

Buy five-spice powder at an Oriental food market or prepare the homemade version using the instructions below—

- 2 1- to 1½-pound Cornish game hens
- 8 whole fresh mushrooms
- 2 lemon slices
- 2 tablespoons water
- 2 tablespoons hoisin sauce
- 2 teaspoons five-spice powder
- ½ teaspoon finely shredded lemon peel
- 1 red *or* green sweet pepper, cut into strips
- 2 cups bok choy cut crosswise into 2-inch pieces

Rinse hens; pat dry. Make four ½-inch-deep slashes in breasts of Cornish hens. Place 4 mushrooms and a lemon slice into each hen cavity. Tie legs together.

For glaze: combine water, hoisin sauce, five-spice powder, and lemon peel. Brush *two-thirds* of the glaze over hens, rubbing it into the slashes.

Place hens on the rack of a steamer. Position hens over, but not touching, boiling water in steamer. Cover and steam for 50 minutes.

Add pepper strips and bok choy to steamer. Cover; steam about 10 minutes more or till hens and vegetables are tender. Before serving, brush with remaining glaze. Makes 2 servings.

Homemade Five-Spice Powder: Stir together 1 teaspoon ground *cinnamon;* 1 teaspoon crushed *aniseed;* ¼ teaspoon crushed *fennel seed;* ¼ teaspoon freshly ground *pepper;* and ⅛ teaspoon ground *cloves.* Store in a tightly covered container.

Per serving: 453 cal., 62 g pro., 15 g carbo., 16 g fat, 261 mg chol., 194 mg sodium. USRDA: 166% vit. A, 322% vit. C, 25% thiamine, 93% riboflavin, 104% niacin, 17% calcium, 42% iron, 75% phosphorus.

BEEF GOULASH

In Hungary, this staple stew is known as Szekely Gulyas—

- 1 pound beef stew meat, cut into 1-inch cubes
- 1 medium onion, chopped (½ cup)
- 2 tablespoons cooking oil
- 1 12-ounce can (1½ cups) beer
- ¾ cup water
- ¼ cup tomato paste
- 1 tablespoon paprika
- ¼ teaspoon salt
- ¼ teaspoon caraway seed
- ¼ teaspoon pepper
- 3 medium potatoes (about 1 pound)
- 1 8-ounce can sauerkraut
- 2 tablespoons snipped parsley

In a Dutch oven cook meat and onion in hot oil till meat is brown and onion is tender. Add beer, water, tomato paste, paprika, salt, caraway seed, and pepper. Bring to boiling; reduce heat. Cover and simmer for 1¼ to 1½ hours or till meat is tender,

Meanwhile, cut potatoes into 1-inch pieces. Add potatoes, *undrained* sauerkraut, and parsley to pan. Cook, covered, about 20 minutes or till the vegetables are tender. Cook, uncovered, about 10 minutes more or till mixture is thickened and most of the liquid is evaporated. Makes 4 servings.

Microwave directions: In a 2-quart nonmetal casserole combine the beef, onion, beer, *2 tablespoons* tomato paste, paprika, salt, caraway seed, and pepper. (Omit oil, water, and the remaining 2 tablespoons tomato paste.)

Micro-cook, covered, on 100% power (HIGH) about 5 minutes or till bubbly. Stir. Micro-cook, covered, on 50% power (MEDIUM) for 20 minutes.

Stir in the cut-up potatoes, sauerkraut, and parsley. Micro-cook, covered, on 50% power (MEDIUM) about 30 minutes more or till meat and vegetables are tender, stirring after every 10 minutes.

Per serving: 461 cal., 26 g pro., 28 g carbo., 25 g fat, 77 mg chol., 652 mg sodium. USRDA: 15% vit. A, 69% vit. C, 17% thiamine, 19% riboflavin, 40% niacin, 28% iron, 32% phosphorus.

FRIED CHEESE

  ¼ cup butter *or* margarine
  ⅓ cup all-purpose flour
  ¼ teaspoon ground nutmeg
  ⅛ teaspoon pepper
1½ cups milk
  3 beaten egg yolks
  2 cups shredded natural Gruyère
     or natural Swiss cheese
     (8 ounces)
  ½ cup grated Parmesan cheese
     (2 ounces)
  1 6-ounce package frozen cooked
     shrimp, thawed, drained, and
     chopped
  3 egg whites
  1 tablespoon water
  1 cup fine dry bread crumbs
Cooking oil for deep-fat frying
Spinach Mayonnaise

In a 2-quart saucepan melt butter or margarine. Stir in flour, nutmeg, and pepper. Add milk. Cook and stir till thickened and bubbly. Cook and stir for 1 minute more. Stir ½ cup of the hot mixture into beaten egg yolks. Return all to pan. Cook and stir till bubbly.

Add Gruyère or Swiss, and Parmesan cheese; stir till melted. Remove from heat. Stir in shrimp. Line a 9x9x2-inch baking pan with clear plastic wrap or foil. Spread mixture in pan. Cover with clear plastic wrap; freeze till firm.

Lift ends of plastic wrap or foil to remove the frozen mixture from pan. Cut mixture into 1-inch squares. Beat egg whites and water till frothy. Dip the shrimp squares into egg white mixture, then into bread crumbs. Transfer squares to a moisture- and vaporproof container, then freeze till needed or cook immediately.

At serving time, arrange cheese squares on a platter. At the dinner table, pour oil to no more than half full into a saucepan set over a hot plate or an electric fondue pot. Heat oil to 365°.

Have each person spear a cheese square on the end of a long wooden skewer or fondue fork. Immerse in hot oil and cook about 2 minutes or till golden. Transfer the cooked squares to dinner plates and serve with Spinach Mayonnaise. Makes 6 servings.

Per serving (without sauce): 576 cal., 28 g pro., 22 g carbo., 42 g fat, 248 mg chol., 644 mg sodium. USRDA: 25% vit. A, 29% riboflavin, 59% calcium, 14% iron, 49% phosphorus.

Spinach Mayonnaise: In a blender container combine 1 cup *mayonnaise* or *salad dressing;* ¼ cup finely snipped fresh *spinach leaves,* 2 tablespoons snipped *parsley,* 2 tablespoons *milk,* 1 tablespoon snipped *chives,* 1 tablespoon *lemon juice,* and ¼ teaspoon dried *tarragon;* crushed. Cover and blend till smooth. Cover and chill till serving time. Makes 1¼ cups.

Per tablespoon: 81 cal., 0 g pro., 0.5 g carbo., 9 g fat, 8 mg chol., and 67 mg sodium.

SHABU-SHABU

1½ pounds lean boneless beef
     (sirloin *or* tenderloin)
  4 medium carrots
  4 cups Chinese cabbage cut
     into 2-inch squares
  2 leeks, bias-sliced ¼ inch thick
  8 ounces tofu, cut into 1-inch
     cubes
  6 cups chicken broth
  1 4-inch square dried kelp
     (seaweed), scored (optional)
  1 recipe Sesame Sauce (optional)
  1 recipe Soy-Lemon Dipping
     Sauce (optional)
Hot cooked rice
Condiments such as vinegar,
     bias-sliced green
     onions, grated gingerroot,
     and crushed garlic cloves
     (optional)

Partially freeze meat; cut across the grain into very thin pieces. Cut carrots into ribbons by cutting lengthwise with a vegetable peeler. Arrange meat, carrots, cabbage, leeks, and tofu cubes on 6 individual plates. Cover and chill till serving time.

To serve, place an electric wok, electric skillet, or hot pot in the center of the dinner table. Add the chicken broth. Bring to boiling. Add kelp. Simmer, uncovered, for 3 minutes. Remove and discard kelp.

Using chopsticks or wooden tongs, have each person immerse a few pieces of meat, vegetables, and tofu in the simmering broth. (Allow 30 seconds for each meat strip; 30 seconds for cabbage; 30 to 60 seconds for leeks; 1 minute for tofu; and 1 to 2 minutes for carrots.)

Using a small Mongolian skimmer, chopsticks, or tongs, transfer the cooked foods to dinner plates. Dip the cooked pieces into Sesame Sauce or Soy-Lemon Dipping Sauce. Serve with hot cooked rice.

After the meat, vegetables, and tofu are cooked, ladle the hot cooking liquid into 6 individual soup bowls. Let each diner garnish his soup serving with vinegar, green onions, gingerroot, or garlic. Makes 6 servings.

Per serving (without sauces): 530 cal., 26 g pro., 33 g carbo., 32 g fat, 81 mg chol., 658 mg sodium. USRDA: 109% vit. A, 30% vit. C, 19% thiamine, 15% riboflavin, 33% niacin, 12% calcium, 31% iron, 31% phosphorus.

Sesame Sauce: In a blender container blend ½ cup toasted *sesame seed* or ¼ cup *tahini* till smooth. Add 3 tablespoons *dashi* or *chicken broth,* 2 tablespoons *soy sauce,* 1 tablespoon *mirin* or *dry sherry,* and 1 teaspoon *sugar.* Cover and blend till smooth. Serve the sauce at room temperature. Makes ⅔ cup sauce.

Per tablespoon: 43 cal., 1 g pro., 2 g carbo., 3 g fat, and 226 mg sodium.

Soy-Lemon Dipping Sauce: In a small bowl stir together ¼ cup *soy sauce* and 3 tablespoons *lemon juice.* Serve the sauce at room temperature. Makes about ½ cup sauce.

Per tablespoon: 8 cal., 1 g pro., 1 g carbo., 0 mg chol., 664 mg sodium.

MARCH

By Diana McMillen

SPRING LAMB
FOR YOUR HOLIDAY FEASTS

Delicate flavor and tenderness plus a better-than-ever supply make lamb a specialty you won't want to miss.

PASTRY-WRAPPED LAMB CHOPS

- 1½ cups all-purpose flour
- ⅓ cup butter *or* margarine
- 4 to 5 tablespoons cold water
- 1½ cups finely chopped mushrooms
- 2 tablespoons chopped green onion
- 2 tablespoons butter *or* margarine
- 1 teaspoon lemon juice
- 4 lamb loin chops, cut 1 inch thick and boned
- Garlic salt
- 4 thin slices fully cooked ham
- 1 slightly beaten egg yolk

Combine flour and ¼ teaspoon *salt.* Cut in ⅓ cup butter or margarine till mixture resembles small peas. Sprinkle *1 tablespoon* of the water over part of the mixture; gently toss. Repeat till all is moistened. Form a ball. Wrap; chill.

Cook the mushrooms and onion in *1 tablespoon* of the remaining butter till tender. Remove from skillet; stir in the lemon juice. Sprinkle with salt and pepper; set aside. Using a meat mallet, pound meat to slightly flatten. Brown in remaining butter. Sprinkle meat with garlic salt and pepper.

On a floured surface, roll pastry into a 12-inch square. Cut into 4 squares. Place *1* slice of ham on *each* square, then a lamb chop, and *one-fourth* of the mushroom mixture. Moisten edges of dough; fold dough over meat, envelope-style. Press to seal. Decorate with additional pastry (optional). Combine egg yolk and 1 tablespoon *water;* brush over pastry. Place on an ungreased baking sheet. Bake in a 400° oven for 25 minutes. Makes 4 servings.

Per serving: 616 cal., 26 g pro., 26 g carbo., 45 g fat, 446 mg sodium.

GARLIC LAMB SHANKS

- 4 lamb shanks (about 3½ pounds)
- 2 tablespoons cooking oil
- 1 cup finely chopped onions
- 1 cup finely chopped carrots
- 1 cup chopped celery
- 1 cup dry white wine
- 30 unpeeled garlic cloves

Cut fell from lamb. Season lamb with salt and pepper. Brown in hot oil; drain off fat. Add onions, carrots, celery, wine, 1 teaspoon *salt,* and ¼ teaspoon *pepper.* Top with unpeeled garlic. Bring to boiling; reduce heat. Cover; simmer 1½ hours. Transfer to serving plate. Skim fat from juices; spoon vegetables and juices over lamb. Makes 4 servings.

Per serving: 521 cal., 48 g pro., 17 g carbo., 24 g fat, 707 mg sodium.

Photograph: Ernie Block

PASTRY-WRAPPED LAMB CHOPS

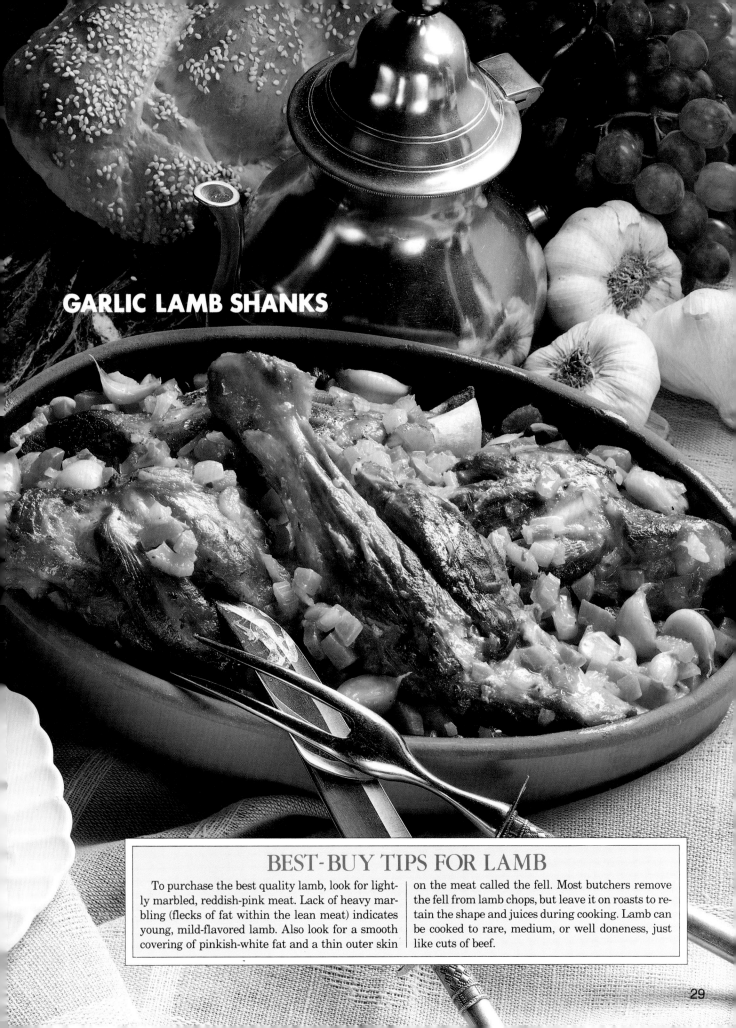

GARLIC LAMB SHANKS

BEST-BUY TIPS FOR LAMB

To purchase the best quality lamb, look for lightly marbled, reddish-pink meat. Lack of heavy marbling (flecks of fat within the lean meat) indicates young, mild-flavored lamb. Also look for a smooth covering of pinkish-white fat and a thin outer skin on the meat called the fell. Most butchers remove the fell from lamb chops, but leave it on roasts to retain the shape and juices during cooking. Lamb can be cooked to rare, medium, or well doneness, just like cuts of beef.

TIPS TO LIGHT AND TASTY BREADS

1. Kneading dough gives the bread even texture. To knead, press the dough using a folding and pushing motion.

2. Pressing fingertips into a dough determines when it's doubled. If the indentation remains, the dough has doubled.

3. Punching dough down makes it easy to shape. Punch in the center first, then the sides of the dough.

REDISCOVER GREAT ·HOME· BAKING

By Nancy K. Wall

When it comes to baking pies, cakes, and breads, the basics never change. As proof, we dusted off antique cookbooks to bring you recipes that employ techniques of yesteryear. Use these basics for successful baking today.

POCKETBOOK ROLLS

According to the cookbook *La Cuisine Creole* of 1885, these irresistible rolls flecked with orange peel are shaped to resemble old-time pocketbooks. Just as the antique recipe says, these rolls are "very much liked" for tea or any special time with friends or family.

TIPS TO MOIST AND TENDER CAKES

1. Creaming butter and sugar gives tender texture. Cream the butter mixture till fluffy and sugar dissolves.

2. Beating well after each alternate addition of flour and milk combines the flour mixture and gives light structure.

3. Gently folding egg whites into the batter using an up-down-and-over motion yields increased volume.

CHEWY FUDGE "CARAMEL CAKE"

"Let all things be done decently and in order." That's the secret for perfect cakes according to *Buckeye Cookery and Practical Housecooking.* This example of a perfect cake gets its name from the fudge frosting. Follow our "orderly" steps to moist, tender cakes.

Photographs, top rows: Bill Hopkins, Hopkins Associates
Photographs, bottom: William Sladcik

DELICATE AND FLUFFY CREAM PUFFS

1. Adding flour all at once while cooking ensures quick blending. Beat vigorously to combine the flour and butter.

2. Cooking the dough till it forms a ball helps make a light pastry. The ball forms as the mixture pulls from the pan.

3. Beating in the eggs one at a time builds airy texture. Cool slightly before adding the eggs to prevent them from cooking.

REDISCOVER GREAT ·HOME· BAKING

NUN'S PUFFS

Cream puff batter that bakes like a popover best describes a Nun's Puff. The directions in this recipe, from the cookbook *Housekeeping in Old Virginia*, 1879, say the muffin-size treats are ready when they puff like balloons! Follow these tips when you make cream puffs, too.

TIPS TO RICH AND FLAKY PASTRY

1. Gently cutting in the shortening yields a tender, flaky pastry. Blend till the ingredients are the size of small peas.

2. Forming the dough into a ball makes it easy to handle. When the mixture is moistened, form a ball with a fork.

3. Preparing a top crust adds a decorative finish. Fold the dough in half, then make slits to form mirror images.

APPLE POT PIE

The earliest cookbooks, such as *La Cuisine Creole,* assure us that a pie's success lies in the pastry. Here, the pastry trimmings are used to make dumplings that bake inside a deep-dish pie. And like any old-fashioned dessert—this one is best when eaten with a spoon and a splash of cream!

33

PURE AND SIMPLE
DAIRY GOODNESS
YOU MAKE YOURSELF

Years ago, a cow in the backyard was as common as a pump at the kitchen sink. The young and old alike in those days took a turn at making wholesome, homemade dairy products.

Today, you can discover the pleasure of making these basic foods with ease in your own kitchen. Without any special equipment, we'll show you how to make old-fashioned buttermilk, crème fraîche (a special treat not widely available), cottage cheese, and sour cream. Although we can't guarantee that these delicious dairy products are cheaper than their commercial counterparts, we *can* guarantee their fresh flavors.

BUTTERMILK

No more leftover buttermilk! Prepare a quart, or just one cup, by doubling or halving this recipe. Commercial buttermilk serves as the starter for this tangy beverage—

- **2 cups skim *or* whole milk**
- **2 tablespoons commercial buttermilk**

Combine the skim milk and the commercial buttermilk, mixing well. Let stand, covered with plastic wrap, in a warm place (similar to where you would place bread to rise) for 16 to 24 hours or till thickened. Refrigerate in a covered container. Shake well or mix in blender container before using. Store in refrigerator for up to 2 weeks. Makes 2 cups.

To replenish: Use 2 tablespoons of your Buttermilk for commercial buttermilk.

These easy-to-make dairy treats get their quick start from ingredients you already have on hand.

CRÈME FRAÎCHE

This thickened soured cream is reminiscent of the French specialty made from raw cream that is allowed to mature naturally, but not to sour. Crème fraîche is great as a substitute for sour cream in cooking because it is less likely to curdle when added to hot mixtures. Or, serve it chilled over sliced fruits for a refreshing dessert—

- **2 cups whipping cream**
- **¼ cup commercial buttermilk**

In a small saucepan heat whipping cream to between 90° and 100°. Pour into a small bowl. Stir in the buttermilk. Cover and let stand at room temperature for 18 to 24 hours or till mixture is thickened. Do not stir. Store in a covered container in refrigerator up to one week. Makes 2 cups.

To replenish supply: Substitute ¼ cup of your Crème Fraîche for the buttermilk in this recipe.

COTTAGE CHEESE

You'll find the rennet tablets in the baking section of the grocery store—

- **¼ tablet rennet**
- **½ cup water**
- **1 gallon skim milk**
- **¼ cup buttermilk**
- **½ cup light cream**

Crush rennet tablet and dissolve in the ½ cup water. In large stainless steel kettle or Dutch oven heat skim milk to 70°. Remove from heat and stir in the buttermilk and rennet tablet solution. Cover with towel; let stand at room temperature for 12 to 20 hours or till a firm curd forms. With a knife, cut curd into ½-inch pieces. Transfer curd and

whey to large stainless steel bowl or saucepan that fits securely over a Dutch oven filled with 1 to 2 inches of water. Heat curd slowly over hot water till temperature reaches 120° to 130° (do not overheat). Hold curd at this temperature for 20 to 30 minutes. Stir gently every 5 minutes to heat curd uniformly. Pour mixture into fine cheesecloth-lined colander and allow whey to drain off. Occasionally shift curd on cloth by lifting corners of cloth. After the whey has drained (8 to 10 minutes), lift curd in cheesecloth and immerse in pan of cold water for 1 or 2 minutes. Then immerse in ice water for 1 to 2 minutes. Return curd in cloth to colander; drain the curd until it is free from moisture. (This could take several hours.) Put cheese in a bowl and gently stir in cream and ½ teaspoon *salt*. Cover and chill. Use within 3 weeks. Makes 4 cups.

HOMEMADE SOUR CREAM

- **2 cups light cream**
- **2 tablespoons buttermilk**

Combine cream with buttermilk in hot, clean glass jar with screw lid. (A canning jar that has been heated in boiling water works.)

Cover tightly and shake gently to thoroughly mix the buttermilk and the cream. Let stand in a warm place (similar to where you would place bread to rise) till thickened (24 to 48 hours). Store, covered, in refrigerator. Stir before serving. Use within 3 weeks. Makes 2 cups.

Photograph: William Sladcik

34

CHEWY FUDGE FROSTING

- ¼ cup butter *or* margarine
- 1 cup packed brown sugar
- ½ cup milk
- 2 squares (2 ounces) unsweetened chocolate, cut up
- 2 tablespoons light cream *or* milk
- 2 teaspoons vanilla

In a heavy 1½-quart saucepan melt butter or margarine. Add brown sugar; stir to combine. Add ½ cup milk and chocolate; stir constantly till mixture boils. Cook over medium heat, stirring occasionally, to 245° (firm-ball stage), 20 to 30 minutes (mixture should boil gently over surface). Remove from heat; stir in cream or milk and vanilla. Quickly pour and spread on cake.

CHEWY FUDGE "CARAMEL CAKE"
pictured on page 27

This old-fashioned cake relies on 1 cup of cornstarch as well as all-purpose flour for structure—

- 1½ cups all-purpose flour
- 1 cup sifted cornstarch
- 1 tablespoon baking powder
- 1 cup butter *or* margarine
- 2 cups sugar
- 1 cup milk
- 7 egg whites
- 1 recipe Chewy Fudge Frosting (see recipe above)

Grease and lightly flour two 9x1½-inch round cake pans or one 13x9x2-inch baking pan; set aside. In a mixing bowl stir together flour, cornstarch, and baking powder; set aside.

In a large mixer bowl beat butter or margarine with an electric mixer on medium speed for 30 seconds. Add sugar and beat till fluffy. Add dry ingredients and milk alternately to beaten mixture, beating on low speed after each addition till just combined.

Transfer the batter to a large mixing bowl. Wash the beaters and mixer bowl. Beat egg whites till stiff peaks form (tips stand straight). Gently fold egg whites into batter.

Turn batter into prepared pan(s). Bake in a 350° oven for 25 to 30 minutes for the 9x1½-inch pans or 40 to 45 minutes for the 13x9x2-inch pan. Cool on wire racks for 10 minutes. Remove from pans. Cool thoroughly. Pour frosting over cake and spread evenly. Makes 12 servings.

Per serving: 505 cal., 6 g pro., 76 g carbo., 21 g fat, 59 mg chol., 361 mg sodium. USRDA: 15% vit. A, 11% riboflavin, 10% phosphorus.

NUN'S PUFF

- ½ cup butter *or* margarine
- 1 cup milk
- ¾ cup all-purpose flour
- 4 eggs
- 1 to 2 tablespoons sugar

Generously grease twelve 2½-inch muffin cups, greasing well on edge and around top of the cup; set aside.

In a 2-quart saucepan melt butter or margarine. Add milk; bring to boiling. Add flour all at once; stir vigorously. Cook and stir till mixture forms a ball that doesn't separate. Remove mixture from heat and cool slightly, about 5 minutes.

Add eggs, one at a time, beating with a wooden spoon after each addition about 1 minute or till smooth. Fill the prepared muffin cups half full; sprinkle with sugar. Bake in a 375° oven for 40 to 45 minutes or till golden brown and puffy. Serve immediately. Makes 12 servings.

Note: Nun's Puffs will fall slightly when removed from the oven.

Per puff: 141 cal., 4 g pro., 8 g carbo., 10 g fat, 111 mg chol., 124 mg sodium. USRDA: 11% vit. A.

APPLE SNACK BARS

Looking for a wholesome treat to beat the lunch box blahs? Pack up these snack bars chock-full of mixed fruit, cereal, and nuts—

- 1 cup whole wheat flour
- 1 cup quick-cooking rolled oats
- ¾ teaspoon baking soda
- ½ teaspoon ground cinnamon
- 1 8½-ounce can (1 cup) applesauce
- ½ cup honey
- ⅓ cup cooking oil
- 1 teaspoon vanilla
- 1 6-ounce package chopped mixed dried fruit
- ½ cup chopped nuts
- ¾ cup crushed bran flakes
- 2 tablespoons butter *or* margarine, melted

Grease a 13x9x2-inch baking pan; set aside. In a large mixing bowl stir together whole wheat flour, oats, baking soda, and cinnamon. In a small mixing bowl combine applesauce, honey, cooking oil, and vanilla. Stir applesauce mixture into dry ingredients. Stir in fruit and nuts.

In a small mixing bowl combine bran flakes and butter or margarine. Sprinkle *half* of the bran mixture over the bottom of the prepared pan.

Drop the batter over bran; spread evenly. Sprinkle with remaining bran mixture. Bake in a 350° oven for 25 to 30 minutes or till done. Cool in pan on a wire rack. Cut into bars. Makes 28 bars.

Per bar: 125 cal., 2 g pro., 20 g carbo., 5 g fat, 3 mg chol., 36 mg sodium.

APPLE POT PIE

One secret for tender, flaky pastry is measuring accurately. Too much flour can make the pastry tough. Too much shortening will make pastry greasy and mealy. Too much water makes pastry tough and soggy—

- 2 **cups all-purpose flour**
- ½ **teaspoon salt**
- ⅔ **cup lard *or* shortening**
- 6 **to 7 tablespoons cold water**
- 12 **medium cooking apples, peeled, cored, and quartered**
- ½ **cup sugar**
- ½ **cup water**
- ¼ **cup raisins**
- 2 **tablespoons molasses**
- 1 **tablespoon butter *or* margarine**
- 1 **tablespoon all-purpose flour**
- 1 **teaspoon ground cinnamon**
- ¼ **teaspoon ground mace**
- ⅛ **teaspoon ground ginger**
- **Milk**
- **Sugar**
- **Light cream (optional)**

In a medium mixing bowl stir together 2 cups flour and salt. Cut in lard or shortening till pieces are the size of small peas. Sprinkle *1 tablespoon* water over part of mixture; gently toss with a fork. Push to side of bowl. Repeat with remaining water till all is moistened. Form dough into a ball. Set aside *one-third* of the dough.

On a lightly floured surface flatten the remaining dough with hands. Roll dough from center to edge, forming a shape 1 inch larger than a deep 2-quart casserole. Fold dough in half. Cut decorative slits in the fold and into top of dough for escape of steam. Roll remaining *one-third* dough ¼ inch thick; cut into 1-inch squares for dumplings.

In a 3-quart saucepan combine apple pieces, ½ cup sugar, ½ cup water, raisins, molasses, butter or margarine, 1 tablespoon flour, cinnamon, mace, and ginger. Cook and stir till slightly thickened and bubbly.

Pour hot mixture into the casserole. Drop dumplings atop; stir. Gently place crust on top of fruit; trim top crust ½ inch beyond edge of casserole. Fold under extra pastry. Brush pastry with milk; sprinkle sugar atop.

Bake in a 375° oven for 30 to 35 minutes or till crust is golden. Serve warm with cream, if desired. Makes 6 to 8 servings.

Per serving: 372 cal., 3 g pro., 57 g carbo., 16 g fat, 17 mg chol., 125 mg sodium. USRDA: 15% thiamine.

POCKETBOOK ROLLS

Old-time bread recipes were based first on softening the yeast. We've updated this antique recipe using the easy-mix method. This method omits the yeast softening step and lets you waste no time in making these delicious rolls—

- 4 **to 5 cups all-purpose flour**
- 2 **packages active dry yeast**
- 1 **cup milk**
- ¾ **cup sugar**
- 3 **tablespoons butter *or* margarine**
- 1 **teaspoon finely shredded orange peel**
- ½ **teaspoon salt**
- 2 **eggs**
- 4 **tablespoons butter *or* margarine, softened**
- 1 **beaten egg**
- 1 **tablespoon cooking oil**
- 1 **tablespoon sugar**

In a large mixer bowl combine *2 cups* of the flour and yeast. In a medium saucepan heat milk, ¾ cup sugar, 3 tablespoons butter or margarine, orange peel, and salt just till warm (115° to 120°) and butter is almost melted, stirring constantly. Add to flour mixture. Add 2 eggs.

Beat with an electric mixer on low speed for 30 seconds, scraping sides of bowl constantly. Beat for 3 minutes on high speed. Using a wooden spoon, stir in as much of the remaining flour as you can.

Turn the dough out onto a lightly floured surface. Knead in enough of the remaining flour to make a moderately soft dough (3 to 5 minutes total). Shape into a ball. Place dough in a greased bowl; turn once to grease surface. Cover; let rise in a warm place till nearly double (45 to 60 minutes).

Punch dough down; divide in half. Cover and let rest for 10 minutes. Roll *each* portion of dough into a 12x6-inch rectangle. Spread *each* rectangle with 2 *tablespoons* of the softened butter or margarine. Fold the dough, lengthwise, into thirds; moisten and pinch seam to seal. Flatten dough slightly to a 3-inch width. Cut, crosswise, into 1-inch slices.

Place rolls, seam side down, in a greased 15x10x1-inch baking pan. Cover and let rise till nearly double (about 30 to 45 minutes). Stir together 1 beaten egg and oil. Brush over rolls; sprinkle with sugar. Bake in a 375° oven for 15 to 18 minutes or till done. Makes 24.

Per serving: 155 cal., 4 g pro., 23 g carbo., 5 g fat, 44 mg chol., 99 mg sodium. USRDA: 10% thiamine.

STEAMED ASPARAGUS MEDLEY

GAZPACHO-STYLE ARTICHOKES

EARLY BIRD SPRING VEGETABLES

By Nancy K. Wall

It's spring! Vegetable bins are brimming with colorful, fresh vegetables to enjoy. Spring vegetables are packed with vitamins and they're so quick and easy to cook.

NEW POTATO SALAD

SELECTION TIPS

- Artichokes—compact size with tightly closed green leaves
- Asparagus—firm and straight stalks with compact, closed tips
- New potatoes—firm, small, and smooth with shallow eyes
- Peas—bright green with fresh-looking stem ends
- Radishes—firm; medium-size

STEAMED ASPARAGUS MEDLEY

- ½ cup whole radishes
- 3 tablespoons olive *or* salad oil
- 2 tablespoons wine vinegar
- 2 teaspoons snipped chives
- 1 teaspoon dried oregano, crushed
- 1 pound fresh asparagus

Rinse the radishes; remove ends and cut into thick slices. Place radishes in a steamer basket. Place over, but not touching, boiling water. Cover; reduce heat. Steam for 8 to 10 minutes. Drain.

For dressing, in screw-top jar combine oil, vinegar, chives, oregano, ⅛ teaspoon *salt,* and ⅛ teaspoon *pepper.* Cover; shake well. Combine radishes and dressing. Cover; chill.

Meanwhile, wash asparagus. Break off woody ends; place asparagus in steamer basket. Place over, but not touching, boiling water. Cover; reduce heat. Steam 10 to 12 minutes. Drain. Cover; chill. Arrange on serving platter. Top with radishes and dressing. Makes 6 servings.

GAZPACHO-STYLE ARTICHOKES

- 2 medium artichokes
- 2 medium tomatoes
- ¼ cup chopped green pepper
- ¼ cup chopped cucumber
- 2 tablespoons chopped onion
- 2 tablespoons olive *or* salad oil
- 2 tablespoons lemon juice
- 1 teaspoon mustard seed
- 1 small clove garlic, minced
- Dash hot pepper sauce

Wash artichokes; trim stems and remove loose outer leaves. Cut off 1 inch of tops; snip off sharp leaf tips. Brush cut edges with lemon juice. In a large kettle cook artichokes, covered, in 2 inches of boiling salted water for 20 to 30 minutes. Drain. Chill thoroughly.

For relish: Peel tomatoes and coarsely chop. Combine tomatoes, green pepper, cucumber, onion, oil, lemon juice, mustard, garlic, pepper sauce, ¼ teaspoon *salt,* and ⅛ teaspoon *pepper.* Cover and chill for several hours, stirring occasionally. To serve, pull leaves off *one* artichoke; remove choke. Chop artichoke heart and stem. Stir into relish. Remove center leaves and choke of remaining artichoke to form cup; fill with relish. Place on platter. Arrange leaves around the artichoke cup. Spoon relish onto base of each leaf. Serves 8 to 10.

NEW POTATO SALAD

- 1 pound tiny new potatoes
- 2 cups fresh pea pods, bias-sliced
- ¼ cup dairy sour cream
- ¼ cup mayonnaise *or* salad dressing
- 1 tablespoon snipped parsley
- 1 teaspoon dried dillweed
- Bibb *or* romaine lettuce

Peel a strip from the center of each potato. Halve potatoes lengthwise. Cook potatoes, covered, in a small amount of boiling salted water for 8 minutes. Add pea pods. Cover and cook for 2 to 4 minutes. Drain well; cool.

For dressing: Combine sour cream, mayonnaise, parsley, dill, and ¼ teaspoon *salt.* Cover and chill. Line salad plates with lettuce leaves. Spoon potato mixture in center. Drizzle dressing over each. Makes 8 servings.

Photograph: William Sladcik

AFTER-WORK COOKING
SOLVE YOUR DINNER DILEMMAS!

By Diana McMillen

You can juggle dinnertime and your family's ever-changing routine with finesse! Five terrific-tasting recipes fit the most frustrating schedules. When time and energy are at a premium, turn to these solutions—you'll knock your family's socks off!

My family partici-pates in a million activities every week—many over the dinner hour. I'm tired of being a short-order cook!
Working mother of three, San Diego, Calif.

READY IN 30 MINUTES!
THE ON-CALL SALAD

Here's a recipe idea you're sure to love—the meal that's ready anytime, for one or all. Stack and store these single-serving main-dish salads; they'll keep fresh in the refrigerator from first supper shift to last.

Photographs: Ernie Block

40

READY IN 25 MINUTES!

OFF-THE-SHELF ITALIAN DINNER

Turn to your pantry for inspiration when you're in a jam. Keep cans of tomato soup, tomato paste, minced clams, and frozen tortellini on hand. They go together for a family-pleasing meal in minutes.

We worry about leaving the kids alone to fend for themselves at dinner. What can we fix that's good that they can self-serve?

**Concerned parents,
Bangor, Maine**

JUST-FOR-KIDS CALZONE

With this freeze-ahead sandwich on hand, enjoy your parents' night out.
Armed with hot pads, your child can bake and serve it. With a salad
you've stashed in the refrigerator and with milk, the meal is complete.

RUSH-HOUR SIMMER DINNER

From the time you open the cupboard door, it takes just 10 minutes to assemble this skillet meal, then it simmers unattended for 20. But, the real bonus comes when it's time to clean up—there's only one pan.

READY IN 30 MINUTES!

There never seems to be enough time to prepare a special treat for my family when one of us brings home some good news.

**Proud, but busy, parent,
Garden City, N.J.**

CELEBRATION COOKIE

A jumbo chocolate chip cookie topped with some peanut butter and bananas—what a great way to celebrate! It takes just 15 minutes to assemble this tasty sweet to mark a promotion or a good grade at school.

Top this fun dessert with your choice of jam or jelly—strawberry, raspberry, grape, currant, apricot, or cherry. You also can use double-chocolate refrigerated cookie dough instead of the dough with the chocolate pieces—

- 1 **15- or 16-ounce roll chocolate chip refrigerated cookie dough**
- 1 **5-ounce can vanilla pudding**
- ⅓ **cup peanut butter**
- ¼ **cup plain yogurt**
- 1 **medium banana**
- ¼ **cup desired jam or jelly**
- 3 **tablespoons chopped dry roasted peanuts**

Cut *two-thirds* of the chocolate chip cookie dough into ½-inch-thick slices.

Chill the remaining dough in the refrigerator for later use or slice and bake according to package directions.

On an ungreased baking sheet arrange and press together the ½-inch-thick slices of cookie dough to form an 8-inch circle. Bake in a 400° oven about 10 minutes or till the cookie crust is done. Cool the crust for 5 minutes on the baking sheet. Using a spatula, loosen the edges of the crust and transfer to a wire rack; cool thoroughly.

Meanwhile, in a small mixing bowl combine vanilla pudding and peanut butter; stir till the mixture is smooth. Fold in the plain yogurt.

Spread the pudding mixture over the cooled cookie crust. Bias-slice the ba-

nana.* Arrange the banana slices over the pudding mixture on the crust.

Just before serving, heat a little jam or jelly over low heat till melted and drizzle over the big cookie. Sprinkle with peanuts. Cut into wedges to serve.

Store any remaining cookie, covered with clear plastic wrap or in a covered container, in the refrigerator. Makes 6 servings.

Per serving: 405 cal., 8 g pro., 48 g carbo., 22 g fat, 24 mg chol., and 268 mg sodium. USRDA: 18% niacin and 15% phosphorus.

*Note: Brush the banana slices with lemon juice or ascorbic acid color-keeper before arranging on the cookie to prevent browning.

ON-CALL SALAD

Lahvosh, Lebanese-style crackers, are available in most large supermarkets. You can serve this stacked salad immediately or save it in the refrigerator up to 4 hours. The cracker softens as it sits—

  1 **15-ounce can garbanzo beans, drained**
  ¼ **cup mayonnaise *or* salad dressing**
  ¼ **cup bottled green goddess salad dressing *or* other creamy salad dressing**
 12 **3-inch individual whole wheat lahvosh rounds**
 1½ **cups shredded lettuce**
  1 **cup shredded cheddar cheese (4 ounces)**
  ⅓ **cup sliced almonds**

In a blender container or food processor bowl combine garbanzo beans, mayonnaise or salad dressing, and green goddess salad dressing. Cover and blend till mixture is smooth.

Spread about *2 tablespoons* of the mixture over *each* lahvosh cracker. Sprinkle shredded lettuce, shredded cheddar cheese, and sliced almonds over each cracker.

Layer lahvosh, 3 in a stack, to form 4 stacks. Cover the salads with clear plastic wrap; refrigerate up to 4 hours. Makes 4 servings.

Note: To serve salads immediately, place lahvosh under gently running water to soften slightly. Pat dry with paper towels. Assemble as directed.

Per serving: 490 cal., 16 g pro., 28 g carbo., 36 g fat, 41 mg chol., 483 mg sodium. USRDA: 11% vit. A, 11% thiamine, 16% riboflavin, 28% calcium, 18% iron, 32% phosphorus.

JUST-FOR-KIDS CALZONE

Refrigerate or freeze these sandwiches—

  ½ **pound ground beef**
  ¼ **cup chopped onion**
  1 **8-ounce can pizza sauce**
  2 **tablespoons chopped pitted ripe olives**
  1 **teaspoon dried basil, crushed**
  ½ **teaspoon dried oregano, crushed**
  3 **individual French rolls (about 8 inches long)**
 1½ **cups shredded mozzarella cheese (6 ounces)**
Fresh Fruit Plate (see recipe, page 46)

In a saucepan cook meat and onion till meat is brown. Remove from heat. Drain off fat. Stir in the pizza sauce, olives, basil, and oregano.

Cut a thin slice from top of each roll. Hollow out bottom of roll to within ½ inch of edges. Sprinkle about *3 tablespoons* of the cheese into the bottom of *each* roll. Spoon meat mixture over each. Sprinkle with remaining cheese. Replace roll tops. Wrap individually in foil. Refrigerate for 3 to 24 hours or freeze for longer storage.

To serve, place foil-wrapped sandwiches on a baking sheet. Bake in a 375° oven till heated through, about 40 minutes if refrigerated, or 60 to 70 minutes if frozen. Serve with Fresh Fruit Plate. Makes 3 servings.

Note: You can prepare Just-for-Kids Calzone using club rolls, also. Prepare the sandwiches as directed above. Bake sandwiches till heated through, about 25 minutes if chilled; about 45 minutes if frozen.

Microwave directions: Crumble meat into a 1-quart nonmetal casserole; add onion. Micro-cook, covered, on 100% power (HIGH) for 5 minutes; stir once to break up meat. Drain off fat. Stir in the pizza sauce, olives, basil, and oregano. Assemble the sandwiches. Refrigerate or freeze. Bake conventionally as directed. Makes 3 servings.

Per serving: 501 cal., 33 g pro., 40 g carbo., 23 g fat, 97 mg chol., 1,152 mg sodium. USRDA: 23% vit. A, 23% thiamine, 26% riboflavin, 33% niacin, 34% calcium, 22% iron, 43% phosphorus.

OFF-THE-SHELF ITALIAN DINNER

For a more colorful dish, use half green and half regular tortellini. You can use packaged dried tortellini also; the cooking time will be slightly longer—

  1 **12-ounce package frozen tortellini**
  1 **tablespoon snipped parsley**
  1 **10½-ounce can ready-to-serve low-sodium tomato soup with tomato pieces**
  ½ **of a 6-ounce can (⅓ cup) tomato paste**
  ½ **teaspoon dried marjoram, crushed**
Dash bottled hot pepper sauce
  1 **6½-ounce can minced clams**
Grated Parmesan cheese

In a saucepan cook tortellini in boiling unsalted water according to package directions; drain. Toss the cooked tortellini with parsley.

Meanwhile, in another saucepan combine soup, tomato paste, marjoram, and hot pepper sauce; cook till bubbly. Add *undrained* clams; heat through.

To serve, spoon hot clam mixture over hot tortellini. Sprinkle with Parmesan. Makes 4 servings.

Microwave directions: In a saucepan on the range top cook tortellini in boiling unsalted water according to package directions; drain. Toss the tortellini with parsley.

Meanwhile, in a 1-quart nonmetal casserole combine soup, tomato paste, marjoram, and hot pepper sauce. Micro-cook, covered, on 100% power (HIGH) for 3 to 4 minutes or till bubbly, stirring once. Add *undrained* clams; micro-cook, covered, for 2 to 3 minutes more or till heated through.

Serve hot clam mixture over hot tortellini. Sprinkle with Parmesan.

Per serving: 427 cal., 17 g pro., 74 g carbo., 6 g fat, 97 mg chol., 306 mg sodium. USRDA: 26% vit. A, 30% vit. C, 55% thiamine, 27% riboflavin, 35% niacin, 10% calcium, 30% iron, 25% phosphorus.

FRESH FRUIT PLATE

Use canned or fresh fruit for this make-ahead salad. Toast the shredded coconut and wrap it in plastic wrap. Your child can sprinkle the coconut over his salad before eating—

- ½ of a 3-ounce package cream cheese, softened
- 1 tablespoon honey
- ⅛ teaspoon ground cinnamon
- 2 cups assorted fresh fruit (choose from chopped apples, orange slices, grapefruit sections, cut-up pineapple, pear slices, grapes, *and* strawberries)
- Butterhead *or* iceberg lettuce leaves
- *Shredded coconut, toasted (optional)

In a small mixer bowl beat the softened cream cheese, honey, and ground cinnamon on high speed of an electric mixer till fluffy.

Brush apple and pear pieces with lemon juice or ascorbic acid color-keeper to prevent the cut edges from browning. Place lettuce leaves on 3 individual salad plates. Arrange the desired fruit on lettuce. Spoon the cream cheese mixture to the side.

Cover well with clear plastic wrap. Refrigerate for 3 to 24 hours. Before serving, sprinkle toasted coconut atop, if desired. Makes 3 servings.

Note: To toast coconut, place the shredded coconut in a shallow baking pan. Bake in a 350° oven for 5 to 10 minutes or till light brown. Stir once or twice during baking to ensure even browning.

Per serving: 128 cal., 2 g pro., 19 g carbo., 6 g fat, 16 mg chol., 38 mg sodium. USRDA: 54% vit. C.

RUSH-HOUR SIMMER DINNER

This savvy one-dish meal takes only 10 minutes to assemble and just 20 minutes to cook. It's a super simple way to create a delicious supper—

- 4 bundles nested vermicelli pasta (5½ ounces)
- 2 6¾-ounce cans chunk-style chicken
- 1 cup frozen peas
- 1 8-ounce can whole small carrots, drained
- 1 small onion, thinly sliced
- 1¼ cups chicken broth
- 1 teaspoon dried tarragon, crushed

In a 10-inch skillet arrange the nested vermicelli, *undrained* chicken, frozen peas, carrots, and sliced onion. Add the chicken broth and sprinkle with tarragon. Bring the mixture to boiling; reduce heat. Cover and simmer for 15 to 20 minutes or till vermicelli are just tender. Serve immediately. Makes 4 servings.

Per serving: 399 cal., 30 g pro., 40 g carbo., 13 g fat, 77 mg chol., 861 mg sodium. USRDA: 175% vit. A, 22% vit. C, 34% thiamine, 19% riboflavin, 42% niacin, 21% iron, 35% phosphorus.

SALMON-STUFFED MANICOTTI

Salmon is an all-around good choice for low-cholesterol meals—

- 4 manicotti shells
- 1 cup low-fat cottage cheese, drained
- 2 teaspoons prepared horseradish
- 1 7¾-ounce can salmon, drained, flaked, and skin and bones removed
- 1 tablespoon butter *or* margarine
- 4 teaspoons all-purpose flour
- ⅛ teaspoon salt
- ⅛ teaspoon pepper
- ¾ cup milk
- ½ cup seeded and shredded cucumber (½ medium)
- Few dashes bottled hot pepper sauce

Cook manicotti according to package directions; drain. Rinse with cold water; drain. In a mixing bowl combine cottage cheese and horseradish. Add salmon; toss.

In a saucepan melt butter or margarine. Stir in flour, salt, and pepper. Add milk. Cook and stir till thickened and bubbly. Stir *1 tablespoon* of sauce into salmon mixture.

Fill *each* manicotti shell with ½ *cup* of the salmon mixture. Place each in an individual casserole or arrange manicotti shells in a 10x6x2-inch or 12x7½x2-inch baking dish.

Stir the cucumber and hot pepper sauce into remaining sauce. Spoon over manicotti. Cover and bake in a 350° oven about 25 minutes or till heated through. Makes 4 servings.

Per serving: 241 cal., 23 g pro., 19 g carbo., 7 g fat, 25 mg chol., 566 mg sodium. USRDA: 14% thiamine, 21% riboflavin, 28% niacin, 21% calcium, 32% phosphorus.

MAY

RAZZLE-DAZZLE
RHUBARB PIES

By Diana McMillen

Rhubarb flavors the spirit of Americana with as much gusto as apple pie! Bake up one of these delicious homespun desserts and you'll understand why some folks also call rhubarb "pieplant."

To harvest, grasp stalks by the base and pull gently with a twisting motion. Use only the reddish-pink stalk of the plant for cooking—the leaves are inedible.

GLAZED RHUBARB ALMOND PIE

You'll find Danish-style dessert mix in the baking section of your grocery store. Choose between the raspberry and strawberry flavors.

- 1 4¾-ounce package Danish-style dessert mix
- ¼ cup sugar
- 4 cups rhubarb cut into 1-inch pieces
- 1 8-ounce package cream cheese, softened
- ¼ cup sugar
- 1 tablespoon milk
- ½ teaspoon vanilla
- ¼ cup toasted, slivered almonds
- 1 9-inch baked pastry shell

Prepare mix according to package directions. Cover the surface with waxed paper; set aside. Bring ¼ cup sugar and 1 cup *water* to boiling; add rhubarb. Return to boiling; reduce heat. Simmer, covered, 4 to 5 minutes or till just tender. Carefully remove with a slotted spoon; set aside.

Beat the cream cheese, ¼ cup sugar, milk, and vanilla till fluffy. Fold in almonds. Spread over bottom and sides of pastry. Spoon *half* of the glaze over cheese layer. Arrange rhubarb over. Pour on remaining glaze. Chill. Before serving, sprinkle with additional almonds, if desired. Makes 8 servings.

RHUBARB CUSTARD PIE

- 4 cups fresh rhubarb cut into ½-inch pieces
- 1 unbaked 9-inch pastry shell
- 1 cup sugar
- 1 tablespoon all-purpose flour
- ¼ teaspoon ground nutmeg
- 4 slightly beaten eggs

Place rhubarb in pastry shell. Combine sugar, flour, and nutmeg. Add eggs; beat well. Pour into pastry shell.

To prevent overbrowning, cover edge with foil. Bake in 375° oven 25 minutes. Remove foil; bake 20 minutes or till nearly set (pie appears soft in center but sets upon cooling). Cool. Cover; store in refrigerator. Top with whipped cream, if desired. Serves 8.

RHUBARB LATTICE PIE

- 1¼ cups sugar
- ⅓ cup all-purpose flour
- Dash salt
- 4 cups rhubarb cut into 1-inch pieces
- Pastry for a 2-crust 9-inch pie
- 2 tablespoons butter *or* margarine
- Milk
- Sugar

Combine 1¼ cups sugar, flour, and salt. Stir in rhubarb pieces. Let mixture stand for 15 minutes.

Meanwhile, prepare pastry and roll out *half* of it; line a 9-inch pie plate. Trim pastry to edge of plate. Transfer rhubarb mixture to pie plate. Dot with butter or margarine.

Roll out remaining pastry; cut into six ¾-inch-wide strips. Weave strips on top of filling to make a loose lattice crust. Cut remaining pastry into ¾-inch squares. Moisten edge of pastry; overlap the squares around rim of dish, pressing to seal.

Brush the pastry with milk; sprinkle with additional sugar. To prevent overbrowning, cover edge of pie with foil. Bake in a 375° oven 25 minutes. Remove foil; bake about 25 minutes more or till golden. Serve warm or cool. Makes 8 servings.

Photograph: Ernie Block

E ven folks with a brown thumb can raise perennial rhubarb! You'll have the best luck starting your rhubarb with roots purchased from a reliable nursery, or take root divisions from an established clump. Plant the rhubarb in full sun. Keep weeds under control, especially during the first year.

RHUBARB LATTICE PIE

GLAZED RHUBARB ALMOND PIE

RHUBARB CUSTARD PIE

FISH
FAST AND EASY TO FIX!

SOLE

delicate taste and texture

firm texture; mild taste

ROCKFISH

chewy, snowy white flesh

WHITEFISH

gray flesh; chewy

TILEFISH

tender with mild flavor

COD

By Joy Taylor

Broil it! Poach it! Micro-cook it! These healthful and simple cooking methods are ideal for fish—and for your family's meals. Nationwide, an impressive variety of fresh and frozen fish is now available. And here, you'll learn how to prepare fish with the greatest of ease. For perfect results, follow our tips to prepare your prized purchase or catch.

Photographs: Ron Crofoot
Food stylist: Judy Tills

Italian-Style Fish with Stuffed Squash

◄ GRILL-OUT

While grilling, use butter or a marinade to keep the fish moist and prevent sticking.

OH, SO LEAN!

One 3-ounce serving of a whitefish such as flounder (brushed lightly with butter while cooking) contains less than 200 calories! And it adds only 78 mg cholesterol and 201 mg sodium to your diet.

Citrus Fish Steaks with Fruit Kabobs

After marinating, save the seasoned liquid to brush on the fish during cooking.

▲ MARINATE

A marinade serves two roles: it enhances taste and adds juiciness—without adding many calories. Marinate fresh or frozen fish for several hours in the refrigerator and turn the portions often so all sides absorb the marinade. Allow extra time when marinating frozen fish; the fish needs to partially thaw before it acquires the marinade flavor.

Use a dinner fork as described below to check if the fish is done.

▲ TEST FLAKINESS

To test fish for doneness, place the tines of a table fork into the fish flesh at a 45-degree angle; gently twist the fork and pull up some of the flesh. Fish that flakes easily is properly cooked. If the flesh resists flaking, the fish is not done. Overcooking results in mealy, tough, dry fish.

Also, *look* at the fish—undercooked fish is translucent; cooked fish is opaque. Rely more on the eye test for firm-fleshed fish, such as halibut and swordfish, which do not flake as easily as soft-fleshed fish.

BROIL IT!

Nothing is easier than broiling a steak, fish steak (and fillets) included! The secret to ensuring moistness is to brush the fish occasionally with melted butter, oil, or a marinade while it's broiling. Fish cooks so quickly that portions less than 1 inch thick never need to be turned while broiling.

Grilling is a natural for fish, too, because it seals in flavor and moistness just as broiling does.

FISH
FAST AND EASY TO FIX!

slightly oily taste; soft texture

BUTTERFISH

BLUEFISH

chewy, firm, and moist; gray flesh

RED SNAPPER

rich, sweet taste; firm flesh

CATFISH

very soft, moist flesh; doesn't "flake"

1 Cut along the backbone.

2 Pull away the skin.

3 Remove the top layer of fish.

4 Discard the backbone.

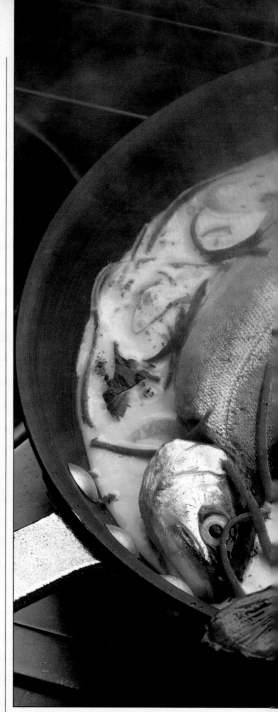

◄ SERVING SAVVY

Whether you're enjoying a single-serving-size cooked fish, or serving a crowd-size salmon, skin and bone a whole fish following these steps:

1 Using the tip of a dinner knife, cut along the center of the backbone from the head to the tail.

2 Using the knife and a fork, loosen and carefully pull the skin toward the stomach to peel it off.

3 With the fork, lift the top piece of fish away from the backbone, and place it on your plate.

4 Pull away the thick backbone and discard. This will expose the bottom layer of fish. Now, enjoy!

Milk-Poached Trout

Add dry sherry and paprika to further flavor and color the poaching liquid.

▲ MAKE A SAUCE

Herbs and vegetables season this poaching liquid. After cooking the fish, make a sauce: strain the broth, return it to the heat, and thicken or reduce it.

CATCHY NAMES

Shopping for fish isn't as much fun as going fishing—but it's quicker! Buy fish with these terms in mind:

Drawn fish: A whole fish minus the internal organs.

Dressed fish: An eviscerated fish with the head, tail, and fins removed. (*Pan-dressed* refers to a small fish.)

Fish steak: A crosscut slice (½ to 1 inch thick) from a large, dressed fish.

Fish fillet: A boneless piece of fish cut lengthwise from the sides and away from the backbone.

POACH IT!

Poaching is as easy as boiling water; all you do is cook fish in a gently boiling liquid such as broth, wine, beer, or, in this case, milk. An oblong fish poacher is handy, but any skillet or roasting pan that's large enough to hold the fish will do. When the liquid (about 1 to 2 inches deep) just begins to simmer (small bubbles appear over the surface), add whole dressed fish, steaks, or fillets. Simmer, covered, till the fish tests done.

MINUTES COUNT

To perfectly cook fish, use these approximate timings in addition to the fork test described on page 51. For complete broiling, grilling, baking, and poaching directions, see page 55.

For fresh fillets and steaks: broil, grill, bake, or poach *4 to 6 minutes* for every half-inch of thickness.

For fresh whole dressed fish: bake or poach the fish *6 to 9 minutes* for every half pound..

Tips: Preheat the broiler or oven; bring the poaching liquid to boiling before adding the fish; timings vary for frozen fish.

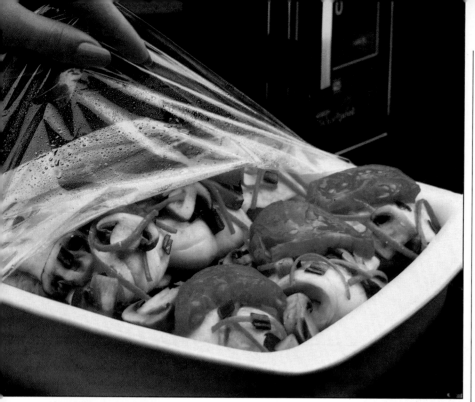

Vegetable-Topped Fillets

MICRO-COOK IT!

For moist, tender fish, the microwave is a sure bet. Micro-cook the fish on HIGH, covered with vented plastic wrap, just till the edges of the fish are done and the center remains slightly translucent. Let the fish stand a few minutes to finish cooking, then uncover and serve.

COHO SALMON — orange/pink flesh; very rich flavor

PIKE — soft flesh; moist, delicate taste

MACKEREL — bold flavor; dark flesh

Fold under only the thin edges.

▲ EVEN COOKING

When micro-cooking fish fillets, turn under any thin portions of the fillets so that the thickness is the same in all pieces. Evenly space the fish in a micro-proof dish.

SERVING-SIZE

How much fish you serve each family member depends on the form of fish. Allow these amounts per serving:
- 8 to 12 ounces dressed fish
- 3 to 4 ounces fish fillets or steaks

FISH
FAST AND EASY TO FIX!

Buying fish

Shopping for fish is as easy as fixing it. Just remember to rely on your nose. Avoid buying any fish with a strong or "fishy" odor. Fresh fish has very little odor.

When buying fresh fish, rely on the expertise of the "fishermen" behind the counter at a fish market or supermarket. They can tell you when the fish was delivered to the store, what part of the world it came from, and what the fish tastes like. They also can suggest fish substitutes when they don't have the variety you had in mind. With over 500 fish and seafood species available in the United States, there's a lot to choose from! When you shop for fresh drawn or dressed fish, consider these characteristics of good quality:
- *Skin*—Shiny, taut skin and bright colors indicate freshness. As a fish begins to deteriorate, the colors fade.
- *Flesh*—When you lightly press the flesh of a fresh fish with your finger, it springs back and feels firm and elastic.
- *Eyes*—Clear, bright, bulging eyes spell freshness. Avoid fish with dull, bloody, or sunken eyes.
- *Gills*—If the gills have not been removed, check to see that they are red and not slippery. As a fish loses quality, the red gills fade in color.

When you shop for fresh fillets or steaks, press the flesh and use your nose to check for freshness. Also, look for moist edges.

Today, you can buy frozen fish that's just as fresh, nutritious, and delicious as fresh-caught. In many cases, fish are cleaned and flash-frozen on board the fishing vessel minutes after being caught. When you shop for frozen fish, look for these characteristics of good quality:
- *Packaging*—Avoid packages that are misshapen, have torn wrappers, or have frost or blood visible inside or out.
- *Temperature*—Check that the package is frozen solid. Frozen fish should be kept at 0° F. or colder.

Types of Fish

Fish fall into one of two categories—lean or fat. All can be prepared any way you choose, provided you use the fat content to determine how best to cook them.

Lean fish with less than 5 percent fat poach well because the liquid keeps them from drying out. When baking, broiling, micro-cooking, or grilling lean varieties, brush them with a sauce, butter, or margarine to replenish moisture. For lean fish, select from Alaska pollock, Atlantic pollock, Atlantic and Pacific cod, croaker, flounder, grouper, haddock, hake, halibut, ocean catfish, ocean perch, orange roughy, sea bass, sea trout, sole, and whiting.

Those fish higher in fat can withstand broiling, grilling, and baking without losing flavor or texture—and without basting. Lake and rainbow trout, whitefish, eel, herring, mackerel, pompano, salmon, and tuna are high-fat varieties.

Storing Fish

The sooner after the catch fresh fish is cooked, the better. And the faster fresh-caught fish is refrigerated or frozen, the more you'll enjoy your fish.

Refrigerator storage: Wrap the uncooked fish loosely in plastic wrap. Cook the fish within 2 days of catch or purchase. Use fish thawed in refrigerator within 2 days. Store leftover cooked fish in foil or a plastic bag in the refrigerator and use within 2 days.

Freezer storage: Store fish at 0° F. or lower in moisture- and vaporproof wrap. Keep fat fish for no more than 3 months, lean fish up to 6 months.

To thaw fish for cooking with a sauce or stuffing, place fish in the refrigerator for 6 to 8 hours. Fish that is left at room temperature either on the counter or in water will not thaw evenly and may spoil.

When poaching, micro-cooking, or baking fish, there's no need to thaw. Do thaw for grilling, broiling, and stuffing. Never refreeze thawed fish.

Cooking Methods

Fish is among the most delicate of foods. It cooks quickly with a minimum of preparation. Although the general cooking guidelines on pages 50 to 54 are useful, actual cooking time depends on the heat setting and the starting temperature and texture of the fish.

Cooking times for fillets and steaks depend on thickness; cooking times for whole dressed fish depend on weight. Check the fish at the minimum cooking time and frequently after that because fish can easily become overcooked.

To bake fillets and steaks: Preheat the oven to 450°. Place fish fillets or steaks, skin side down, in a single layer in a shallow, greased baking pan. Tuck under thin edges to make an even layer. Brush with melted butter or margarine. Season with salt and pepper.

Bake, uncovered, in a 450° oven till fish flakes easily when tested with a fork. Allow 4 to 6 minutes for each ½ inch of thickness. If fish is 1 inch thick, turn over halfway through baking.

Note: For frozen fish fillets or steaks, allow 9 to 11 minutes baking time for each ½ inch of thickness.

To bake dressed fish: Place fish in a greased baking pan. Brush outside and cavity of fish with butter and season with salt and pepper. Bake, uncovered, in a 350° oven till fish flakes easily when tested with a fork. Allow 6 to 9 minutes for each half pound.

To poach fillets and steaks: Place fish in simmering liquid such as broth or wine. Bring to boiling; reduce heat. Cover and simmer till fish flakes easily when tested with a fork. Allow 4 to 6 minutes for each ½ inch of thickness. Remove fish with a slotted spoon. Use the poaching liquid to make a sauce.

Note: For frozen fish fillets or steaks, allow 6 to 9 minutes poaching time per ½ inch of thickness.

To poach dressed fish: Place fish in a large roasting pan or fish poaching pan. Pour in enough water, broth, wine, or combination of liquids to cover half of the fish. Remove fish. Bring liquid to boiling.

Carefully add fish. Return to boiling; reduce heat. Cover and simmer till fish flakes easily when tested with a fork. Allow 6 to 9 minutes cooking time for each half pound.

To broil fillets and steaks: Preheat the broiler. Place fish in a single layer on the greased rack of an unheated broiler pan. Tuck under thin edges of fish. Brush with butter and season.

Broil 4 inches from heat till fish flakes easily when tested with a fork. Allow 4 to 6 minutes for each ½ inch of thickness. Turn once during cooking if fish is 1 inch or thicker.

Note: For frozen fish fillets or steaks, allow 6 to 9 minutes broiling time for each ½ inch of thickness.

To grill fillets and steaks: Place fish in a well-greased wire grill basket or directly on the greased grill. Steaks can be turned easily without a basket, but fillets may break apart if turned.

Grill over *medium-hot* coals till fish flakes easily when tested with a fork. Allow 4 to 6 minutes for each ½ inch of thickness. Turn over the grill basket halfway through grilling.

Note: Frozen fish are not recommended for grilling.

CITRUS FISH STEAKS

Be sure to marinate frozen fish for at least 8 hours. It takes this long for the fish to thaw and begin absorbing the marinade flavor. To cut this time in half, you can thaw the fish in the micro-wave oven first—

- 3 **fresh *or* frozen salmon, halibut, shark, *or* swordfish steaks, cut 1 inch thick (about 1½ pounds)**
- 1 **grapefruit**
- ¼ **cup dry white wine**
- 2 **tablespoons snipped parsley**
- 2 **tablespoons cooking oil**
- 1 **green onion, sliced**
- 1 **teaspoon dried marjoram, crushed**
- ½ **teaspoon paprika**
Cooking oil
- 1 **recipe Fruit Kabobs (optional, see recipe at right)**

Arrange fish steaks in a shallow dish. Finely shred enough grapefruit peel to make *1 teaspoon.* Halve grapefruit. Squeeze out juice (should have ⅔ cup).

For marinade, combine grapefruit peel, juice, wine, parsley, cooking oil, green onion, marjoram, and paprika. Pour over fish. Marinate fresh fish in the refrigerator, covered, for 4 to 6 hours. (Or, for frozen fish steaks, marinate overnight.)

Drain fish, reserving marinade. To prevent fish from sticking, brush the rack of an unheated broiler pan with cooking oil. Place fish on rack. (Or, place in a greased shallow baking pan.) Brush fish with reserved marinade.

Broil fish 4 inches from heat till fish flakes easily when tested with a fork. Allow 4 to 6 minutes for each side. Using a wide spatula, carefully turn fish when half done. Brush often with marinade to prevent drying out. Broil Fruit Kabobs with fish as directed in kabob recipe. Serve immediately. Makes 3 servings.

Grilling directions: Marinate fish steaks as directed above. Drain fish, re-serving marinade. Brush grill with cooking oil. Place fish steaks on the grill or in a grill basket over *medium-hot* coals. Brush with marinade.

Cover and grill fish about 6 min-utes or till light brown. Brush with marinade. Using a wide spatula, care-fully turn the steaks. Grill, covered, about 6 minutes more or till fish flakes easily when tested with a fork, brush-ing often with the marinade.

Citrus Fish Fillets: Substitute 1 pound *fish fillets* such as sole, flounder, red snapper, *or* trout for the fish steaks. Cut fillets into 4 or 6 serving-size por-tions. Marinate fillets in the refrigera-tor for 2 to 4 hours.

Place fillets in a single layer on a greased rack of an unheated broiler pan or in a greased baking pan. Tuck under any thin edges. Brush fish with marinade.

Broil fish 4 inches from heat till fish flakes easily when tested with a fork; allow 4 to 6 minutes for each ½ inch of thickness. Brush fish with mari-nade during cooking to prevent drying. If fish is more than 1 inch thick, turn when half done.

Per serving: 481 cal., 48 g pro., 8 g carbo., 28 g fat, 146 mg chol., 125 mg sodium. USRDA: 25% vit. A, 50% vit. C, 13% thiamine, 11% riboflavin, 95% niacin, 12% iron, 49% phosphorus.

FRUIT KABOBS

- 1 **small apple, cored and cut into wedges**
- 1 **small pear, cored and cut into wedges**
Lemon juice
- 1 **cup fresh pineapple chunks *or* one 8¼-ounce can pineapple chunks**
Orange marmalade *or* pineapple preserves

Brush cut sides of apple and pear with lemon juice. Alternate the apple, pear, and pineapple on 4 wooden skewers. Brush with marmalade.

Broil kabobs alongside fish 4 inch-es from heat for 5 to 8 minutes or till heated through and slightly tender; turn once. Makes 3 servings.

Per serving: 118 cal., 1 g pro., 30 g carbo., 1 g fat, 4 mg sodium.

ITALIAN-STYLE FISH

Use the herb butter on broiled fish, too—

- 4 **fresh *or* frozen halibut, salmon, shark, *or* swordfish steaks, cut 1 inch thick (about 2 pounds)**
- ½ **cup butter *or* margarine**
- 2 **tablespoons snipped parsley**
- 1 **tablespoon snipped fresh basil *or* 1 teaspoon dried basil, crushed**
- 2 **teaspoons lemon juice**
Cooking oil
- 1 **recipe Stuffed Squash (optional, see recipe at right)**

Thaw fish, if frozen. In a small mixing bowl beat together butter or marga-rine, parsley, basil, and lemon juice.

To prevent the fish from sticking, brush the grill with cooking oil. Place fish steaks on the grill or in a grill bas-ket over *medium-hot* coals. Brush fish lightly with some of the butter mixture.

Cover and grill fish about 6 min-utes or till light brown. Brush steaks with butter mixture. Using a wide spat-ula, carefully turn the steaks. Grill, covered, about 6 minutes more or till fish flakes easily when tested with a fork, brushing often with the butter mixture.

Before serving, top each fish steak with a dollop of the remaining butter mixture. Grill Stuffed Squash along-side fish steaks as directed in the squash recipe. Serve immediately. Makes 4 servings.

Per serving: 618 cal., 48 g pro., 0 g carbo., 49 g fat, 216 mg chol., 403 mg sodium. USRDA: 42% vit. A, 11% thia-mine, 94% niacin, 48% phosphorus.

STUFFED SQUASH

2 medium zucchini
1 large tomato, cut into 8 wedges
2 teaspoons snipped chives
½ teaspoon garlic salt
½ cup shredded cheddar cheese (2 ounces)

Tear off two 18-inch-square pieces of heavy-duty foil. Fold each piece in half.

Make 4 crosswise V-shape grooves about ¼ inch wide in each zucchini, cutting to, but not through, the opposite side. Place a zucchini on each piece of foil. Place a tomato wedge in each zucchini groove. Sprinkle each zucchini with chives and garlic salt. Fold edges of foil to enclose vegetables, leaving space for expansion of steam.

Grill over *medium-hot* coals about 30 minutes. Roll foil back around zucchini. Carefully puncture bottom of foil packet with a fork to release excess liquid. Sprinkle cheese over top of each. To serve, cut through each zucchini. Makes 4 servings.

Per serving: 80 cal., 5 g pro., 5 g carbo., 5 g fat, 14 mg chol., 332 mg sodium. USRDA: 17% vit. A, 42% vit. C, 13% calcium, 10% phosphorus.

CLAM SAUCE

¼ cup thinly sliced celery
1 tablespoon butter *or* margarine
2 teaspoons cornstarch
1 6½-ounce can minced clams, drained
1 6-ounce can hot-style vegetable juice cocktail
1 tablespoon snipped parsley

In a saucepan cook celery in butter or margarine till tender. Stir in cornstarch. Stir in clams, vegetable juice cocktail, and parsley. Cook and stir till thickened and bubbly. Cook and stir for 2 minutes more. Serve hot with fish. Makes 1 cup.

Per 2 tablespoons: 32 cal., 2 g pro., 2 g carbo., 2 g fat, 12 mg chol., and 83 mg sodium.

MILK-POACHED TROUT

2 6- to 8-ounce fresh *or* frozen pan-dressed trout
¾ cup milk
½ cup water
¼ cup celery leaves
1 small onion, sliced into rings
1 small carrot, sliced into thin julienne strips
2 sprigs parsley
4 peppercorns
¾ teaspoon dried dillweed
½ teaspoon salt
⅛ teaspoon pepper
1 tablespoon cold water
1½ teaspoons cornstarch
1 tablespoon dry sherry
⅛ teaspoon paprika

Let frozen fish stand at room temperature about 20 minutes. In a 10-inch skillet combine milk, ½ cup water, celery leaves, onion, carrot, parsley, peppercorns, dillweed, salt, and pepper. Bring to boiling; reduce heat. Cover and simmer for 10 minutes.

Place fish in simmering broth. Return to boiling; reduce heat. Simmer, covered, 12 minutes or till fish flakes easily when tested with a fork. (Allow 5 to 10 minutes more for frozen fish.) Remove from skillet. Cover; keep warm.

For sauce, line a sieve with a small piece of cheesecloth. Pour the cooking liquid through sieve. Return ½ *cup* of the strained liquid to a small saucepan (add water, if necessary). Combine 1 tablespoon cold water and cornstarch. Stir into the strained liquid. Cook and stir till thickened and bubbly. Cook and stir for 2 minutes more. Remove from heat. Stir in sherry and paprika.

To serve, pull away fins from each fish. Arrange each on a dinner plate. Spoon some sauce onto each dinner plate by fish. Pass remaining sauce.

To eat, cut along the center of the backbone from head to tail with the tip of a sharp knife. The knife tip should just touch the rib cage. Peel off the top skin, pulling toward the belly. Run a fork along the backbone over ribs and under meat; lift off top half of fish. Pull away backbone and discard. Turn over the bottom half of the trout; remove skin. Makes 2 servings.

Per serving: 246 cal., 21 g pro., 15 g carbo., 10 g fat, 60 mg chol., 665 mg sodium. USRDA: 124% vit. A, 19% vit. C, 13% thiamine, 18% riboflavin, 15% niacin, 17% calcium, 35% phosphorus.

VEGETABLE-TOPPED FILLETS

1 pound fresh *or* frozen fish fillets (sole, flounder, orange roughy, *or* haddock)
¼ teaspoon garlic powder
1 cup sliced fresh mushrooms
½ cup julienne carrot strips
1 green onion, sliced
1 tablespoon butter *or* margarine
1 small tomato

Arrange fish fillets in a 12x7½x2-inch nonmetal baking dish. Sprinkle with salt, pepper, and garlic powder. For even cooking, turn under any thin portions so fillets are all about the same thickness.

In a 1½-quart nonmetal casserole combine mushrooms, carrot strips, green onion, and butter or margarine. Micro-cook, covered, on 100% power (HIGH) for 2 to 3 minutes or till onion is tender.

Meanwhile, rub the back of a knife across tomato skin to loosen. Peel and slice. Spoon vegetable mixture over fillets. Arrange tomato slices atop.

Cover with vented clear plastic wrap. Micro-cook on 100% power (HIGH) for 5 to 7 minutes or till fish is opaque, white, and tender when tested with a fork, rotating the dish a half-turn after 3 minutes. Let stand for 1 minute. Remove the clear plastic wrap. Makes 4 servings.

Per serving: 120 cal., 18 g pro., 4 g carbo., 4 g fat, 69 mg chol., 178 mg sodium. USRDA: 37% vit. A, 13% vit. C, 15% niacin, 25% phosphorus.

Lemon-Garlic Sauce (on fish), Sweet-Sour Sauce (front), Clam Sauce (center), and Tomato Dill Sauce (back).

TOMATO DILL SAUCE

Our taste panel suggested serving this full-flavored condiment with sea bass or other firm-flesh fish—

- ¼ cup chopped onion
- ½ teaspoon dried dillweed
- 1 tablespoon butter *or* margarine
- 1 7½-ounce can tomatoes, cut up
- 3 tablespoons chili sauce

In a small saucepan cook onion and dillweed in butter or margarine till onion is tender but not brown.

Stir in *undrained* tomatoes and chili sauce. Bring to boiling; reduce heat. Simmer, uncovered, for 5 to 7 minutes or till of the desired consistency. Serve hot with fish. Makes 1½ cups.

Per 2 tablespoons: 18 cal., 2 g carbo., 1 g fat, 3 mg chol., and 87 mg sodium.

HERBED SAUCE FOR FISH

Try this cousin of tartar sauce with hot or cold fish—

- ½ cup mayonnaise *or* salad dressing
- ½ cup dairy sour cream
- 2 tablespoons finely chopped sweet pickle
- 1 tablespoon sliced green onion
- 1 tablespoon snipped parsley
- ½ teaspoon dry mustard
- ½ teaspoon paprika
- ¼ teaspoon salt
Dash pepper

In a small mixing bowl combine all ingredients. Cover and chill thoroughly. Serve with fish. Makes about 1 cup.

Per 2 tablespoons: 135 cal., 1 g pro., 2 g carbo., 14 g fat, 16 mg chol., 183 mg sodium.

SWEET-SOUR SAUCE

Serve this Oriental-style condiment with the fish of your choice—

- ¼ cup packed brown sugar
- 2 teaspoons cornstarch
- ½ teaspoon sesame seed (optional)
- ⅓ cup chicken broth
- ¼ cup sliced green onions
- 3 tablespoons red wine vinegar
- 1 tablespoon soy sauce

In a small saucepan combine brown sugar; cornstarch; and sesame seed, if desired. Stir in chicken broth, green onions, wine vinegar, and soy sauce. Cook and stir till thickened and bubbly. Cook and stir for 2 minutes more. Serve hot with fish. Makes ¾ cup sauce.

Per 2 tablespoons: 44 cal., 11 g carbo., 1 mg chol., 263 mg sodium.

LEMON-GARLIC SAUCE

- ¼ cup sliced green onions
- 2 cloves garlic, minced
- ¼ teaspoon dried dillweed *or* tarragon, crushed
- 1 tablespoon olive oil
- 2 tablespoons all-purpose flour
- 1 cup fish broth *or* chicken broth*
- ⅓ cup dairy sour cream
- ½ teaspoon grated lemon peel
- ¼ teaspoon salt

In a saucepan cook green onions, garlic, and herb in oil till onion is tender but not brown. Stir in *1 tablespoon* of the flour. Add broth.

Stir remaining 1 tablespoon flour into sour cream. Add sour cream mixture, lemon peel, and salt to sauce. Cook and stir till thickened and bubbly. Cook and stir for 1 minute more. Serve hot with fish. Makes 1⅓ cups.

*Note: If using canned chicken broth, you may wish to decrease or omit the salt.

Per 2 tablespoons: 36 cal., 2 g carbo., 3 g fat, 3 mg chol., 164 mg sodium.

Herbed Sauce for Fish complements a chilled cooked fish and vegetables.

CHUTNEY MARINADE

Salmon steaks are just one choice for using this versatile marinade—

½ cup cooking *or* olive oil
⅓ cup white wine vinegar
¼ cup finely chopped chutney
1 green onion, thinly sliced
2 teaspoons curry powder
1 teaspoon sugar
¼ teaspoon salt
⅛ teaspoon ground red pepper
Fish fillets *or* steaks

For marinade, in a small mixing bowl combine oil, vinegar, chutney, green onion, curry powder, sugar, salt, and red pepper.

To marinate fish, place fish in a shallow baking dish. Pour marinade over fish. Cover and refrigerate for 4 to 6 hours or overnight, turning fish occasionally. Remove fish from marinade.

Broil or grill fish, brushing occasionally with marinade. Makes about 1 cup (enough for 2 pounds fish).

Per 2 tablespoons: 145 cal., 7 g carbo., 14 g fat, 83 mg sodium.

Save Chutney Marinade to brush over fish fillets or steaks during cooking.

ORIENTAL BASTE

Brush this sauce on fillets or steaks during grilling or broiling. Spoon more on before serving—

3 tablespoons butter *or* margarine
1 tablespoon soy sauce
1 tablespoon dry sherry
1 tablespoon vinegar
½ teaspoon sesame oil
⅛ teaspoon ground ginger

In a small saucepan melt butter or margarine. Remove from heat. Stir in remaining ingredients. Makes ⅓ cup.

Per 2 tablespoons: 360 cal., 4 g carbo., 37 g fat, 108 mg chol., 1740 mg sodium.

Oriental Baste seasons fish and keeps it moist during grilling or broiling.

RICE-STUFFED VEGETABLES

½ cup quick-cooking rice
½ teaspoon instant chicken bouillon granules
⅛ teaspoon fennel seed, crushed
½ cup boiling water
¼ cup shredded carrot
2 tablespoons thinly sliced green onion
½ cup shredded American cheese (2 ounces)
4 medium tomatoes *or* 2 green peppers

Combine rice, bouillon granules, and fennel seed. Pour boiling water over; let stand 5 minutes. Stir in carrot, green onion, and cheese.

Cut a thin slice off the top of each tomato. Using a spoon, hollow out the tomato, leaving a ¼-inch shell. (Or, cut peppers in half lengthwise. Remove seeds and membranes.) Spoon the hot rice mixture into each vegetable shell.

Place each stuffed vegetable on a large piece of heavy-duty foil. Fold edges of foil to enclose tomato, leaving space for expansion of steam.

Grill over *medium-hot* coals 20 to 25 minutes for tomatoes or till heated through; 30 to 45 minutes for the green pepper halves or till crisp-tender. To serve, roll foil back. Makes 4 servings.

Per serving: 121 cal., 5 g pro., 15 g carbo., 4 g fat, 13 mg chol., 227 mg sodium. USRDA: 35% vit. A, 37% vit. C, 12% calcium, 15% phosphorus.

Cook foil packets of Rice-Stuffed Vegetables alongside fish on the grill.

YORKSHIRE BEEF PIE

A take-off on the British classic Yorkshire Pudding, this main-dish beef pie sports a crust similar to a popover—

- ¾ pound ground beef
- 1 small onion, thinly sliced
- ½ cup cooked cut-up vegetables
- 1 10¼-ounce can beef gravy
- ½ cup water
- 1 tablespoon Worcestershire sauce
- 2 tablespoons butter *or* margarine
- 2 beaten eggs
- 1 cup milk
- 1 cup all-purpose flour
- ¼ teaspoon salt
- ⅛ teaspoon pepper

In a large skillet cook ground beef and onion till meat is brown and onion is tender; drain off fat. Add vegetables and ¼ *cup* of the beef gravy. Stir water and Worcestershire sauce into remaining gravy. Set aside.

In a 10-inch quiche or pie plate place butter or margarine and put in oven; set oven to 425°.

Meanwhile, in small mixer bowl combine eggs and milk. Add flour, salt, and pepper. Beat on low speed of an electric mixer till smooth.

Remove dish from oven. Pour egg mixture into hot dish. Spoon meat mixture evenly over bottom, keeping 1 inch from the edge. Bake for 25 to 30 minutes or till brown and puffed. Heat gravy mixture and pass with pie. Serve immediately. Makes 4 servings.

DATE MACAROON PIE

Orange slices decorate the top of this cheesecakelike pie pictured above—

- 1 3-ounce package cream cheese, softened
- 2 tablespoons sugar
- ¼ cup milk
- 1 cup crumbled soft macaroons (4 or 5 cookies)
- ½ cup chopped pitted dates
- ½ cup chopped pecans
- 1 cup whipping cream
- 1 9-inch graham cracker crumb pie shell
- 1 orange, peeled and sectioned

In a small mixer bowl combine cream cheese and sugar; beat on low speed of an electric mixer till mixed. Gradually add milk, beating till smooth. Stir in macaroons, dates, and pecans.

In a medium mixer bowl beat whipping cream till soft peaks form (tips curl). Fold whipped cream into cheese mixture. Transfer to pie shell. Chill in the refrigerator till firm. Before serving, garnish top of pie with orange slices. Makes 8 servings.

CRANBERRY ICE CREAM PIE

Ice cream and cranberry sauce star in this no-bake pie pictured above—

- 1 16-ounce can jellied cranberry sauce
- 1 baked 9-inch pastry shell
- 1 pint vanilla ice cream
- 1 4-serving-size package *instant* vanilla pudding mix
- ¼ cup frozen orange juice concentrate, thawed
- ½ cup whipping cream
- Ground nutmeg (optional)

Cut cranberry sauce crosswise into ½-inch-thick slices; arrange in the bottom of pastry shell, trimming slices to fit as necessary.

In a medium mixing bowl stir ice cream with a wooden spoon to soften. Add *dry* pudding mix and orange juice concentrate; mix well.

In a small mixer bowl beat whipping cream till soft peaks form (tips curl). Fold whipped cream into ice cream mixture; spoon over cranberry slices. Sprinkle with nutmeg, if desired.

Freeze pie till firm, several hours or overnight. Before serving, let frozen pie stand at room temperature for 10 to 15 minutes to soften. Makes 8 servings.

JUNE

June 1985 • $1.50

Better Homes
and Gardens.

Super Scrumptious
BERRIES 'N CREAM TORTE
You Make It In Minutes! See page 116

OUTDOOR
LIVING 15 Super New
Projects For Yard, Deck, Porch,
and Patio...BUILD 'EM,
ENJOY 'EM!

GOOD DESIGN
AT A **GOOD PRICE**
Snazzy NEW Bath
Accessories

CAMPING IN
AMERICA'S BEST
STATE PARKS

3 FABULOUS,
AFFORDABLE
FAMILY ROOM
ADD-ONS

BERRIES

By Nancy K. Wall

Photograph: de Gennaro Studios
Food stylist: Mable Hoffman

Strawberries, blueberries, raspberries, blackberries, boysenberries—any way you serve them, they make summer vibrant and fun. Add a natural freshness to summertime eating with these choose-a-berry dessert ideas.

BERRIES 'N' CREAM TORTE

Try your favorite purchased ice cream to shortcut this already quick dessert—

- 1 11-ounce package 3-inch soft cookies such as apple spice *or* oatmeal
- 1 recipe Strawberries 'n' Cream (see recipe, page 75)
- 1 recipe Strawberry Sauce
- 2 cups desired berries

Line a 1½-quart soufflé dish with plastic wrap, extending wrap 1 to 2 inches above dish. Gently press 7 or 8 cookies around side of dish, overlapping as necessary to form a scalloped edge. Place about *half* of the remaining cookies onto bottom of dish, breaking cookies as necessary to fit.

Stir ice cream to soften. Spoon *half* of the ice cream into dish. Place remaining cookies atop. Top with remaining ice cream. Cover; freeze 4 hours or till firm. To serve, lift out torte by pulling up on plastic wrap. Carefully remove plastic wrap; transfer with large spatulas to platter. Top with berries and sauce. Serves 8 to 10.

Strawberry Sauce: In a saucepan combine 3 tablespoons *sugar* and 2 teaspoons *cornstarch*. Stir in ½ cup *pineapple juice*. Cook and stir

Attention berry lovers! Choose from Berry Clafouti, Berries 'n' Cream Torte, and berries drenched in Almond Pudding.

till the mixture bubbles. Cook and stir 2 minutes more. Remove from heat; stir in 1 tablespoon *brandy* and several drops *red food coloring*. Cover surface with clear plastic wrap. Cool. Pour over berries on Berries 'n Cream Torte.

ALMOND PUDDING WITH BERRIES

Almond pudding and berries are naturally good together. Choose a pretty mixture of raspberries and blackberries for this one—

- ¼ cup sugar
- 2 teaspoons cornstarch
- 1½ cups milk
- 3 beaten egg yolks

- 2 tablespoons amaretto *or* ⅛ teaspoon almond extract
Desired berries

In a heavy small saucepan combine the sugar and cornstarch. Stir in the milk. Cook and stir over medium heat till thickened and bubbly. Cook 2 minutes more. Stir a little of the hot mixture into the yolks; return all to saucepan. Cook and stir till bubbly. Remove from heat. Stir in the amaretto.

Pour pudding into a medium bowl. Cover the surface with clear plastic wrap; chill. Serve the pudding spooned on top of desired berries. Makes 6 servings.

BERRY CLAFOUTI

Pancakelike clafouti is a simple French dessert. Top the batter with fresh berries before baking—

- 3 eggs
- 1¼ cups milk
- ⅔ cup all-purpose flour
- ⅓ cup sugar
- 2 teaspoons vanilla
- ¼ teaspoon nutmeg
- ⅛ teaspoon salt
- 1½ cups desired berries

In a small mixer bowl beat the eggs with electric mixer till foamy. Add remaining ingredients *except* the berries; beat on low speed till smooth. Pour batter into a buttered 9-inch quiche dish or pie plate. Top batter with berries. Bake in a 350° oven 40 to 45 minutes or till knife inserted off-center comes out clean. Let stand 15 minutes. Makes 8 servings.

BERRIES AT THEIR BEST

Berries are among the summer's favorite fruits. Serve them plain or added to breads, salads, sauces, pies, or other desserts.

- **Rinse berries with cool water just before serving.**

- **Refrigerate berries, lightly covered.**

- **Enjoy fresh-picked or purchased berries within three days.**

BRING ON THE BARBECUE

TWO EXPERTS SHARE THEIR SECRET RECIPES

 By Nancy K. Wall

North, south, east, west—everyone loves barbecue! But
the South claims it has the best barbecue
around. We visited award-winning backyard chefs in
Memphis—home of the International Barbecue Contest. Try their recipes in your own backyard.

BILL'S SUPER SAUCES

Bill Horrell, a veteran barbecue contestant, takes a strong stand on what constitutes "true" barbecue. "It's pork, slow-cooked outdoors, pure and simple," says Bill. Bill usually cooks a pork shoulder, but for smaller gatherings, he suggests cook-ing a Boston butt pork roast. "The flavor," Bill notes, "comes from the combination of the meat and the hickory smoke."

Bill has tested his cooking know-how in more than 50 southern barbecue contests! And from the first contest, called Dad's Cookout, the outdoor events have become a family affair. Cecelia, Bill's wife, helps with the preparation of the tasty sauces. Their 14-year-old son, Trey, serves his dad's prize pork to the judges and helps with the cleanup.

"There's no two bones about it; a great way to serve pork barbecue is on a bun with slaw, *Old-Style Potato Salad*, and *Favorite Baked Beans*," claims Bill.

"Even the hot sauce is not a scorcher," says Bill. "A touch of sweet comes first, then herbs and spices roll in, then the hot eases in, peaks, and rolls off." Bill prefers his meat without sauce so the smoked pork flavor predominates. For guests, he offers three sauces—*Sweet and Sour, Medium Hot*, and *Oh-So-Hot!*

Photographs: Jim Hedrich, Hedrich-Blessing

Bill credits much of his barbecue success to his father-in-law's secret *Basting Sauce.* To baste, use a sturdy brush (a new paintbrush will do) and slather sauce on every 30 minutes.

"The meat is done when you can gently pull it apart into bite-sized pieces," explains Bill. "The job is especially easy when you use tongs." Another way of serving the meat is to chop it into smaller pieces—some Southerners call it "chopped barbecue."

BRING ON THE
BARBECUE

RAY'S COUNTRY RIBS

Unless he serves blue-ribbon barbecue every time, Ray's not satisfied. His meat must be tender, flavorful, juicy, and mouth-watering to be a real winner. Ray's sauce has to be just right, too. "Without combining all five qualities, you come up short!" explains Ray.

The focal point of Ray's barbecue is his custom-made grill, 40 feet long and big enough to cook five whole hogs. While the grill is part of his "whole hog" success, it's the barbecue sauce that keeps the judges coming back. "My southern-style HOT sauce is based on whiskey, lemon, and a dash of red pepper. It's sure to make anyone's meat taste great!" exclaims Ray. "Another secret is that I use only top-quality ingredients." Ray even raises his own hogs and makes his own charcoal from the hickory trees that grow on his farm.

"I've been cooking barbecue for the family get-togethers ever since I was young," says Ray Jamieson, a busy attorney in Memphis. On weekends, Ray heads to his farm to cook the best pork ribs south of the Mason-Dixon line! "As a boy, summer fun meant a Tennessee country barbecue," Ray says. "Entertaining is my whole reason for barbecuing."

Ray always serves his favorite Old South recipes along with the barbecued meat. While Ray stands watch over the ribs, his friends join right in and help. Guests have fun shucking their own corn-on-the-cob as well as frying their own Cheese-and-Pepper Corn Cakes.

Guest participation is a must at Ray's gatherings.

MENU

Ray's Country Ribs
Roasted Corn on the Cob
Country-Style Turnip Greens
Cheese-and-Pepper Corn Cakes
Fresh Melon Salad
White Bean Soup
Breads
Southern Fried Peach Pies

BARBECUE BUTT ROAST

To test for medium heat, hold your hand palm down above the coals at the height the meat will be cooked. Count the seconds; you should need to remove your hand on the count of four—

 1 **4- to 6-pound pork shoulder blade Boston (butt) roast**
 2 **teaspoons garlic salt**
 2 **teaspoons garlic pepper**
 2 **teaspoons lemon pepper**
 1 **recipe Basting Sauce (see recipe at right)**
 12 **to 15 hamburger buns, split**
    Sweet-and-Sour Sauce, Medium Hot Sauce, *or* Oh-So-Hot Sauce (see recipes at right and on page 69)

Rub meat with garlic salt, garlic pepper, and lemon pepper. In a covered grill arrange preheated coals in a circle, leaving a hole in the center. Test for *medium* heat over the center where there are no coals.

Place meat on a rack in a shallow roasting pan; place the roasting pan on the grill over the center, not over coals. With a long-tined fork, pierce meat in several places. Brush with some of the Basting Sauce.

Lower the grill hood. Grill for 2 to 2½ hours or till meat thermometer registers 180°, brushing meat with sauce every 30 minutes. Add more coals as necessary.

Remove the roasting pan; drain off fat. Pour enough Basting Sauce into the pan to cover the bottom; cover with foil. Return the pan to the grill. Lower the hood. Grill meat for 1 to 1½ hours more or till it will shred; add more Basting Sauce after 1 hour to cover the bottom of the pan, if necessary.

Transfer meat to a large platter or board. Using meat forks, shred meat by gently pulling. Spoon shredded meat onto bottom half of each bun. If desired, top with slaw. Add your choice of Sweet-and-Sour Sauce, Medium Hot Sauce, or Oh-So-Hot Sauce and bun tops. Makes 12 to 15 servings.

Per serving of barbecued pork with Basting Sauce: 536 cal., 26 g pro., 23 g carbo., 37 g fat, 90 mg chol., 1,535 mg sodium. USRDA: 24% vit. C, 83% thiamine, 21% riboflavin, 36% niacin, 23% iron, 29% phosphorus.

MEDIUM HOT SAUCE

Lots of vegetables give a new twist to this barbecue sauce—

 ¾ **cup finely chopped fresh mushrooms**
 1 **medium onion, finely chopped (½ cup)**
 1 **medium green pepper, finely chopped (½ cup)**
 1 **stalk celery, finely chopped (½ cup)**
 5 **cloves garlic, minced**
 1 **tablespoon olive oil *or* cooking oil**
 1½ **cups tomato juice**
 1½ **cups bottled barbecue sauce**
 ½ **cup bottled hickory smoke-flavored barbecue sauce**

In a large saucepan cook mushrooms, onion, pepper, celery, and garlic in hot olive or cooking oil till tender but not brown. Stir in tomato juice, barbecue sauce, and smoke-flavored barbecue sauce. Bring to boiling; reduce heat.

Cover and simmer for 1 hour, stirring occasionally. Uncover and simmer about 50 minutes more or till sauce reaches desired consistency, stirring occasionally. Makes 3 cups sauce.

Per tablespoon: 15 cal., 0.3 g pro., 2 g carbo., 1 g fat, 102 mg sodium.

BASTING SAUCE

Southerners use a thin liquid, such as this lemon-flavored sauce, for brushing during cooking—

 3 **cups water**
 2 **tablespoons salt**
 ½ **teaspoon finely shredded lemon peel**
 2 **tablespoons lemon juice**
 1½ **teaspoons dried minced onion**
 1½ **teaspoons dried diced bell pepper**
 ½ **teaspoon garlic salt**
 ½ **teaspoon crushed red pepper**
 ½ **teaspoon garlic pepper**
 ½ **teaspoon lemon pepper**

In a large saucepan combine all ingredients. Bring to boiling; reduce heat. Simmer, covered, for 30 minutes. Stir before brushing. Makes about 3 cups.

SWEET-AND-SOUR SAUCE

Double this recipe, using an 8-ounce can of crushed pineapple. Store leftovers in the refrigerator for basting burgers—

 ½ **cup crushed pineapple (juice pack)**
 ½ **cup catsup**
 ½ **cup unsweetened pineapple juice**
 ¼ **cup packed brown sugar**
 ¼ **cup vinegar**

Place *undrained* pineapple in a blender container. Cover and blend till finely chopped. In a medium saucepan stir together pineapple, catsup, pineapple juice, brown sugar, and vinegar. Cook and stir just till mixture boils; reduce heat. Simmer, uncovered, about 5 minutes or until sauce reaches desired consistency. Makes 1⅔ cups.

Per tablespoon: 20 cal., 0 g pro., 5 g carbo., 0 g fat, 53 mg sodium.

OH-SO-HOT SAUCE

Crushed red pepper helps this sauce live up to its name—

- 1 **medium onion, finely chopped (½ cup)**
- 5 **cloves garlic, minced**
- 2 **tablespoons crushed red pepper**
- 1 **tablespoon olive oil *or* cooking oil**
- 1 **cup beef broth**
- 1 **6-ounce can tomato paste**
- ¾ **cup honey**
- 1 **teaspoon salt**
- 1 **teaspoon dried thyme, crushed**
- 1 **teaspoon dried oregano, crushed**
- 2 **bay leaves**

In a medium saucepan cook onion, garlic, and red pepper in hot oil till onion is tender but not brown. Stir in broth, tomato paste, honey, salt, thyme, oregano, and bay leaves. Bring to boiling; reduce heat. Simmer, uncovered, for 20 minutes. Strain through a sieve; discard solids. Makes 1⅔ cups.

Per tablespoon: 43 cal., 0.5 g pro., 10 g carbo., 0.6 g fat, 117 mg sodium.

FAVORITE BAKED BEANS

Bill says no barbecue get-together is complete without a pot of these all-time favorite beans—

- 3 **slices bacon, halved crosswise**
- 2 **16-ounce cans pork and beans in tomato sauce**
- 1 **cup packed brown sugar**
- 1 **cup catsup**
- 1 **medium onion, chopped (½ cup)**
- ¼ **cup Worcestershire sauce**
- 2 **tablespoons prepared mustard**

In a small skillet partially cook bacon; drain and set aside.

In a large mixing bowl stir together pork and beans, sugar, catsup, onion, Worcestershire sauce, and mustard. Tranfer mixture to a 2-quart casserole. Lay partially cooked bacon slices atop. Bake, uncovered, in a 350° oven about 2 hours or till of desired consistency. Makes 10 servings.

Per serving: 256 cal., 8 g pro., 49 g carbo., 4 g fat, 2 mg chol., 899 mg sodium. USRDA: 10% vit. A, 11% vit. C, 16% iron, 12% phosphorus.

OLD-STYLE POTATO SALAD

Mashing the potatoes slightly is an old-time trick that helps bring out more potato flavor—

- 5 **medium red potatoes, peeled and quartered (about 2 pounds)**
- 4 **hard-cooked eggs, chopped**
- ½ **cup chopped dill pickle**
- 1 **medium onion, chopped (½ cup)**
- ¼ **cup chopped celery**
- 1 **2-ounce jar diced pimiento, drained**
- ⅓ **cup mayonnaise *or* salad dressing**
- 2 **tablespoons tarragon vinegar**
- 2 **tablespoons prepared mustard**
- ¼ **teaspoon salt**
- ⅛ **teaspoon pepper**

Hard-cooked egg slices (optional)

In a large saucepan cook potatoes in boiling salted water, covered, about 20 minutes or until tender; drain. Mash potatoes *slightly*.

In a medium mixing bowl combine potatoes, 4 chopped hard-cooked eggs, dill pickle, onion, celery, and pimiento.

For dressing, in a small mixing bowl stir together mayonnaise or salad dressing, tarragon vinegar, mustard, salt, and pepper.

Add dressing to potato mixture. Stir gently to coat. Turn into a serving bowl. If desired, garnish with hard-cooked egg slices. Serve warm. Makes 10 servings.

Per serving: 153 cal., 5 g pro., 15 g carbo., 8 g fat, 106 mg chol., 494 mg sodium. USRDA: 36% vit. C.

RAY'S HOT SAUCE

Ray says the corn whiskey (which you'll find in any liquor store) gives this zippy sauce its Southern personality. It's different from most tomato-based sauces— it's savory, not sweet—

- 1 **large onion, chopped (1 cup)**
- 1 **medium green pepper, chopped (¾ cup)**
- ½ **stalk celery, chopped (¼ cup)**
- 2 **cloves garlic, minced**
- 2 **tablespoons butter *or* margarine**
- 1 **15-ounce can tomato-herb sauce**
- 1 **cup tomato juice**
- ½ **of a 6-ounce can (⅓ cup) tomato paste**
- 3 **to 4 tablespoons lemon juice**
- 1 **lemon slice**
- 2 **teaspoons crushed red pepper**
- ¼ **teaspoon pepper**

Few drops bottled hot pepper sauce
- ¼ **cup corn whiskey (optional)**

In a 3-quart saucepan cook chopped onion, green pepper, celery, and garlic in hot butter or margarine till vegetables are tender but not brown. Stir in the tomato-herb sauce, tomato juice, and tomato paste. Bring to boiling, then reduce heat. Simmer the mixture, uncovered, for 15 minutes.

Stir lemon juice, lemon slice, red pepper, pepper, and hot pepper sauce into the hot mixture. Cook, uncovered, for 15 minutes more. Stir in corn whiskey, if desired. Cover and cook about 5 minutes more or till the mixture is heated through.

Cool the sauce slightly. Strain through a sieve; discard solids. Brush sauce onto Ray's Country Ribs (see recipe, page 70). Makes about 2 cups.

Per tablespoon: 18 cal., 0.5 g pro., 3 g carbo., 1 g fat, 2 mg chol., 122 mg sodium. USRDA: 15% vit. C.

RAY'S COUNTRY RIBS

When the pork ribs are nearly done, reheat Ray's Hot Sauce on the side of the grill—

- 6 cups hickory wood chips
- 4 pounds pork loin back ribs
- 1 cup dry white wine
- 1 cup vinegar
- 1 cup water
- 1 medium onion, finely chopped (½ cup)
- 1 teaspoon pepper
- 1 recipe Ray's Hot Sauce (see recipe, page 69)

Soak wood chips in enough water to cover about 1 hour before cooking time.

Meanwhile, with a long-tined fork, pierce ribs all over. Place ribs in a roasting pan.

In a small mixing bowl stir together wine, vinegar, water, onion, and pepper. Pour over ribs. Cover; let stand at room temperature about 1 hour.

In a covered grill arrange preheated coals on both sides of a foil drip pan. Test for *slow* heat by holding hand over drip pan where ribs will be and counting the seconds you can hold position; count 6 seconds for slow coals. Drain the wood chips. Sprinkle some of the drained wood chips over the coals.

Drain ribs; reserve wine mixture for basting. Place ribs in a rib rack, if desired. Then, place ribs on the grill rack over the drip pan but not over the coals. Lower the grill hood. Grill for 45 minutes. Add more drained wood chips. Turn ribs and grill, covered, about 45 minutes more or till ribs are well-done, brushing with wine mixture during the last 20 minutes. Pass Ray's Hot Sauce with ribs. Makes 8 servings.

Per serving: 524 cal., 20 g pro., 4 g carbo., 45 g fat, 85 mg chol., 72 mg sodium. USRDA: 64% thiamine, 14% riboflavin, 26% niacin, 19% iron, 23% phosphorus.

COUNTRY-STYLE TURNIP GREENS

Long, slow simmering is the secret to the full-bodied flavors in this traditional vegetable dish—

- ½ pound sliced bacon
- 1 pound turnip greens *or* mustard greens
- 1 medium turnip
- 3 cups water
- 1 smoked *or* plain pork hock
- 1½ teaspoons sugar
- 1 teaspoon crushed red pepper
- ¼ teaspoon salt

In a large skillet cook bacon till crisp; drain, reserving drippings. Crumble bacon and set aside.

Discard stems of turnip or mustard greens and any damaged portions. Tear up any large leaves. Peel turnip and cut into bite-size pieces.

In a Dutch oven bring water to boiling. Add bacon, reserved drippings, turnip or mustard greens, turnip, pork hock, sugar, red pepper, and salt. Cover and simmer for 1½ hours. Uncover and simmer for 45 minutes more.

Remove pork hock. When it is cool enough to handle, cut meat from hock and return to greens mixture. Serve with a slotted spoon. Makes 8 servings.

Per serving: 310 cal., 10 g pro., 5 g carbo., 28 g fat, 42 mg chol., 605 mg sodium. USRDA: 86% vit. A, 138% vit. C, 31% thiamine, 19% riboflavin, 12% niacin, 15% calcium, 13% iron, 12% phosphorus.

ROASTED CORN ON THE COB

Fresh ears of corn
Butter *or* margarine
Salt
Pepper

Remove husks from corn. Remove silks with a stiff brush or by hand. Spread *each* ear with about *1 tablespoon* butter or margarine. Sprinkle corn with a little salt and pepper. Wrap securely in heavy-duty foil. Roast corn over *medium-hot* coals about 30 minutes or till corn is tender, turning several times.

Per ear of corn: 172 cal., 3 g pro., 16 g carbo., 12 g fat, 36 mg cholesterol, 1,846 mg sodium. USRDA: 16% vit. A, 12% vit. C.

FRESH MELON SALAD

Use cantaloupe, honeydew, or additional watermelon to make this cool, colorful salad—

- 1 small watermelon
- 4 cups assorted fresh melon balls
- ¼ cup melon liqueur *or* orange liqueur
- 3 tablespoons lime juice *or* lemon juice

If desired, hollow watermelon and cut edge of watermelon shell in a sawtooth design; set aside.

In a large mixing bowl combine melon balls, melon or orange liqueur, and lime or lemon juice. Cover and place in the refrigerator for 2 to 4 hours, stirring occasionally. To serve, fill melon shell with fruit mixture. Makes 8 servings.

Per serving: 105 cal., 2 g pro., 20 g carbo., 0.5 g fat, 12 mg sodium. USRDA: 30% vit. A, 72% vit. C.

WHITE BEAN SOUP

You can make a whole meal of this hearty bean soup—

2⅓ cups dry navy beans (1 pound)
  8 cups cold water
  6 cups cold water
  1 large onion, chopped (1 cup)
  1 stalk celery, chopped (½ cup)
  1 clove garlic, minced
  2 tablespoons butter *or* margarine
  1 meaty ham bone *or* 3 smoked
     pork hocks
 ¼ pound salt pork
  2 bay leaves
  4 teaspoons sugar
  1 teaspoon crushed red pepper

Rinse beans. In a heavy 3-quart saucepan combine beans and 8 cups cold water; cover and let stand overnight. (Or, bring mixture to boiling; reduce heat and simmer 2 minutes. Remove from heat. Cover and let stand 1 hour.)

Drain beans; rinse. Cover with 6 cups cold water. Bring beans and water to boiling; reduce heat. Cover and simmer for 1 hour.

Meanwhile, in a small saucepan cook onion, celery, and garlic in butter or margarine till onion is tender but not brown. Add onion mixture, ham bone or pork hocks, salt pork, bay leaves, sugar, and red pepper to the saucepan with beans. Bring to boiling; reduce heat. Cover and simmer 1 hour.

Remove salt pork and bay leaves; discard. Remove ham bone or pork hocks. When cool enough to handle, cut meat from bone; discard bone. Chop meat and return to bean mixture. Simmer bean mixture, uncovered, about 1 hour or till of desired consistency, stirring occasionally. Makes 12 side-dish servings (or 6 main-dish servings).

Per side-dish serving: 429 cal., 21 g pro., 26 g carbo., 27 g fat, 60 mg chol., 749 mg sodium. USRDA: 50% thiamine, 13% riboflavin, 19% niacin, 27% iron, 27% phosphorus.

CHEESE-AND-PEPPER CORN CAKES

Remember these peppery cheese-studded pancakes for a Southern-style brunch—

1½ cups cornmeal
 ¼ cup whole wheat flour
  2 teaspoons baking powder
 ½ teaspoon baking soda
 ½ teaspoon salt
  2 beaten eggs
1¼ cups buttermilk
 ½ cup cooking oil
  1 tablespoon honey
  1 8-ounce can cream-style corn
  1 4-ounce can green chili peppers,
     rinsed, seeded, and chopped
  1 cup sliced green onion
  1 cup shredded sharp cheddar
     cheese (4 ounces)

In a large mixing bowl stir together cornmeal, whole wheat flour, baking powder, soda, and salt.

In a medium mixing bowl combine eggs, buttermilk, oil, and honey. Stir in corn, chili peppers, green onion, and cheese. Add all at once to cornmeal mixture, stirring just till moistened.

For *each* pancake, spoon about ¼ *cup* of the cornmeal batter onto a hot, lightly greased griddle or skillet. Cook on each side for 2 to 3 minutes or till golden brown. Serve pancakes immediately. Makes 18 to 20.

Per cornmeal pancake: 161 cal., 4 g pro., 16 g carbo., 9 g fat, 36 mg chol., 232 mg sodium. USRDA: 11% vit. C, 10% phosphorus.

SOUTHERN FRIED PEACH PIES

When fresh peaches aren't available, you can substitute frozen unsweetened sliced peaches—

  3 cups sliced, peeled fresh
     peaches (about 5 peaches)
 ½ cup sugar
  2 tablespoons butter *or* margarine
1½ teaspoons vanilla
 ½ teaspoon ground nutmeg
1½ cups all-purpose flour
 ¾ teaspoon salt
 ½ cup lard *or* shortening
  5 tablespoons cold water
Shortening *or* cooking oil for
     shallow frying

For filling, in a large heavy saucepan combine peaches, sugar, butter or margarine, vanilla, and nutmeg. Bring to boiling; reduce heat. Simmer gently, uncovered, about 1 hour or till of jam consistency, stirring occasionally. Cool for 1 hour.

Meanwhile, for pastry, in a medium mixing bowl combine flour and salt. With a pastry cutter or 2 knives, cut in ½ cup lard or shortening till pieces are the size of small peas. Sprinkle *1 tablespoon* cold water over part of mixture; gently toss with a fork. Push to side of the bowl. Repeat till all is moistened. Form dough into a ball.

On a lightly floured surface, roll dough to ⅛-inch thickness. Cut dough into 5-inch circles. Place about *1 rounded tablespoon* of the cooled peach mixture on half of *each* circle. Fold circle in half over filling; seal well with the tines of a fork.

In a 12-inch skillet heat ¼ inch shortening or cooking oil till hot. Fry pies for 3 to 4 minutes or till golden, turning once. Drain on paper towels. Serve pies warm or cool. Makes 8 to 10 fried pies.

Per serving of peach pie: 304 cal., 3 g pro., 36 g carbo., 17 g fat, 9 mg chol., 236 mg sodium. USRDA: 19% vit. A, 11% thiamine.

ICE CREAM! ICE CREAM! WE ALL SCREAM FOR ICE CREAM!

By Diana McMillen

I DULGE!

Dip into one—or all—of our nine drippingly delicious flavors! They're the latest ice creams you can crank up at home. As a bonus, some recipes fit into the new smaller ice cream freezers and some don't need a machine at all! To complete this tasty project, we've supplied you with the necessary know-how on ice cream making.

Photograph: Jim Hedrich, Hedrich-Blessing
How-to photographs: George Ceolla. Food stylist: Fran Paulson

FROZEN TROPICAL PARADISE

CAFÉ AU LAIT SHERBET

DOUBLE CHOCOLATE CHUNK ICE CREAM

STRAWBERRIES 'N' CREAM

THE REAL STUFF!
HOMEMADE ICE CREAM

GETTING STARTED: ICE CREAM MAKING

Pour ice cream ingredients into a freezer can to no more than ⅔ capacity. Under-filling the can allows room for your ice cream mixture to expand as air is beaten into it and for the ice cream to get creamy and fluffy.

Fit can into freezer bucket. Adjust dasher (the paddle) to stand up straight; cover with lid. Now, add layers of crushed ice and rock salt to outer container. (Use 6 cups ice to 1 cup salt.)
continued

GRANOLA
SUNDAE
SCOOP

VERY
BOYSENBERRY
SORBET

PEANUT BUTTER
'N' JELLY
ICE CREAM

APPLE-PIE-
IN-A-SCOOP

GINGERBREAD
COOKIE
ICE CREAM

THE REAL STUFF!

HOMEMADE ICE CREAM!

STEP 2

FREEZING THE ICE CREAM

Fit the handle or motor into place; secure. For hand-crank machines, turn the handle till there's a slight pull, then gradually turn it faster. Continue until turning becomes impossible. Add some ice and salt occasionally as the ice melts. (It takes 20 to 30 minutes before the ice cream is ready—no matter what size ice cream freezer you use.)

Remove the ice to below the level of the can lid so that no salty ice can seep into the can. Wipe the can and lid with a damp cloth to remove salt. Remove lid and dasher; scrape ice cream from the dasher back into the can.

STEP 3

GETTING GOOD TEXTURE

Don't eat the ice cream yet! It needs to ripen. This is how it gets a creamy texture. Some say ripening is the hardest part—it means you have to wait!

To ripen the ice cream, cover can with waxed paper or foil and plug hole in lid with a cork. Cover can with lid. Return to freezer bucket. Next, pack additional layers of ice and salt into outer container; this time, use 4 cups ice to 1 cup salt. (You need more salt here because you want the ice cream to get cold and to harden.) Cover freezer with a heavy cloth or newspapers to keep it cold. Ripen 4 hours.

STEP 4

IT'S READY!

Uncover; remove ice to below the level of can lid of the ice cream freezer. Wipe can and lid to remove salt and ice. Remove lid.

Now, dig in!

INDULGE!

GET YOUR LICKS!

Whether you stir up homemade ice cream the old-fashioned way with a hand-crank freezer, or use one of the gourmet electric ice cream makers, the basics are the same.

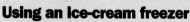

Using an ice-cream freezer

You'll have creamier ice cream when you use an ice cream freezer versus placing it in a refrigerator-freezer. The paddling motion helps smaller ice crystals form, creating a smooth dessert. Paddling also beats air into the mixture, adding smoothness and volume.

Combining salt and ice

Use rock salt and crushed ice according to the proportions specified in the step-by-step instructions above. Combining these two ingredients lowers the freezing temperature and freezes your ice cream fast while it's being beaten with the paddle.

Why is it smooth?

The more butterfat in the ice cream itself, the creamier it will feel on your tongue. Milk and cream contain the butterfat that makes for a smooth frozen dessert. That's why ice cream tends to be smoother than no-milk or low-milk sherbet.

STRAWBERRIES 'N' CREAM

This recipe fills the Berries 'n' Cream Torte pictured on pages 61 and 62—

- 1 14-ounce can (1¼ cups) *sweetened condensed* milk
- ⅓ cup lemon juice
- 1 pint fresh strawberries, mashed (1 cup)
- 1 cup whipping cream
- ½ cup coarsely chopped almonds, toasted

In a large mixing bowl combine milk and lemon juice; stir just till mixture begins to thicken. Stir in strawberries.

In a medium mixer bowl beat cream just till it mounds. Fold whipped cream into strawberry mixture. Freeze in refrigerator-freezer till firm.

Break frozen mixture into chunks with a wooden spoon; transfer to a chilled large mixer bowl. Beat with an electric mixer till smooth. Fold in nuts. Makes 1 quart ice cream.

Per ½-cup serving: 370 cal., 8 g pro., 43 g carbo., 20 g fat, 56 mg chol., 86 mg sodium. USRDA: 13% vit. A, 46% vit. C, 23% riboflavin, 23% calcium, 21% phosphorus.

APPLE-PIE-IN-A-SCOOP

You won't even miss a piecrust—

- 1¼ cups sugar
- ¼ cup all-purpose flour
- 4 cups milk
- 4 beaten eggs
- 4 cups whipping cream
- 1 21-ounce can apple pie filling
- 3 tablespoons vanilla
- 1 teaspoon ground cinnamon

In a large saucepan combine sugar and flour. Stir in milk. Cook and stir till slightly thickened and bubbly. Stir about *1 cup* of the hot mixture into eggs. Return all to saucepan. Cook and stir 2 minutes more. Cover and chill.

Stir whipping cream, pie filling, vanilla, and cinnamon into chilled mixture. Freeze in a 4- or 5-quart ice cream freezer according to manufacturer's directions. Makes 4 quarts ice cream.

Per ½-cup serving: 346 cal., 5 g pro., 33 g carbo., 23 g fat, 138 mg chol., 68 mg sodium. USRDA: 22% vit. A, 13% riboflavin, 14% calcium, 12% phosphorus.

DOUBLE CHOCOLATE CHUNK ICE CREAM

Attention chocolate lovers! Here's a rich and creamy treat especially for you—

- 2 cups sugar
- 2 envelopes unflavored gelatin
- 4 cups light cream
- 4 squares (4 ounces) unsweetened chocolate, chopped
- 2 beaten eggs
- 4 cups whipping cream
- 1 cup finely chopped milk chocolate (about 6 ounces)

In a large saucepan combine sugar and gelatin. Stir in light cream and unsweetened chocolate. Cook and stir over medium heat till mixture almost boils, sugar dissolves, and chocolate melts. Stir *1 cup* of the hot mixture into eggs; return all to saucepan. Cook and stir 2 minutes more. (If chocolate flecks appear, beat till smooth.) Cover; chill.

Stir whipping cream and milk chocolate into chilled mixture. Freeze in a 4- or 5-quart ice cream freezer according to manufacturer's directions. Makes about 2½ quarts ice cream.

Per ½-cup serving: 405 cal., 5 g pro., 30 g carbo., 31 g fat, 112 mg chol., 53 mg sodium. USRDA: 22% vit. A, 11% riboflavin, 12% calcium, 12% phosphorus.

CAFÉ AU LAIT SHERBET

You can make this smooth sherbet without an ice cream machine—

- ¼ cup sugar
- 1 envelope unflavored gelatin
- 2 tablespoons instant coffee crystals
- 2 cups milk
- ¼ cup cold water
- 2 egg whites
- ¼ cup sugar

In a medium saucepan combine ¼ cup sugar, gelatin, and coffee crystals. Stir in milk and cold water. Cook and stir over low heat to dissolve gelatin, sugar,

and coffee crystals. Transfer to an 8x8x2-inch pan. Cover and freeze about 4 hours or just till firm.

In a small mixer bowl beat egg whites till soft peaks form (tips curl). Gradually add ¼ cup sugar, beating till stiff peaks form (tips stand straight).

Break frozen mixture into chunks with a wooden spoon; transfer to a chilled large mixer bowl. Beat with an electric mixer till smooth. Fold in beaten egg whites. Return mixture to cold pan. Cover and freeze overnight or till firm. Makes 1 quart ice cream.

Per ½-cup serving: 96 cal., 4 g pro., 16 g carbo., 2 g fat, 9 mg chol., and 44 mg sodium.

FROZEN TROPICAL PARADISE

Made with or without an ice cream freezer, this ice cold novelty comes out just as heavenly—

- 3 beaten eggs
- 1 cup milk
- ¾ cup sugar
- 1¼ cups chopped fresh pineapple *or* one 20-ounce can crushed pineapple, well drained
- ½ cup coconut, toasted
- 1 teaspoon vanilla
- 2 cups whipping cream

In a heavy medium saucepan combine eggs, milk, and sugar. Cook and stir over medium heat till mixture thickens and coats a metal spoon. To cool mixture quickly, place the saucepan in a bowl of ice water; stir till cold. Stir in pineapple, coconut, and vanilla.

In a large mixer bowl beat cream till soft peaks form (tips curl).* Gently fold whipped cream into pineapple mixture. Transfer to a 9x9x2-inch pan. Cover; freeze at least 6 hours or till firm. Let stand at room temperature 20 minutes before serving. (Or, freeze in a 3- or 4-quart ice cream freezer according to manufacturer's directions.) Makes 1 quart ice cream.

*If using an ice cream freezer, *do not* beat whipping cream first; just stir it into cold custard mixture.

Per ½-cup serving: 332 cal., 5 g pro., 26 g carbo., 24 g fat, 165 mg chol., 61 mg sodium. USRDA: 21% vit. A, 11% riboflavin, 10% calcium, 11% phosphorus.

VERY BOYSENBERRY SORBET

Taste panel members loved this sorbet and gave it an outstanding rating—

⅔ cup water
¼ cup sugar
1½ cups fresh *or* frozen
    boysenberries
½ teaspoon finely shredded lemon
    peel
1 tablespoon lemon juice

In a small saucepan combine water and sugar. Bring to boiling; remove from heat. Cover and chill.

Place boysenberries in a blender container or food processor bowl. Cover and blend till smooth. Press pureed boysenberries through a sieve to remove seeds.

In a medium mixing bowl combine chilled sugar mixture, sieved boysenberries, lemon peel, and lemon juice; stir till well blended. Transfer to an 8x4x2-inch loaf pan; cover and freeze till firm.

Break frozen mixture into chunks with a wooden spoon; transfer to a chilled medium mixer bowl. Beat with an electric mixer till smooth. Return to the cold pan; cover and freeze till firm. Let stand at room temperature for 5 minutes before serving. Makes about 1 pint sorbet.

Per ½-cup serving: 72 cal., 0.6 g pro., 18 g carbo., 0.2 g fat, 0.7 mg sodium. USRDA: 14% vit. C.

GINGERBREAD COOKIE ICE CREAM

½ cup raisins, chopped
2 tablespoons rum
4 beaten eggs
2 cups milk
1 cup sugar
3 cups whipping cream
2 tablespoons light molasses
1 tablespoon vanilla
1 cup broken gingersnaps
    (about 10 cookies)

In a small mixing bowl combine raisins and rum; set aside.

In a medium saucepan combine eggs, milk, and sugar. Cook and stir over medium heat just till mixture coats a metal spoon. Cover and chill.

Stir raisin-rum mixture, whipping cream, molasses, and vanilla into chilled mixture. Stir in gingersnaps. Freeze in a 4- or 5-quart ice cream freezer according to manufacturer's directions. Makes 2 quarts ice cream.

Per ½-cup serving: 265 cal., 4 g pro., 24 g carbo., 17 g fat, 119 mg chol., 73 mg sodium. USRDA: 15% vit. A.

GRANOLA SUNDAE SCOOP

If you scoop this treat into a bowl, sprinkle with additional granola—

1 envelope unflavored gelatin
¼ cup milk
2 cups vanilla yogurt
1 ripe large banana, mashed
    (1 cup)
¼ cup honey
1 teaspoon vanilla
1 cup granola
2 egg whites
½ cup sugar

In a saucepan combine gelatin and milk; cook and stir over low heat till gelatin dissolves. Cool 10 to 15 minutes.

In a medium mixer bowl combine gelatin mixture, yogurt, banana, honey, and vanilla; beat till smooth. Transfer to a 9x9x2-inch pan. Cover and freeze for 1 hour.

Transfer the partially frozen mixture to a large mixer bowl. Beat with an electric mixer till fluffy. Stir in granola.

Wash beaters. In a small mixer bowl beat egg whites till soft peaks form (tips curl). Gradually add sugar, beating till stiff peaks form (tips stand straight). Fold egg whites into yogurt mixture. Return to the pan. Cover and freeze 6 hours or until firm. Makes 5 cups ice cream.

Per ½-cup serving: 134 cal., 5 g pro., 24 g carbo., 3 g fat, 4 mg chol., and 53 mg sodium.

PEANUT BUTTER 'N' JELLY
ICE CREAM

¾ cup sugar
1 envelope unflavored gelatin
2 cups light cream
1 beaten egg
½ cup chunk-style peanut butter
2 cups light cream
2 teaspoons vanilla
½ cup grape jelly

In a medium saucepan combine sugar and gelatin. Stir in 2 cups light cream. Cook and stir over medium heat till mixture almost boils and sugar dissolves. Stir ½ cup hot mixture into egg; return all to saucepan. Cook and stir 2 minutes more. Remove from heat. Add peanut butter; stir till melted. Cool.

Add 2 cups light cream and vanilla. Freeze in a 2- or 3-quart ice cream freezer according to manufacturer's directions. Remove the lid and the dasher. Insert a spatula into the center of ice cream to form a hole. Pour in jelly. Swirl the spatula to marble. Makes 5 cups ice cream.

Per ½-cup serving: 388 cal., 7 g pro., 32 g carbo., 27 g fat, 89 mg chol., 129 mg sodium. USRDA: 17% vit. A, 11% riboflavin, 11% calcium, 14% phosphorus.

JULY

LAID-BACK SUMMER MEALS

By Diana McMillen

Entertain this summer in a way that puts everyone at ease—in your own backyard! Hosting's a pleasure when the food's as simple and smart as the menus featured here.

To add dash at little cost (in time or money), borrow from our bright table-setting ideas for serving the food in style. Then sit back and enjoy your party!

BRATWURST PICNIC

Gather your young ones and come on over! This backyard bratwurst buffet for 10 has the elements of the perfect event: so-easy-to-make food that's sure to bring shouts of "seconds, please." You and your family can cook and chop, and assemble the condiments, relish, and salads hours (or even a day) before the get-together. Spread out blankets for casual seating and dining. All that's left to do is grill the bratwurst, then dig in!

MENU

GRILLED BRATWURST ON BUNS*
RAISIN-KRAUT RELISH*
YOUR FAVORITE CONDIMENTS
TARRAGON POTATO SALAD*
ROWS OF SALAD*
SPARKLING FRUIT BOWL*
FROZEN FRUIT POPS*

Serve Frozen Fruit Pops to kids of all ages. Mix up the ingredients and freeze in 3-ounce paper cups topped with wooden sticks. Let your guests serve themselves by tearing off the paper cup.

LAID-BACK SUMMER MEALS

EASY-GOING GRILLOUT

Fire up the mesquite (or the hickory chips)... anytime! This ready-when-you-are barbecue menu combines the slickest of hosting tricks.

First, assemble the kabob makings with the lime marinade and the tomato bake; then, prepare the rest of the meal for the barbecue in advance. Finally, come kabob-grilling time, put guests in charge of cooking their own meals on a stick!

MENU

CHICKEN AND BEEF KABOBS*
GREEK TOMATO BAKE*
PEPPERCORN DIP* WITH CRUDITES
FRESH SUMMERTIME PLUM TART*

Our tart is not only tasty, it goes together fast. Arranging plum slices over the filling is probably the trickiest part. Begin with the outside row, and place slices to form concentric circles.

LAID-BACK SUMMER MEALS

NO-COOK BUFFET

Serve these party foods chilled—it's a great way to impress your guests while you keep your cool! Make the beef roll-ups several hours ahead; the rest of the menu, the day before.

There's no last-minute cooking—guaranteed! Just set out the food smorgasbord style in your backyard so that guests can help themselves when the day's activities bring pangs of hunger.

MENU

TORTILLA BEEF ROLL-UPS*
AMBROSIA TOSSED SALAD*
BROWN RICE AND VEGETABLE SALAD*
CHOCOLATE-NECTARINE SHORTCAKE*

You need only four ingredients to assemble Tortilla Beef Roll-Ups. Put the horseradish dip and beef on the tortillas, then add lettuce and more dip. Roll up and chill the tortillas till serving time.

Bratwurst Picnic

Grilled Bratwurst on Buns
Raisin-Kraut Relish
Your Favorite Condiments
Tarragon Potato Salad
Rows of Salad
Sparkling Fruit Bowl
Frozen Fruit Pops

Timetable:
One day before serving:
● Fix and freeze the Frozen Fruit Pops. Get your kids involved in the fun!
● Put together the Tarragon Potato Salad; cover and chill.
● Prepare the Raisin-Kraut Relish; cover and chill.
● Marinate bratwurst in beer overnight in the refrigerator.
Day of picnic:
● Decoratively arrange the Rows of Salad on a platter; cover and chill.
● Stir together the ingredients for Sparkling Fruit Bowl and spoon into a serving container; cover and chill.
● Fire up the coals 30 minutes before guests arrive.
● Arrange the food in buffet style.
● Grill the bratwurst. Heat the Raisin-Kraut Relish just before eating, if desired. Dig in!

FROZEN FRUIT POPS

These desserts have no added sugar—

3 **large ripe bananas, peeled and cut up**
1 **6-ounce can frozen tangerine juice *or* orange juice concentrate, thawed**
1 **cup water**

In a blender container or food processor bowl combine bananas, tangerine or orange juice concentrate, and water. Cover and blend or process till smooth. Pour into ten 3-ounce paper drink cups. Cover each with aluminum foil. Freeze for 1 hour.

Insert a wooden stick through foil into each cup. Freeze about 3 hours more or till firm. To serve, tear off the paper cups or remove from pop molds. Makes 10 pops.

Per pop: 69 cal., 1 g pro., 17 g carbo., 1 mg sodium. USRDA: 41% vit. C.

GRILLED BRATWURST ON BUNS

For hearty appetites, plan two bratwurst sandwiches for each person—

10 **fully cooked bratwurst**
Beer
1 **recipe Raisin-Kraut Relish (see recipe at right)**
10 **individual French-style rolls, halved lengthwise**
Desired condiments (such as German-style mustard, catsup, sweet pickle relish, *or* pickled chili peppers)

To marinate, place bratwurst in a plastic bag set in a large mixing bowl. Add enough beer to cover. Seal tightly and marinate overnight in the refrigerator, turning the bag occasionally.

Light the coals. Drain bratwurst. Grill bratwurst, uncovered, over *medium-hot* coals* for 4 minutes. Turn and grill for 3 to 4 minutes more or till heated through. If desired, heat Raisin-Kraut Relish with bratwurst.

Serve bratwurst in French-style rolls with chilled or reheated Raisin-Kraut Relish and desired condiments. Makes 10 sandwiches.

*Note: To check the coal temperature, hold your hand above the coals at the height where the bratwurst will be cooking. If you need to withdraw your hand after 3 seconds, then the coals are medium-hot.

Per sandwich: 353 cal., 15 g pro., 33 g carbo., 17 g fat, 46 mg chol., 1,077 mg sodium. USRDA: 23% thiamine, 17% riboflavin, 18% niacin, 15% iron, 15% phosphorus.

RAISIN-KRAUT RELISH

Cooking the cabbage and apple in vinegar gives this easy-to-make relish a sauerkraut-flavor—

⅓ **cup water**
⅓ **cup vinegar**
2 **tablespoons brown sugar**
½ **teaspoon salt**
⅛ **teaspoon pepper**
5 **cups shredded red *or* green cabbage (about 1 pound)**
2½ **cups finely chopped unpeeled apple (about 3 apples)**
⅓ **cup raisins**

In a 3-quart saucepan combine water, vinegar, brown sugar, salt, and pepper. Cook and stir till sugar dissolves. Add red or green cabbage, apple, and raisins; stir to coat.

Bring to boiling; reduce heat. Cover and simmer over low heat about 30 minutes or till cabbage is very tender. Cover and chill. Serve relish chilled or reheat on range top or grill. Makes 8 to 10 servings.

Microwave directions: In a 3-quart nonmetal casserole combine water, vinegar, brown sugar, salt, and pepper. Micro-cook, uncovered, on 100% power (HIGH) for 2½ to 3½ minutes or till brown sugar is dissolved, stirring once.

Add cabbage, apple, and raisins, stirring to coat. Cover and micro-cook on 100% power (HIGH) for 12 to 15 minutes or till cabbage is very tender. Cover and chill.

Serve chilled or reheat in covered casserole. To reheat, micro-cook on 100% power (HIGH) 10 to 11 minutes or till heated through, stirring twice.

Per serving: 69 cal., 1 g pro., 17 g carbo., 151 mg sodium. USRDA: 61% vitamin C.

TARRAGON POTATO SALAD

The peel on the red potatoes adds color to the salad—

10 medium red potatoes (about 3 pounds)
½ teaspoon instant beef bouillon granules
¼ cup warm water
½ cup mayonnaise *or* salad dressing
¼ cup vinegar
¼ cup thinly sliced green onions
2 tablespoons snipped parsley
2 teaspoons snipped fresh tarragon *or* ½ teaspoon dried tarragon, crushed
½ to 1 teaspoon pepper
Leaf lettuce (optional)

Scrub potatoes well. In a 4½-quart Dutch oven or kettle cook potatoes, covered, in boiling salted water for 20 to 25 minutes or just till tender; drain. Cool slightly. Cut into ¼-inch-thick slices.

For dressing, in a medium mixing bowl dissolve the bouillon granules in warm water. Stir in mayonnaise or salad dressing, vinegar, green onions, parsley, tarragon, and pepper.

Pour dressing over sliced potatoes, then toss gently to coat. Cover and chill. If desired, serve in a lettuce-lined salad bowl. Makes 8 to 10 servings.

Per serving: 232 cal., 4 g pro., 30 g carbo., 11 g fat, 10 mg chol., 118 mg sodium. USRDA: 50% vit. C, 11% thiamine, 13% niacin.

ROWS OF SALAD

The colorful rows of ingredients will brighten your buffet table—

6 hard-cooked eggs
1 2¼-ounce can sliced pitted ripe olives, drained (½ cup)
4 ounces cheddar cheese, cubed
4 ounces Swiss cheese, cubed
3 medium carrots, shredded
¼ cup raisins
5 ounces fresh mushrooms, coarsely chopped (2 cups)
2 tablespoons snipped chives
Spinach *or* leaf lettuce
3 cups alfalfa sprouts
3 medium tomatoes, chopped
½ cup sweet pickle juice *or* ½ cup vinegar *and* 2 teaspoons sugar
¼ cup salad oil
¼ cup lemon juice

Coarsely chop eggs. Toss chopped eggs with sliced olives. Toss together cheddar and Swiss cheeses. Toss together carrots and raisins. Toss together the mushrooms and chives.

On a large serving platter arrange spinach or lettuce to cover. Divide the sprouts in half; arrange at each end of platter. Form 5 rows of vegetables or cheese crosswise on platter. Arrange egg-olive mixture first, then chopped tomatoes. Arrange the cheeses in the center of the platter. Place carrots and raisins on the platter next, then mushrooms and chives to form the last row. Cover and chill up to 4 hours.

Meanwhile, for dressing, in a screw-top jar combine pickle juice, salad oil, and lemon juice. Cover and chill. To serve, shake dressing and drizzle over salad. Makes 8 to 10 servings.

Per serving: 362 cal., 18 g pro., 15 g carbo., 26 g fat, 232 mg chol., 432 mg sodium. USRDA: 100% vit. A, 30% vit. C, 25% riboflavin, 41% calcium, 15% iron, 35% phosphorus.

SPARKLING FRUIT BOWL

Choose a fruit combination that's not only tasty, but colorful, too—

1 teaspoon shredded orange peel
2 oranges
6 cups fresh fruit (choose 2 cups each of 3 fruits): peeled and cubed mangoes, melons, papayas, and pineapple; sliced kiwi fruit; whole berries (halve large strawberries); halved and pitted dark sweet cherries; *or* halved and seeded grapes
1 cup chilled carbonated water
¼ cup honey
1 tablespoon lemon juice

Peel oranges and slice crosswise. In the bottom of a 2-quart glass serving bowl arrange orange slices. Top with 3 layers of desired fresh fruits. Cover and chill in the refrigerator until serving time.

In a 2-cup measure stir together the orange peel, carbonated water, honey, and lemon juice, then pour over chilled fruit. Serve immediately.

To serve, spoon into individual dessert dishes. Makes 8 to 10 servings.

Per serving: 100 cal., 1 g pro., 26 g carbo., 5 mg sodium. USRDA: 58% vit. A, 90% vit. C.

Easy-Going Grillout

Chicken and Beef Kabobs
Greek Tomato Bake
Peppercorn Dip with Crudités
Fresh Summertime Plum Tart
Iced Tea

Timetable:
One day before serving:
● Assemble Greek Tomato Bake; cover and chill.
● Prepare Peppercorn Dip; chill in a covered container.
● Prepare and bake Fresh Summertime Plum Tart; cover and chill.
Day of the grillout:
● Marinate the chicken and beef for the kabobs; cover and chill.
● Cut up the vegetables for the kabobs and for the dip; cover and chill.
● Soak the mesquite chips 1 hour before grilling.
● 30 minutes before the guests arrive, fire up the barbecue grill.
Before serving:
● Bake the tomatoes 15 minutes before serving time.
● Drain chicken and beef and make the glaze for kabobs.
● Attractively arrange the food buffet style on a table.
● As your guests build up an appetite, sit back, and let them thread and grill their own kabobs!

CHICKEN AND BEEF KABOBS

A sweet sesame-lime glaze coats these kabobs. You can easily double the recipe if your guests are hefty eaters—

  1 tablespoon finely shredded lime
    peel
⅓ cup lime juice
  3 tablespoons cooking oil
  1 tablespoon sesame oil
¼ teaspoon salt
  1 whole large chicken breast,
    skinned, boned, and halved
    lengthwise
½ pound boneless beef sirloin
    steak, cut 1 inch thick
  2 cups mesquite *or* hickory chips
  1 medium red *or* green sweet
    pepper (*or* half of each), cut
    into 1-inch squares
  1 small yellow summer squash,
    halved lengthwise and cut into
    ½-inch-thick slices
  1 medium onion, cut into wedges
  2 tablespoons honey
  1 teaspoon sesame seed

For marinade, combine lime peel, juice, cooking oil, sesame oil, and salt. Cut chicken and beef into 1-inch pieces. In a plastic bag set in a mixing bowl, combine chicken, beef, and marinade. Close bag and chill for 1 to 4 hours, turning twice to distribute marinade. About 1 hour before cooking, soak wood chips in enough water to cover.

Drain chicken and beef, reserving marinade. On four 10-inch skewers thread chicken, beef, pepper, squash, and onion pieces. For glaze, combine ¼ *cup* of the reserved marinade with honey and sesame seed.

Drain mesquite chips and sprinkle over coals. Grill kabobs, uncovered, over *medium-hot* coals for 6 minutes. Turn kabobs and brush with glaze. Grill for 4 to 6 minutes more or till done. Brush with glaze again before serving. Makes 4 servings.

Per serving: 433 cal., 29 g pro., 14 g carbo., 29 g fat, 39 mg chol., 162 mg sodium. USRDA: 18% vit. A, 78% vit. C, 15% riboflavin, 46% niacin, 14% iron, 29% phosphorus.

GREEK TOMATO BAKE

Tomatoes form an edible container for a Greek-style cheese filling. This recipe easily can be doubled for a crowd—

  4 small tomatoes
½ of a small onion, thinly sliced and
    separated into rings
⅓ cup sliced pitted ripe olives
⅓ cup crumbled feta cheese
  2 tablespoons olive *or* salad oil
  2 tablespoons red wine vinegar
  2 teaspoons snipped fresh basil *or*
    ½ teaspoon dried basil, crushed
  1 teaspoon sugar
¼ teaspoon garlic salt

Cut off tops of tomatoes. Remove centers, leaving shells; invert to drain. Divide onion and olives among tomato shells. Place in a 10x6x2-inch baking dish. Sprinkle with feta cheese. Cover and chill.

In a screw-top jar combine olive or salad oil, vinegar, basil, sugar, and garlic salt. Shake well to mix. Store at room temperature.

Before serving, drizzle *each* stuffed tomato with *1 tablespoon* of the olive oil mixture. Bake, uncovered, in a 400° oven about 15 minutes or till heated through. Makes 4 servings.

Microwave directions: Prepare and chill the stuffed tomatoes as directed. Before serving, place in a 10x6x2-inch nonmetal baking dish. Cover with waxed paper and micro-cook on 100% power (HIGH) for 2 to 3 minutes or till heated through, giving the dish a half-turn once during cooking.

Per serving: 138 cal., 3 g pro., 8 g carbo., 11 g fat, 8 mg chol., 308 mg sodium. USRDA: 19% vit. A, 42% vit. C.

FRESH SUMMERTIME PLUM TART

Can't find plums? Try using peaches or nectarines instead—

- 1 **9-inch folded refrigerated *or* frozen unbaked piecrust**
- 5 **large plums *or* 3 medium peaches**
- **Lemon juice**
- ½ **cup peach preserves**
- ½ **cup vanilla yogurt *or* dairy sour cream**
- 1 **tablespoon lemon juice**

Thaw piecrust, if frozen. Pit and thinly slice plums or peaches. Brush cut edges with lemon juice.

Unfold piecrust (or remove from pie plate) onto an ungreased baking sheet. Roll the edges of the piecrust inward (about 1 inch) to make a 10-inch circle. Crimp edge to form a ½-inch-high rim. Prick bottom. Bake in a 450° oven for 11 to 12 minutes or till done.

In small mixing bowl stir together *half* of the preserves and the yogurt or sour cream, then spread over hot crust. Arrange plums or peaches over yogurt mixture, starting with the outside row and placing slices to form concentric circles (see photo, page 80). Bake in a 350° oven for 12 to 15 minutes or till done. Transfer to a wire rack.

In a small saucepan stir together the remaining preserves and 1 tablespoon lemon juice. Heat till preserves are melted. Spoon over fruit on tart to glaze. Cool tart completely before serving. Makes 8 servings.

Per serving: 193 cal., 2 g pro., 30 g carbo., 8 g fat, 1 mg chol., 148 mg sodium. USRDA: 14% vit. A.

PEPPERCORN DIP

For a fun presentation, serve the dip in red pepper bottoms on each plate—

- 1 **8-ounce package Neufchâtel cheese, softened**
- 1 **teaspoon cracked peppercorns**
- ¼ **teaspoon garlic powder**
- ¼ **cup milk**
- **Assorted vegetable dippers (jicama sticks, carrot sticks, green onions, broccoli flowerets, fresh mushrooms, *or* sliced green *or* red sweet pepper)**

In a small mixer bowl combine cheese, peppercorns, and garlic powder. Beat with an electric mixer till blended. Gradually beat in the milk till mixture is fluffy. Cover and chill. Serve with assorted vegetable dippers. Makes about 1 cup dip.

Per tablespoon: 40 cal., 2 g pro., 3 g fat, 11 mg chol., 59 mg sodium.

No-Cook Buffet

Tortilla Beef Roll-Ups
Ambrosia Tossed Salad
Brown Rice and Vegetable Salad
Chocolate-Nectarine Shortcake
Fruit Juice

Timetable:
One day before serving:
● Prepare Ambrosia Tossed Salad; cover and chill.
● Assemble Brown Rice and Vegetable Salad; cover and chill.
● Bake the shortcake, if serving cooled. Wrap to store.
Day of the outdoor buffet:
● Prepare Tortilla Beef Roll-Ups; cover and chill.
● Bake the shortcake, if serving warm.
● Slice the nectarines.
Before serving:
● Cut the tortilla roll-ups into thirds.
● Whip cream for shortcake.
● Arrange the food buffet-style and call everyone to dinner.

TORTILLA BEEF ROLL-UPS

Combine just four ingredients to make this tortilla-wrapped sandwich. It's quick for a hungry crowd—

- 4 **12-inch flour tortillas**
- 1 **8-ounce container sour cream dip with bacon and horseradish**
- 10 **to 12 ounces thinly sliced cooked beef**
- **Leaf lettuce**

Spread 1 side of each tortilla with about 2 tablespoons of the bacon and horseradish dip, covering the whole surface of tortilla. Top with 1 or 2 slices of cooked beef. Top with lettuce leaves. Spread another 2 tablespoons of the dip onto the lettuce. Roll up each tortilla jelly-roll style (see photo, page 82).

Place assembled tortilla roll-ups, seam side down, on a serving platter. Cover and chill in the refrigerator till serving time.

Before serving, cut each roll-up crosswise into thirds. Makes 6 servings, 2 pieces each.

Per serving: 251 cal., 17 g pro., 14 g carbo., 14 g fat, 60 mg chol., 58 mg sodium. USRDA: 14% riboflavin, 16% niacin, 15% iron, 17% phosphorus.

BROWN RICE AND VEGETABLE SALAD

This colorful salad packs a lot of crunch and vitamins, yet it's easy to make. Use either regular or quick-cooking brown rice, depending on your schedule—

- ⅔ cup brown rice
- ½ of a 16-ounce package loose-pack frozen broccoli, corn, and red peppers (about 2½ cups)
- 2 tablespoons snipped parsley
- 2 tablespoons sliced green onion
- ⅓ cup bottled Italian salad dressing

In a medium saucepan cook *uncooked* brown rice according to package directions, then drain. Cook frozen mixed vegetables according to package directions, then drain.

In a medium mixing bowl combine the cooked brown rice, cooked vegetables, snipped parsley, and green onion. Pour Italian salad dressing over all; toss gently to coat.

Transfer the salad to a colorful serving bowl, then cover and chill in the refrigerator till serving time. Makes 6 servings.

Per serving: 222 cal., 4 g pro., 30 g carbo., 10 g fat, 278 mg sodium. USRDA: 14% vit. A, 29% vit. C, 14% thiamine.

CHOCOLATE-NECTARINE SHORTCAKE

Choose bright-looking nectarines that are firm and rounded—

- 1⅔ cups all-purpose flour
- ½ cup sugar
- ⅓ cup unsweetened cocoa powder
- 2 teaspoons baking powder
- ¼ teaspoon baking soda
- ½ cup butter *or* margarine
- 1 beaten egg
- ⅔ cup milk
- 6 medium nectarines
- Lemon juice
- 1 cup whipping cream (optional)
- 2 tablespoons sugar (optional)
- ½ teaspoon vanilla (optional)

In a large mixing bowl stir together flour, ½ cup sugar, cocoa powder, baking powder, and baking soda. Cut in the butter or margarine till mixture resembles coarse crumbs. Combine the egg and milk, then add all at once to the dry ingredients. Stir just to moisten.

Spread dough into a greased 5-cup ovenproof ring mold or a 9x1½-inch round baking pan. Bake in a 450° oven for 15 to 18 minutes or till done.

Cool for 10 minutes on a wire rack. Remove shortcake from pan and place on a serving platter. Serve warm or cover and store at room temperature.

Before serving, pit and slice nectarines. In a medium mixing bowl combine nectarine slices and lemon juice. Toss to coat cut edges; set aside.

If desired, in a small mixer bowl combine the whipping cream, 2 tablespoons sugar, and vanilla, then beat on medium speed of an electric mixer till soft peaks form.

Serve sliced nectarines with warm or cooled shortcake and whipped cream mixture, if desired. Makes 8 servings.

Per serving: 466 cal., 6 g pro., 63 g carbo., 23 g fat, 103 mg chol., 1,955 mg sodium. USRDA: 53% vit. A, 23% vit. C, 14% thiamine, 15% riboflavin, 13% niacin, 11% calcium, 10% iron, 15% phosphorus.

AMBROSIA TOSSED SALAD

Be sure to chill the colorful fruit-spinach mixture separately from the dressing to prevent watering out—

- 1 medium apple
- Lemon juice
- 4 cups torn spinach *or* leaf lettuce
- 1 11-ounce can pineapple tidbits and mandarin orange sections, drained
- ½ of an 8-ounce container (½ cup) soft-style cream cheese with strawberries
- ¼ cup orange juice
- 1 tablespoon lemon juice
- 2 tablespoons sunflower nuts
- ⅓ cup coconut

Core and slice apple. Brush cut edges with lemon juice. In a salad bowl combine spinach, pineapple-orange mixture, and apple. Toss gently to mix. Cover and chill till serving time.

For dressing, in a small mixing bowl stir together cream cheese, orange juice, and 1 tablespoon lemon juice. Cover and chill till serving time.

Top each serving with 1 teaspoon of the sunflower nuts, some of the dressing, and 1 tablespoon of the coconut. Makes 6 servings.

Per serving: 240 cal., 5 g pro., 20 g carbo., 17 g fat, 42 mg chol., 123 mg sodium. USRDA: 76% vit. A, 51% vit. C, 11% riboflavin.

BEST of SEASON

Smooth, sparkling, sprightly, and satisfying! When warm weather hits, sip our refreshing rainbow of drinks!

SUPER SUMMER DRINKS

By Joy Taylor

SWISS MALT

- 2 cups vanilla ice milk
- 1 cup milk
- 2 tablespoons instant malted milk powder
- 2 tablespoons instant Swiss-style coffee powder

In blender combine ingredients. Cover; blend till smooth. Makes 3 (8-ounce) servings.

Per serving: 281 cal., 10 g pro., 40 g carbo., 10 g fat, 45 mg chol., 168 mg sodium. USRDA: 27% riboflavin, 16% niacin, 32% calcium, 29% phosphorus.

COCO-BERRY CALYPSO

- 2 cups fresh strawberries
- ½ cup cream of coconut
- 12 ice cubes

In blender combine berries and cream of coconut. Cover; blend till smooth. With blender running, add ice cubes, one at a time, through opening in lid. Blend till slushy. Serve in chilled glasses. Makes 3 (6-ounce) servings.

Per serving: 170 cal., 2 g pro., 12 g carbo., 13 g fat, 0 mg chol., 3 mg sodium. USRDA: 99% vit. C, 10% iron.

90

ALMOND COOLER

2 cups boiling water
3 almond herbal tea bags
1 pint lemon *or* orange sherbet

Pour the boiling water over tea bags. Let stand for 5 minutes. Remove tea bags; discard. Chill tea *at least* 2 hours. At serving time, spoon sherbet into 4 chilled glasses; pour in chilled tea. Stir just till combined. Makes 4 (8-ounce) servings.

Per serving: 129 cal., 1 g pro., 30 g carbo., 1 g fat, 10 mg sodium.

SCARLET SIPPER

4 cups cranberry-apple drink
1 cup orange juice
¼ cup lemon juice
1 28-ounce bottle carbonated water
Ice cubes

In a large pitcher combine cranberry-apple drink, orange juice, and lemon juice. Slowly pour the carbonated water down the side of the pitcher; stir gently. Serve in wineglasses. Makes 8 (8-ounce) servings.

Per serving: 98 cal., 0 g pro., 25 g carbo., 0 g fat, 0 mg cholesterol, 2 mg sodium. USRDA: 65% vit. C.

Photo: Jim Hedrich, Hedrich-Blessing. Food stylist: Fran Paulson

MICROWAVE COOKING

TIPS FROM OUR TEST KITCHEN

By Joy Taylor

Go ahead—let your meals be care-free, cool, and fast, fast, fast! It's a cinch when you explore microwave cooking beyond "defrost" and "reheat." Need help? Starting with this season's fresh fruits and vegetables, follow these tips from the *BH&G Test Kitchen.* You'll find your summer harvest never tasted so good!

Peaches, Berries, and Cream

■ Some "rules" of microwave cooking are similar to those for conventional cooking. For example, this saucy dessert must be stirred during cooking to prevent lumps. Stir the berries once or twice from the outside of the dish to the center to evenly distribute the heat.

92

AT ITS BEST

Photographs: William K. Sladcik, Inc.
Food stylist: Fran Paulsen

■ "We've tested microwave recipes for more than 13 years, and each recipe offers great flavor and eye appeal while saving time," says Sharon Stilwell, Test Kitchen Director. Here, Sharon (*center*) evaluates a recipe with Marge Steenson (*left*), Dianna Nolin (*standing*), and Lynelle Munn (*right*).

Squash Sunflowers

■ These carrot-puree-filled patty-pan squash demonstrate a basic microwave cooking lesson: To ensure even doneness, select foods that are about equal in shape and weight.

Triple-Peppered Sausage

■ Sausage tends to expand and split during cooking, so the Test Kitchen recommends slashing each piece. "Use a sharp knife to cut through the skin and about ¼ inch into the meat. Be careful not to cut too deep," says Dianna Nolin, a Test Kitchen veteran.

MICROWAVE COOKING AT ITS BEST

Variable power settings make today's microwave ovens more versatile than ever. Now you can adjust the power similar to how you adjust the heat of the burner when cooking conventionally. This flexibility means you can serve foods at their peak, neither under- nor overdone.

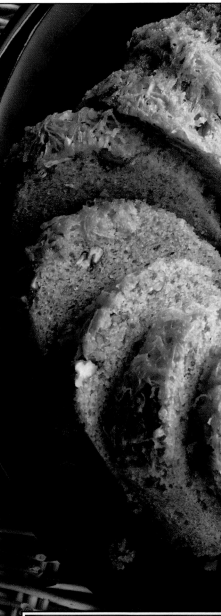

Marinated Vegetable Plate

■ One big microwave timesaver is cooking in measuring cups. For this salad dressing, one ingredient is measured in a larger-than-needed container. Other ingredients can be added and the salad dressing cooked with no fear of its boiling over.

94

■ Appearance, taste, ease of preparation, nutritional value, and cost—our food staff, including **Jean Brekke** (*front*) and **Jennifer Darling** (*back*), considers these and several other factors when evaluating a recipe for publication. Recipes are retested as needed to meet our high standards.

Wheaty Carrot Cake

■ "Check a micro-cooked cake for doneness just as you would a conventional cake," advises Marilyn Cornelius, who's tested *BH&G* recipes for 12 years. "A pick inserted off-center should come out clean."

Custard-in-Squash Pie

■ The Test Kitchen warns that custards continue to cook after micro-cooking. This quichelike main dish (or any micro-cooked custard) is done when a knife inserted *2 inches* from the center comes out clean. Cooking till the *center* tests done is too long.

MICROWAVE COOKING AT ITS BEST

Your microwave oven lets you put nutritious meals on the table—no matter how hectic your schedule. Micro-cooking is more like steaming than boiling, so fruits and vegetables retain more vitamins and minerals. They also keep their fresh color, flavor, and texture.

Three-Fruit Cobbler

■ "To avoid a doughy topping, make sure the fruit mixture is bubbly hot before spooning on the biscuit mixture," says Test Kitchen pro Marge Steenson. To give the micro-cooked dessert a traditional browned topping, she suggests a sprinkling of cinnamon and granola.

PERRY STRUSE

Pasta 'n' Tomatoes

■ Here's a jazzy way to fix an old standby. Fill same-size tomatoes with a pasta mixture, saving some pasta for the bottom of the dish. This provides better heat distribution, and diners get extra stuffing!

One-Dish Turkey Dinner

■ Use a cooking bag to steam the corn and okra alongside the cooking turkey breast. Remember to shake about 1 tablespoon flour in the cooking bag before adding the vegetables. And puncture the bag so that it doesn't explode during micro-cooking.

NEW WAVE
MICROWAVE COOKWARE
GOOD-LOOKING, HARDWORKING

Stocking up on microwave cookware can be mind boggling! With so many new items available, your choices may be harder then ever. Review this lineup of multipurpose utensils that replace earlier, single-purpose microwave equipment.

1. Tupperware Ultra 21® Ovenware Casseroles
2. Taraware® 7-Piece Egg Poacher Set 3. Regal™ Pop 'N' Lite Corn Popper 4. Corning Ware® Covered Casserole 5. Anchor Ovenware Microware® Divided Plate 6. Anchor Ovenware Microware® Spring-Powered Turntable 7. Nordic Ware® Loaf Pan 8. Rubbermaid® Covered Small Entrée Plates 9. Pyrex® Covered Individual Bowl 10. Nordic Ware® Bake 'N' Bacon Sheet

Multiple-Purpose Cookware
■ To make the best use of kitchen cabinet space, find microwave dishes that come with versatile attachments.

All-in-one dishes: Before you buy a bacon rack and a cake ring, consider a dish that's complete with a browning grill, a center stem for cakes, a steaming rack, and a lid/cooking container.

Have your cake and eat eggs, too: Anything's possible with a layer cake pan that comes with egg cups, poaching tray, and steaming rack (see No. 2).

Two-sided grills: Instead of sizzling with a one-sided meat or bacon rack, turn to a dish that has a ribbed side for meats and a flat side for appetizers, reheating, or defrosting (see No. 10).

More than a popper: Microwave popcorn poppers pinch-hit as casseroles and steamers. When popping, follow instructions carefully. For a popper with all the bells and whistles, opt for the version with carousel lights that flash as the corn pops (see No. 3).

Freezer-to-Dishwasher Cookware
■ With your busy lifestyle, you deserve cookware that adapts to the freezer, broiler, range top, conventional and convection ovens, and dishwasher. Thanks to recent innovations, you can have it.

Plastic cookware: Look for plastic cookware made of substances that tolerate conventional heat. One type of thermoset plastic withstands temperatures of up to 600° (see No. 1). Glass-filled thermoset polyesters can be heated to 400° or 410° (see Nos. 5, 7, and 10). Do not subject these plastics to temperatures above the allowed maximum, and do not use them with the range top, broiler, or grill.

Clay cookware: A manufacturer has introduced a microwave clay cookware line that you can use in the conventional oven, but not under the broiler or on the range top.

Glass and glass-ceramic: Other attractive serving containers include heat-resistant glass or glass ceramic cookware that you can use with either range top or broiler, as well as in conventional and convection ovens (see Nos. 4 and 9).

Microwave-safe labels: When you buy micro-cookware, don't assume anything. Look for package labels that indicate whether the dish is safe to use with the freezer, dishwasher, oven, broiler, or range top.

Small-Size Cookware
■ Because so many of you have small families or small microwave ovens, you've prompted a manufacturing trend toward smaller microwave dishes. You can find downsized grilling racks, browning skillets, turntables, popcorn poppers, and casseroles, as well as single-serving cooking dishes (see Nos. 8 and 9).

Active Cookware
■ Newly developed cookware can help you conquer some of the problems inherent in microwave cooking: no browning, lack of crispness, and uneven cooking. This special cookware has been labeled "active," because it relies on both the reflective and redirective properties of metal to activate or heat the dish. Some active cookware you may find on the market includes browning skillets, pizza crispers, egg cookers, coffee makers, and popcorn poppers. You also will see a different kind of "active" utensil—the freestanding microwave turntable that rotates to ensure more even cooking (see No. 6).

Use and Care
■ Besides being more versatile, microwave cookware today is more easily cleaned, handled, and stored.

Nonstick coating: To make your cleaning job easier, several companies coat the inside of their plastic or glass cookware with a Silver-Stone® lining (see Nos. 7 and 10). This keeps foods from sticking and eliminates the need to grease.

PEACHES, BERRIES, AND CREAM

Crème fraîche is a sour-creamlike dairy product found in the refrigerated case of some supermarkets. Or, you can make your own—

- 2 **pints fresh** *or* **frozen blueberries**
- ⅓ **cup sugar**
- 3 **tablespoons all-purpose flour**
- ½ **teaspoon ground allspice**
- 1 **teaspoon lemon juice**
- 2 **peaches**
- **Crème Fraîche (see recipe at right)** *or* **whipped cream (optional)**

Rinse frozen blueberries. In a 9-inch nonmetal quiche dish or cake dish combine sugar, flour, and allspice. Stir in berries and lemon juice. Micro-cook, uncovered, on 100% power (HIGH) for 9 to 10 minutes or till thickened and bubbly, stirring after every 2 minutes.

Peel and pit peaches. Cut each into 6 wedges. Arrange wedges in blueberry mixture. (Peaches should not be completely covered by blueberries.) Micro-cook, loosely covered with waxed paper, on 100% power (HIGH) 3 to 4 minutes more or till peaches are just hot and berry mixture is bubbly. Serve warm. Top with Crème Fraîche or whipped cream, if desired. Makes 4 servings.

Conventional directions: Rinse frozen blueberries. In a medium saucepan combine sugar, flour, and allspice. Stir in berries and lemon juice. Let stand for 5 minutes. Cook and stir over medium heat till thickened and bubbly. Transfer mixture to a 9-inch quiche dish. Peel and pit peaches. Cut each peach into 6 wedges. Arrange peach wedges in the blueberry mixture. Cover with foil. Bake in a 375° oven about 10 minutes or till peaches are just hot and blueberry mixture is bubbly. Serve warm. Top with Crème Fraîche or whipped cream, if desired.

Crème Fraîche: In a small saucepan heat 2 cups *whipping cream* to between 90° and 100° F. Pour into a small bowl. Stir in ¼ cup *commercial buttermilk*. Cover and let stand at room temperature for 18 to 24 hours or till mixture is thickened. Do not stir. Store in a covered container in refrigerator for up to 1 week. Makes 2 cups.

Per serving: 231 cal., 2 g pro., 57 g carbo., 1 g fat, 0 mg chol., 3 mg sodium. USRDA: 17% vit. A, 55% vit. C, 10% riboflavin, 14% iron.

SQUASH SUNFLOWERS

So simple, and so pretty! Highlight a meat, poultry, or fish dinner with this refreshing side dish—

- 4 **large carrots, thinly sliced (2 cups)**
- 3 **tablespoons water**
- 1 **egg yolk**
- 2 **tablespoons butter** *or* **margarine**
- 4 **small (4 to 6 ounces each) patty-pan squash**
- 2 **tablespoons chopped pecans**

In a 1-quart nonmetal casserole combine carrots and 3 tablespoons water. Micro-cook, covered, on 100% power (HIGH) for 6 to 8 minutes or till very tender. *Do not drain.* In a blender container combine carrots and cooking liquid, egg yolk, and butter or margarine. Cover; blend till smooth, stopping occasionally to push mixture into blades.

Cut a thin slice from the top of each squash. Using a small spoon, scoop out squash centers and seeds. (If necessary, cut a thin slice from the bottom of each squash so squash sits flat.) Sprinkle salt and pepper into each squash. Invert squash in a 12x7½x2-inch nonmetal baking dish. Add 2 tablespoons *water* to dish.

Micro-cook, covered, on 100% power (HIGH) for 6 to 8 minutes or till tender, rearranging squash once. Drain. Turn squash over. Spoon carrot mixture into squash. Sprinkle pecans atop. Micro-cook, uncovered, on 100% power (HIGH) for 1 to 2 minutes or till heated through. Makes 4 servings.

Conventional directions: In a 1-quart saucepan combine carrots and 3 tablespoons water. Cover and cook on range-top over medium-high heat for 10 to 12 minutes or till carrots are very tender. *Do not drain.* In a blender container combine carrots and cooking liquid, egg yolk, and butter or margarine. Cover. Blend till smooth, stopping occasionally to push mixture into blades.

Cut a thin slice from the top of each squash. Using a small spoon, scoop out squash centers and seeds. (If necessary, cut a thin slice from the bottom of each squash so squash sits flat.) Sprinkle salt and pepper into each squash. Arrange squash in a 10-inch skillet. Add ⅓ cup *water*.

Cover and cook for 10 minutes or till tender. Spoon carrot mixture into each squash. Cover and cook about 5 minutes more or till carrot puree is hot. Remove from skillet with a slotted spoon. Top with nuts.

Per serving: 146 cal., 3 g pro., 13 g carbo., 10 g fat, 81 mg chol., 107 mg sodium. USRDA: 171% vit. A, 44% vit. C, 10% riboflavin, 10% phosphorus.

August

TRIPLE-PEPPERED SAUSAGE

Look for fully cooked smoked turkey sausage in the refrigerated meat case along with other smoked sausages. To serve this recipe as a sandwich, spread individual French rolls with additional prepared mustard and fill with the sausage mixture—

- 1 **pound fully cooked smoked turkey sausage**
- 1 **medium green pepper, cut into ½-inch strips**
- 1 **medium sweet red pepper, cut into ½-inch strips**
- 1 **banana pepper, seeded and sliced crosswise**
- 1 **medium onion, thinly sliced and separated into rings**
- ¼ **cup beer**
- 1 **tablespoon prepared mustard**

Cut the sausage into 2-inch pieces. Slash each piece with a sharp knife to cut through the skin and about ¼ inch into the meat. Place sausage in a 10x6x2-inch nonmetal baking dish. Arrange all of the peppers and onion rings around and over sausage pieces.

In a screw-top jar combine beer and prepared mustard. Cover and shake well. Pour over mixture in dish. Micro-cook, covered with vented clear plastic wrap, on 100% power (HIGH) for 9 to 11 minutes or till sausage is hot and vegetables are just tender, turning dish once. Serve sausage and onions with a slotted spoon. Makes 4 servings.

Conventional directions: Cut the sausage into 2-inch pieces. Slash each piece with a sharp knife to cut through the skin and about ¼ inch into the meat. Place sausage in a 10-inch skillet. Arrange all of the peppers and onion rings around and over sausage pieces.

In a screw-top jar combine beer and prepared mustard. Cover and shake well. Pour mixture into skillet. Bring to boiling and reduce heat. Cover and simmer for 10 minutes or till vegetables are tender. Serve sausage and onions with a slotted spoon.

Per serving: 249 cal., 36 g pro., 8 g carbo., 7 g fat, 98 mg chol., 1,850 mg sodium. USRDA: 28% vit. A, 156% vit. C, 16% riboflavin, 45% niacin, 15% iron, 32% phosphorus.

MARINATED VEGETABLE PLATE

Colorful! Healthful! Your garden's bounty makes this bright and tasty salad. Precook the vegetables separately before adding the dressing; that way the beets won't discolor the onion and cubed potatoes. Also, the vegetables absorb more flavor when warm—

- 3 **large fresh beets, peeled and coarsely shredded (4 cups)**
- 1 **small onion, sliced and separated into rings**
- 2 **small potatoes, peeled and cubed (about 1½ cups)**
- 1 **small zucchini, shredded (1 cup)**
- ¾ **cup water**
- 2 **tablespoons vinegar**
- 2 **tablespoons lemon juice**
- 2 **tablespoons dry sherry**
- 1 **teaspoon instant chicken bouillon granules**
- ¼ **teaspoon salt**
- ⅛ **teaspoon pepper**
- **Beet leaves, romaine, *or* Boston lettuce leaves**

Place beets in a medium glass bowl with 2 tablespoons *water*. Micro-cook, covered, on 100% power (HIGH) for 6 minutes or till tender; drain well. In a small bowl micro-cook onion with 2 tablespoons *water*, covered, about 2 minutes or till tender; drain well. In another small bowl micro-cook potato with 2 tablespoons *water*, covered, about 6 minutes or till tender; drain well. Place uncooked zucchini in a fourth bowl.

In a 2-cup glass measure combine ¾ cup water, vinegar, lemon juice, sherry, bouillon granules, salt, and pepper. Micro-cook, uncovered, on 100% power (HIGH) for 2 to 3 minutes or till boiling, stirring once. Pour ¼ of the mixture over beets, ¼ over potato, ¼ over onion, and the remainder over zucchini. Cover and chill vegetables for 2 to 6 hours or till serving time.

To serve, line a platter with beet leaves, romaine, or Boston lettuce leaves. Remove vegetables with a slotted spoon and arrange beets, potato, and zucchini over lettuce. Sprinkle onion over all. Toss vegetables to serve. Makes 6 servings.

Conventional directions: In a covered medium saucepan cook beets in a small amount of boiling water for 9 to 10 minutes or till tender. Drain well. Arrange potatoes on 1 side in a steamer. Place over boiling water. Cover and cook about 6 minutes or till almost tender. Add onion to other side of the steamer basket. Cook 4 minutes more or till potatoes and onion are tender. Transfer beets, potatoes, onion, and uncooked zucchini to separate bowls.

In a small saucepan combine the ¾ cup water, vinegar, lemon juice, sherry, bouillon granules, salt, and pepper. Bring to boiling; remove from heat. Pour ¼ of the mixture over beets, ¼ over potato, ¼ over onion, and the remainder over zucchini. Cover and chill vegetables for 2 to 6 hours.

To serve, line a platter with beet leaves, romaine, or Boston lettuce leaves. Remove vegetables with a slotted spoon and arrange beets, potato, and zucchini over lettuce. Sprinkle onion over all. Toss vegetables to serve.

Per serving: 57 cal., 2 g pro., 12 g carbo., 0 g fat, 0 mg chol., 186 mg sodium. USRDA: 34% vit. C.

WHEATY CARROT CAKE

    1 cup all-purpose flour
    1 cup whole wheat flour
   ⅓ cup nonfat dry milk powder
    1 teaspoon baking soda
    1 teaspoon baking powder
   ½ teaspoon salt
   ½ teaspoon ground cinnamon
    2 tablespoons butter *or* margarine
    3 cups finely shredded carrots
   ½ cup chopped pecans
    1 cup cooking oil
    1 cup granulated sugar
    1 cup packed brown sugar
    1 teaspoon vanilla
    4 eggs

In a 12-cup nonmetal fluted tube pan combine butter or margarine and ½ *cup* carrots. Micro-cook, covered, on 100% power (HIGH) for 2 minutes, stirring once. Sprinkle pecans evenly over carrots in pan. Set pan aside.

In a mixing bowl stir together all-purpose flour, whole wheat flour, milk powder, baking soda, baking powder, salt, and cinnamon. Set aside.

In a large mixer bowl beat oil and sugars with an electric mixer on low speed till mixed. Add vanilla. Add eggs, one at a time, beating well after each. Add flour mixture, beating till combined. Stir in remaining carrots by hand. Pour batter into prepared pan.

Micro-cook, uncovered, on 50% power (MEDIUM) for 16 minutes, giving pan a quarter-turn every 4 minutes. (Surface of cake will appear wet, but cake will have risen to top of pan.) Give dish another quarter-turn. Cook, uncovered, on 100% power (HIGH) for 1½ minutes. Give dish a half-turn.

Micro-cook 30 seconds to 1½ minutes more or till surface appears almost dry and a wooden toothpick comes out clean. Place cake on rack. Cool 10 minutes. Invert onto plate. Serve warm. If desired, garnish with additional pecan halves. Makes 12 servings.

Conventional directions: In a saucepan cook ½ *cup* carrots and butter or margarine till carrots are tender. Spoon cooked carrots into the bottom of a 12-cup fluted tube pan. Sprinkle pecans over carrots in pan.

Prepare cake batter as directed. Pour batter into prepared pan. Bake in a 325° oven about 60 minutes or till cake tests done. Place cake on rack. Cool 10 minutes. Invert cake onto plate. Serve as above.

Per serving: 464 cal., 6 g pro., 54 g carbo., 26 g fat, 91 mg chol., 281 mg sodium. USRDA: 66% vit. A.

CUSTARD-IN-SQUASH PIE

    2 small green *or* yellow zucchini *or* yellow summer squash, cut into slices ¼ inch thick (2 cups)
   ½ cup sliced green onion
    2 tablespoons water
    2 eggs
    2 cups cooked rice
    1 5⅓-ounce can evaporated milk
    1 cup shredded Monterey Jack cheese with jalapeño peppers *or* Monterey Jack cheese (4 ounces)
   ¼ teaspoon salt
    1 small tomato, chopped
Sliced green onion tops (optional)

In a 4-cup glass measure micro-cook zucchini and green onions in water, covered, on 100% power (HIGH) for 3 to 4 minutes or just till tender; drain well. Cool slightly. Arrange zucchini slices and onion over bottom and around sides of an ungreased 9-inch nonmetal pie plate, slightly overlapping zucchini pieces on sides.

Lightly beat eggs in a bowl. In the same 4-cup glass measure combine rice and milk. Cook for 1½ to 2 minutes or till heated through. Gradually add to eggs. Stir in cheese and salt. Carefully pour egg mixture into the pie plate. Sprinkle tomato over top.

Micro-cook on 70% power (MEDIUM-HIGH) for 7 to 9 minutes, giving dish a half-turn once. When pie is done, a knife inserted 2 inches from the center will come out clean and the center will still appear wet. Let stand for 5 minutes or till center is set. Serve warm. Sprinkle with green onion, if desired. Makes 6 to 8 servings.

Conventional directions: In a medium saucepan combine zucchini, onions, and ¼ cup *water.* Bring to boiling; reduce heat. Simmer, covered, 5 minutes or till just tender; drain well. Cool slightly. Arrange zucchini and onion over bottom and around sides of an ungreased 9-inch pie plate, slightly overlapping zucchini pieces on sides.

In a mixing bowl combine eggs, rice, milk, cheese, and salt. Pour into a pie plate. Bake in a 325° oven for 28 to 30 minutes or till knife inserted near center comes out clean. Sprinkle tomato over top. Bake for 2 minutes more. Let stand for 10 minutes. Sprinkle with green onion, if desired.

Per serving: 223 cal., 11 g pro., 22 g carbo., 10 g fat, 112 mg chol., 500 mg sodium. USRDA: 18% vit. A, 23% vit. C, 16% riboflavin, 24% calcium, 21% phosphorus.

PASTA 'N' TOMATOES

1 cup tiny bow tie pasta
4 large fresh tomatoes, cored
4 green onions, sliced (¼ cup)
1 clove garlic, minced
1 tablespoon butter *or* margarine
1 tablespoon snipped fresh basil
1 3-ounce package cream cheese, cubed
¼ cup shredded mozzarella, cheddar, *or* Swiss cheese (1 ounce)
¼ cup grated Parmesan cheese
¼ cup milk
⅛ teaspoon pepper
8 ounces fully cooked ham, cut into ½-inch cubes (1½ cups)

Cook pasta according to package directions; drain. Cut a thin slice off stem ends of tomatoes. Hollow tomatoes, leaving ¼- to ½-inch-thick shells. Discard seeds. Chop tomato pulp and tops. Set aside.

In a 2-cup glass measure combine green onions, garlic, butter or margarine, and basil. Micro-cook, covered, on 100% power (HIGH) for 1 minute. Stir together warm pasta, cheeses, milk, and pepper. Stir till cheeses are slightly melted. Stir in onion mixture and ham.

Spoon ½ *cup* pasta mixture into *each* tomato. Spoon remaining pasta mixture into the bottom of an 8x8x2-inch nonmetal baking dish. Sprinkle with the chopped tomato.

Arrange filled tomatoes atop pasta mixture. Cover with vented clear plastic wrap. Micro-cook on 100% power (HIGH) for 5 to 7 minutes or till heated through. Let stand, covered, for 1 minute. Makes 4 servings.

Conventional directions: Cook the pasta according to package directions; drain well. Trim and hollow tomatoes as directed. Chop tomato pulp and tops. Set aside.

In a large saucepan cook onion and garlic in butter or margarine till onion is tender. Stir in warm pasta, cheeses, milk, ham, basil, and pepper. Spoon ½ *cup* of the pasta mixture into *each* tomato. Spoon remaining pasta mixture into the bottom of an 8x8x2-inch baking dish. Sprinkle with chopped tomato. Arrange filled tomatoes atop pasta. Cover loosely with foil. Bake in a 325° oven for 30 minutes.

Per serving: 413 cal., 23 g pro., 30 g carbo., 22 g fat, 97 mg chol., 734 mg sodium. USRDA: 37% vit. A, 51% vit. C, 43% thiamine, 25% riboflavin.

ONE-DISH TURKEY DINNER

1 2½- to 3-pound frozen boneless turkey breast roast, thawed
Melted butter *or* margarine
⅓ cup chili sauce
¼ cup orange marmalade
1 tablespoon all-purpose flour
2 fresh ears of corn, cut into 1-inch pieces
2 cups okra cut crosswise into ½-inch pieces
2 tablespoons butter *or* margarine
½ cup orange juice
2 teaspoons cornstarch

Place turkey on a nonmetal rack in a 12x7½x2-inch baking dish. Cover with waxed paper. Micro-cook on 100% power (HIGH) for 5 minutes. Give dish a quarter-turn. Cook, covered, on 50% power (MEDIUM) for 20 minutes. Give dish a quarter-turn. Brush turkey with melted butter or margarine. Stir together the chili sauce and marmalade. Spread *half* of the marmalade mixture over turkey. Re-cover the turkey with waxed paper.

Sprinkle the inside of a 10x16-inch cooking bag with flour, shaking to coat bag. Add corn, okra, and 2 tablespoons butter or margarine. Tie bag closed with string. Puncture top of bag with a fork. Place bag alongside turkey in dish. Micro-cook, covered, on 50% power (MEDIUM) for 20 to 25 minutes more or till vegetables are tender and turkey reaches an internal temperature of 170°. Remove from microwave oven. Cover turkey with foil, shiny side in. Let stand for 10 minutes.

Meanwhile, in a 2-cup glass measure stir together the remaining marmalade mixture, orange juice, and cornstarch. Cook, uncovered, on 100% power (HIGH) for 2 to 3 minutes or till thickened, stirring after every minute. To serve, transfer turkey and vegetables to a serving platter. Spoon sauce over turkey. Makes 8 servings.

Per serving: 391 cal., 53 g pro., 19 g carbo., 11 g fat, 133 mg chol., 319 mg sodium. USRDA: 31% vit. C, 18% riboflavin, 91% niacin, 46% phosphorus.

THREE-FRUIT COBBLER

¾ cup apricot nectar *or* apple juice
2 teaspoons cornstarch
⅛ teaspoon ground cinnamon
2 pears
2 peaches, peeled, pitted, and sliced
¾ cup seedless red *or* green grapes
¾ cup packaged biscuit mix
3 tablespoons sugar
2 tablespoons milk
3 tablespoons granola, crushed
½ teaspoon ground cinnamon
Vanilla ice cream (optional)

In a 1- or 1½-quart nonmetal casserole stir together nectar or juice, cornstarch, and ⅛ teaspoon cinnamon. Micro-cook, uncovered, on 100% power (HIGH) for 2 to 2½ minutes or till bubbly, stirring after every 30 seconds. Peel and core pears. Finely chop enough pears to make ¼ cup. Set aside. Slice remaining pears. Stir sliced pears, peaches, and grapes into sauce. Micro-cook, uncovered, on 100% power (HIGH) for 2 to 4 minutes or till fruit is almost tender and mixture is bubbly.

Meanwhile, for dumplings, in a medium mixing bowl stir together the chopped pear, biscuit mix, and sugar. Add milk and stir just till moistened. Dollop 6 mounds of the mixture around the edge of hot fruit. Cook, uncovered, on 70% power (MEDIUM-HIGH) for 4 to 7 minutes or till dumplings are set, giving dish a half-turn once. Stir together granola and ½ teaspoon cinnamon. Sprinkle over dumplings. Serve cobbler warm with ice cream, if desired. Makes 6 servings.

Conventional directions: In a saucepan combine nectar or juice, cornstarch, and ⅛ teaspoon cinnamon. Cook and stir till thickened and bubbly. Peel and core pears. Finely chop enough pears to make ¼ cup. Set aside. Slice remaining pears. Stir sliced pears, peaches, and grapes into sauce. Spoon into a 1- or 1½-quart casserole. Bake, covered, in a 350° oven for 20 minutes.

Prepare dumpling batter as directed above. Dollop 6 mounds of the batter atop hot fruit mixture. Bake, uncovered, about 15 minutes more or till dumplings are done. Combine granola and ½ teaspoon cinnamon. Sprinkle over dumplings. Serve as above.

Per serving: 191 cal., 3 g pro., 41 g carbo., 3 g fat, 1 mg chol., 205 mg sodium. USRDA: 19% vit. A, 12% vit. C.

SEPTEMBER

September 1985 ● $1.50

Better Homes and Gardens

DECORATING
GETTING GOOD DESIGN AT A GOOD PRICE!

PROBLEM-SOLVING STORAGE PROJECTS

9 GOURMET-SHOP DISHES YOU CAN MAKE AT HOME

REMODELING
SAME PLACE, MORE SPACE!

CHANGE YOUR DECORATING STYLE WITHOUT BREAKING YOUR BUDGET

MAGIC FROM MUSLIN
25 FABULOUS GIFTS TO MAKE ALL UNDER $10!

Perfect Jam and Jelly

Don't put it off any longer! It's time to put up the summer's fruits. Our step-by-step directions make jelly- and jam-making a cinch. And the results are oh, so nice.

A. After cooking jelly or jam to desired thickness, use a wide-mouth funnel to ladle or pour boiling jelly into jars. Fill jars to within ¼ inch of the top. Immediately wipe rims to ensure perfect seals.

B. Use paraffin or flat metal lids and screw bands for sealing jars of jelly. To complete the sealing of flat metal lids, turn the jars upside down. Hold long enough so the metal lid becomes hot.

C. When processing is complete, turn off heat. Use a jar lifter to transfer hot jars to a rack. When jars are completely cool, check seals by feeling for an indentation in center of lid.

TOMATO—BASIL JAM

Try this special jam with breads or with meats—

- **3½ pounds tomatoes, peeled, cored, and seeded**
- **3 tablespoons snipped fresh basil**
- *or* **1 tablespoon dried basil, crushed**
- **¼ cup lemon juice**
- **3 cups sugar**
- **1 1¾-ounce package *light* powdered fruit pectin**

Finely chop tomatoes to make 3½ cups. In a 6- to 8-quart kettle or Dutch oven simmer tomatoes, covered, for 10 minutes; measure 3⅓ cups. Return tomatoes to kettle.

Add basil and lemon juice. Stir ¼ cup of the sugar into the pectin. Stir pectin mixture into tomato mixture. Bring mixture to a full rolling boil, stirring constantly. Stir in remaining sugar. Return to full rolling boil. Boil hard for 1 minute, stirring constantly. Remove from the heat; skim off foam with a metal spoon.

Ladle jam into 5 hot, clean, half-pint canning jars, leaving a ¼-inch headspace *(Photo A)*. Adjust lids. Process in a boiling water bath for 15 minutes (start timing when water comes to boiling). Immediately remove jars from water bath *(Photo C)*. Makes 5 half-pints.

Per tablespoon: 33 cal., 8 g carbo., 45 mg potassium.

SPICED PEACH JELLY

Choose peaches that are slightly soft at the seam—

- **4 pounds fresh peaches, peeled, pitted, and sliced (8 cups)**
- **1 cup water**
- **1 1¾-ounce package powdered fruit pectin**
- **5 cups sugar**
- **½ teaspoon ground cinnamon**
- **¼ teaspoon almond extract**
- **⅛ teaspoon ground mace**

In a 3-quart saucepan mash peaches; add water. Bring to boiling; reduce the heat. Cover; simmer for 10 minutes or till very soft, stirring occasionally. Strain into a bowl through several thicknesses of cheesecloth lining a colander; let stand for several hours. (Avoid squeezing mixture or pulp will cause cloudy jelly.)

Measure juice, adding enough water to make 3½ cups. In an 8- to 10-quart kettle bring pectin and peach juice to full rolling boil over high heat, stirring constantly. Stir in sugar, cinnamon, extract, and mace. Return to a full rolling boil; boil hard for 1 minute, stirring constantly. Remove from the heat; skim off foam with a metal spoon.

Ladle jelly into 5 hot, clean, half-pint canning jars, leaving ¼-inch headspace *(Photo A)*. Wipe jar rims; seal, using metal lids or paraffin *(Photo B)*. Makes 5 half-pints.

Per tablespoon: 56 cal., 14 g carbo., 40 mg potassium.

GOURMET

Takeout

Secrets From Great Cooks Who've Turned Their Hobby Into A Business

By Joy Taylor, Nancy Byal, and Diana McMillen

Ever dream of opening your own food shop, so others can savor your prize recipes? Many food-loving entrepreneurs have taken the plunge—and succeeded. In talking with shop owners throughout the country, we found four recurring keys to their success: integrity, enthusiasm, creativity, and the most important, a supportive family.

We visited three of the most innovative fancy food haunts to sample their recipes firsthand. Duplicate the specialties featured here from Pasta LaVista, Something Different, and Diane's Desserts in your home. You'll discover why folks return again and again to these shops: quality.

Dan and Sandie Linn, Don Mizock, and Debbie Lobatz rely on a 28-member staff to make fresh pasta daily.

"WE WANT PEOPLE TO WALK OUT OF HERE FEELING WE'VE BEEN CHEATED BECAUSE THEY'VE GOTTEN SO MUCH GOOD FOOD FOR SO LITTLE."

What? Is that any way to run a business? You bet it is! At least so claims Don Mizock, one of the four owners of a wildly successful pasta eatery and take-out store in San Diego's Mission Hills. He and his partners believe this is absolutely the best way to establish a loyal and enthusiastic clientele. And they must be doing something right; in just over a year Pasta LaVista has captured the imagination of this California city. They've done it by providing economical and delicious take-out meals, four kinds of freshly made pastas daily, a

meet-and-greet wine and beer bar, an informal restaurant, and a bimonthly "Pastagram" newsletter.

As with many new ventures, Pasta LaVista involves family commitment. Don formed a partnership with his old friends from the Midwest, Sandie and Dan Linn. After a year of planning and designing the shop (Dan is a practicing architect), the threesome opened their restaurant with room for a small take-out department. The take-out business grew with the reputation of the restaurant; now take-out accounts for about 50 percent of the total. Eventually, Debbie Lobatz, Don's sister, joined the business.

Pasta LaVista's owners clearly don't believe in limitations. They sell pasta in all shapes and flavors, including spinach, tomato, and whole wheat. "Eventually, we'd like to open two or three pasta 'depots' around town with this as the central kitchen," explains Don.

THE FOUR OWNERS SINCERELY BELIEVE IN THEIR PRODUCT, AND WORK TO DISPEL THE NOTION THAT PASTA IS "JUST" ITALIAN AND IS FATTENING.

It's especially enjoyable for these pasta-pushers to introduce new customers to the firm texture and full flavor of freshly made noodles. They also promote pasta's versatility as an ingredient. To that end, their menu includes such innovative dishes as Feta Fettuccine and their customers' favorite, the Szechuan Chicken Pasta.

THE IMPORTANCE OF IMAGE

Pasta LaVista's owners agree that word of mouth is the best advertiser. But they don't rely on it. Conventional advertising and their newsletter help, too.

Don, Debbie, Sandie, and Dan foster additional good will by participating in civic affairs. Last year, Pasta LaVista donated a Christmas tree decorated with pasta to a Historical Society benefit, and the shop annually sponsors a fund raiser for the San Diego Symphony.

"Each pasta recipe that Sandie and I create is more than Italian or a reflection of the new American cuisine," explains Dan. **Szechuan Chicken Pasta** (*left*), **Super Salmon Salad** (*center*), **and Vegetarian Pasta a la Grecque** (*right*) are good examples of their worldly flair with food.

107

GOURMET Takeout

"BEFORE OPENING SOMETHING DIFFERENT, WE VOWED TO SELL ONLY VERY FRESH FOODS MADE FROM SCRATCH."

DREW AND SUSAN GOSS DON'T HAVE A FREEZER, COOK WITH JUST TWO BURNERS AND TWO OVENS, AND SOMEDAY WOULD LIKE TO OWN AN ICE-CREAM MAKER. YET, THEY HAVE CHANGED THE WAY INDIANAPOLIS EATS.

From dawn until dusk six days a week, the Gosses toil in the kitchen of their take-out food store. As they work, they are in full view of the daily customers who stop by to pick up a sandwich for lunch, a cold salad for a quick supper, or a loaf of the Gosses' signature herb bread.

Getting where they are today took months and months of research, scads of determination, and words of encouragement from their parents.

After college graduation, Susan and Drew (high school and college sweethearts) reevaluated their individual career goals so that they could be together more often. Their common belief in small enterprise and their love for cooking launched them into studying the food business. And what better place to learn about food than New York City?

In 1983, Susan and Drew spent five months at Manhattan's New York Restaurant School. While in New York, they supplemented their intense study by eating out three times a week, frequenting the new, trendy food stores, and haunting the specialty shops and old-time ethnic markets. Finally sated with the New York food scene, the two 26-year-olds returned home to start a food business that would be, for Indianapolis, something truly different.

The Gosses first searched for a suitable location—they settled on an upscale mall in the city—then they

Susan and Drew Goss personally prepare every single item they sell.

worked with professionals to design and construct the shop. Next, Susan and Drew began a difficult search for wholesalers who carried the quality ingredients they demanded. "We contacted every wholesaler in the Yellow Pages," Drew remembers, "but since we weren't yet buying, no one would talk to us." Throughout the preliminary, costly planning, Drew's folks supplied financial backing.

Finally, encouraging the early customers to try their rather esoteric menu was challenging, too. Once people tasted, however, they were pleased. Word of mouth rapidly spread about the imaginative food at Something Different in The Fashion Mall at Keystone at the Crossing. **MUCH OF THEIR SPECIALNESS IS THAT THEY MAKE THEIR OWN STOCKS, MAYONNAISES, AND PASTRIES; SMOKE THEIR OWN FISH, POULTRY, AND MEAT; AND ARE FANATICAL ABOUT FRESHNESS.**

Although every day is busy (with a crunch at noon), the Gosses notice a difference in the buying habits of the weekday customer and the weekend shopper, and that affects how much cooking they do. "On the weekends we'll sell three times as many baked goods, pâtés, and salads as we do during the week," says Drew. Most customers fit the yuppie image, seem to be on the go, and appreciate good food. The other major faction is women over 45 who shop at the mall and are delighted to take dinner home.

Where do Susan and Drew go from here? In the next few years, look for another new and different restaurant opening in Indianapolis!

FIGURING FOOD COSTS

To keep the necessary tight control on their expenses, the Gosses "cost out" every dish, which means they calculate, ingredient by ingredient, exactly how much it costs to produce each one. Then, they multiply by a factor to arrive at the retail price. Into that price they must figure overhead and labor as well as a profit. "Making a profit enables us to sell the kind of food we want to," explains Drew.

To keep up with rising food costs, the couple reevaluates each recipe every six months and, if necessary, raises its price. Most items are sold by weight—the Gosses find this is fairer for both buyer and seller.

Drew and Susan's advice for anyone thinking about getting in the food business? Know as much as you can about what you want to do—that includes the business side, first and last.

DIFFERENT DISHES

Try a Something Different specialty at home: **Greek Chicken Salad** (*front*); **Smoked Turkey Sandwich** (*back left*) made with bacon, blue cheese, and watercress; and **Duck Salad** (*right*) with sweet red peppers and cashews.

GOURMET Takeout

DIANE'S DESSERTS

"EVEN THOUGH WE'D WORKED IN RESTAURANTS, WE WEREN'T PREPARED FOR THE TIME COMMITMENT OF OWNING A BUSINESS."

WARMTH. IT'S FOUND EVERYWHERE IN THIS COZY SHOP: FROM THE HEAT OF THE OVENS, FROM THE CHARM OF THE DECOR, AND MOST RADIANTLY FROM THE YOUNG OWNERS, DIANE MARGARITIS AND JOHN DURKIN.

The warmth is just one reason why so many Long Islanders feel lucky to be within driving distance of Diane's Desserts in Roslyn, New York. Another reason is Diane and John's dedication. They are bent on selling only better - than - homemade goods, baked with expertise, love, and care. Their desire to please others demands long, long hours and constant dialogue with their customers.

Every food is created to satisfy customer taste. In fact, customer comments prompted Diane and John to cut a quarter of the sugar in some recipes.

One assistant helps Diane and John bake every day (using seasonal ingredients whenever possible) to fill their sparkling display cases. Depending on the time of year, the fruit tarts may be peach, plum, apple, banana, cranberry, rhubarb, or strawberry! Muffins, cakes, yeast rolls, chocolate delicacies, and cookies of all shapes surround the tarts.

John and Diane admit that their initial eagerness resulted in overextending themselves. "Now we're accustomed to long hours, six days a week. We've started working in two shifts which makes us more productive," explains John.

Even though time is at a premium, Diane and John go out of their way to provide simple pleasures. When they make Linzer bar cookies, they bake the dough remnants into crisp heart shapes as giveaways to every browser. It's little wonder that visitors to this quaint place come back, again and again.

GETTING ORGANIZED, AS *DIANE'S DESSERTS* IS TODAY, WASN'T EASY. JOHN REFERS TO THE CHRISTMAS OF '84 AS THEIR 'MELTDOWN.'

"At that time, Diane and I worked almost nonstop, baked 200 pounds of cookies, and gift-wrapped them in 1-pound boxes. Yet we coordinated our schedules with all of our customers so that orders were warm from the oven when picked up. Our ambitiousness caused problems— we rushed around, spilling and dropping things."

Diane adds, "Some of our past mistakes now seem funny. In particular she remembers the time she left salt out of 40 pounds of bread dough. She discarded the partially kneaded mass in a dumpster behind the shop. "Next thing I knew, my brother Albert came in with the news that the rising dough had lifted the heavy metal top off the dumpster! I sent Albert back out to punch down the dough until the yeast worked out of it!"

Albert has helped in greater ways, too. He built a building, designed by Diane's mother, to house the bakery and an upstairs antique shop—owned and operated by the Margaritis family. The family ties extend even further: both Diane's and John's families provided financial backing so that these energetic bakers could fulfill their dream.

Proprietor Diane Margaritis extends the antique charm of the sweets shop to the outdoors when weather allows.

Irresistible! Strawberry-Rhubarb Tart (left), Pear Custard Tart (back center), and Apple Dumplings (right).

PEAR CUSTARD TART

1 Fit Pastry Dough into the bottom and up the sides of an 8-inch pastry ring placed on a greased baking sheet. Trim, flute edge, and prick. Wrap and freeze or bake immediately.

2 Prepare Pastry Cream. Spoon the warm Pastry Cream into the cooled baked crust. Spread the cream to evenly distribute it in the pastry shell. Cover the surface with clear plastic wrap (this prevents a skin from forming on the filling); chill.

3 Arrange the poached pear slices atop the Pastry Cream. Brush melted currant jelly over the pears to add a glistening finish.

APPLE DUMPLINGS

1 Divide Pastry Dough into fourths. Roll each portion to ⅛-inch thickness; trim into an 8-inch circle. Reroll the trimmings and cut dough into decorative leaf cutouts.

2 Core apples. Place an apple on an 8-inch dough circle. Fill apple with the dried fruit mixture. Wrap dough around the apple to resemble a bundle; press edges together at the top to seal. Trim off excess dough. Repeat with remaining apples and dough.

3 Arrange leaf cutouts on the top of each bundle. Place bundles in a greased, shallow baking pan, and bake.

Takeout

More Secrets From Great Cooks

"Cooking is just one part of operating a successful food business," says Stacy DeLano, owner of **Movable Feast** in Washington, D.C. "Be systemized," she advises, "especially in bookkeeping."

Stacy's organized approach has paid off. Ten years ago, she started cooking and catering part-time at home to supplement her income. Word spread about her catering, and Stacy started making money! She eventually quit a full-time job to operate the business and expand into gourmet takeout.

Chefs now do the cooking, but Stacy still studies the food business at a local college. She's taken courses in sanitation and cost controls, and encourages future entrepreneurs to do the same.

"I have had a love affair with food all of my life," says Christina Rooth of **Christina's—A Food Boutique** in La Mesa, California. "Food was an important part of family life in Sweden, where my parents owned a food business. As an adult, I delved into any food opportunity to learn more. I was determined to own a food business someday." To learn through others, Christina worked four years for a restaurateur/caterer. While there, she confirmed that "busy people want high-quality food at affordable prices," and set out to meet that need.

Christina started her own business from a small commercial kitchen. But the rented space wasn't always available when needed, and scheduling problems developed. That's when she leased an old service station and converted it into a catering center. "I had so much space that I added a few chairs and tables. Before too long I was in the restaurant business, too!"

Long hours, sizable expenses, and thousands of miles to visit food shops across the country—that's what Penny Rembe logged before she opened **The Valley Deli** in Albuquerque, New Mexico. Although making the decision to start a deli was long and hard, success was almost instantaneous. But when you review Penny's inventive, regionalized menu, her success is understandable. Blue corn jalapeño muffins, sherry ginger sauce, southwestern vinegar, and the most popular item, green chili soup, sell, sell, and sell.

What's surprising about The Valley Deli's success is that customers must go out of their way to get there. The deli is tucked away in a group of specialty shops on the outskirts of the city. People make repeat visits because many remember what day of the week the staff bakes rye bread or has banana cake warm and waiting.

Expansion is tempting, but Penny keeps the business small so that the staff can provide "personalized food service," including catered parties and custom cooking.

Can an Italian food shop succeed in a non-Italian neighborhood? The answer is a resounding "yes" say Tom and Molly Broder—the husband/wife team of **Broders' Cucina Italiana.** "I think it's the shop's novelty that helped," says Molly. "There's nothing like it in this part of Minneapolis." Before opening the shop, the Broders studied cooking in Italy. Their love of Italian food and their belief that their neighbors would love it, too, prompted the Broders to set up the shop in its unlikely location. To please Minnesotans even more, they recently hired a cheesemaker from Sicily to make fresh cheeses.

Rhoda Kreamer and Becky Swartz tested their mother-daughter relationship in a unique way: they opened **Viva La Pasta** in Des Moines, Iowa. After analyzing the city and realizing that there was definitely a market for fresh pasta, the women went to work in May 1984. Since then they've delighted central Iowans with homemade pasta, sauces, breads, and biscottis. And as the business flourishes, the family ties strengthen. "Working together can be difficult at times, but no matter what, we always love each other at the end of the day," says Becky. "That's because we share our ideas and frustrations, and work them out together."

VEGETARIAN PASTA A LA GRECQUE

Serve this meatless marvel as a main dish and your guests will never miss the meat; or give your dinner a Greek touch by serving this as a side dish—

- 3 medium zucchini, sliced (about 4½ cups)
- 1 medium onion, sliced and separated into rings
- ¼ cup olive oil *or* cooking oil
- 3 medium tomatoes, peeled and chopped *or* one 16-ounce can tomatoes, cut up
- 2 teaspoons dried mint, crushed
- 1½ teaspoons dried dillweed
- ½ teaspoon salt
- 8 ounces corkscrew macaroni *or* other pasta
- 1 tablespoon all-purpose flour
- 1 cup dairy sour cream *or* plain yogurt
- ½ cup crumbled feta cheese (2 ounces)

In a large saucepan cook zucchini and onion in hot oil for 5 minutes. Add chopped tomatoes or *undrained* tomatoes, mint, dillweed, and salt. Cover and simmer for 8 minutes.

Meanwhile, cook pasta according to package directions; drain. Keep warm. Stir flour into sour cream or yogurt. Stir *1 cup* of the tomato mixture into sour cream or yogurt mixture; return all to saucepan. Heat through but *do not boil.* Transfer warm pasta to a serving platter; spoon on vegetable mixture. Sprinkle feta cheese on top. Makes 4 servings.

Per serving: 550 cal., 14 g pro., 59 g carbo., 30 g fat, 38 mg chol., 463 mg sodium. USRDA: 35% vit. A, 86% vit. C, 44% thiamine, 28% riboflavin, 28% niacin, 21% calcium, 16% iron, 27% phosphorus.

SZECHUAN CHICKEN PASTA

This hot and spicy stir-fry is sure to set your palate ablaze—

- 8 ounces linguine *or* spaghetti
- 3 tablespoons soy sauce
- 1 tablespoon rice wine vinegar
- 1 teaspoon purchased *or* Homemade Chili Oil (see recipe below)
- ½ teaspoon crushed red pepper
- 2 tablespoons cooking oil
- 1 clove garlic, minced
- 1 teaspoon grated gingerroot
- 2 whole medium chicken breasts (1½ pounds total), skinned, boned, and cut into 1-inch pieces
- 2 cups fresh pea pods, coarsely chopped (4 ounces)
- 1 red *or* green sweet pepper, cut into thin strips
- 2 green onions, chopped
- ¼ cup coarsely chopped peanuts
  Orange slice (optional)

Cook linguine or spaghetti according to package directions; drain. To serve hot, keep pasta warm. In a small bowl combine soy sauce, vinegar, chili oil, and crushed red pepper. Set aside.

In a wok or large skillet heat *1 tablespoon* cooking oil. Stir-fry garlic and gingerroot in hot oil for 30 seconds. Add *half* of the chicken and stir-fry for 1 minute. Add pea pods; stir-fry for 1 minute more. Remove mixture from wok or skillet.

Add remaining cooking oil to wok, if necessary. Stir-fry remaining chicken, red or green pepper, and green onion for 2 minutes. Return all to wok. Add soy mixture and hot pasta to mixture in wok. Toss gently to mix. Serve hot or cover and chill. Top with peanuts. Garnish with an orange slice, if desired. Makes 5 servings.

Homemade Chili Oil: In a small saucepan heat ½ cup *sesame oil* till warm (200°). Remove from the heat. Stir in ⅓ cup crushed *red pepper.* Cover; let stand for several hours or overnight. Strain, pressing out oil with the back of a spoon. Store, covered, in the refrigerator. Makes about ⅓ cup.

Per serving: 542 cal., 55 g pro., 46 g carbo., 14 g fat, 107 mg chol., 959 mg sodium. USRDA: 13% vit. A, 90% vit. C, 46% thiamine, 25% riboflavin, 30% iron, 106% niacin, 54% phosphorus.

SUPER SALMON SALAD

This out-of-the-ordinary salad, accented with horseradish, tastes fresh and full of flavor—

- 4 ounces fettuccine
- 1 7¾-ounce can salmon, drained
- 2 hard-cooked eggs, chopped
- ½ cup frozen peas
- ½ cup finely chopped celery
- 2 green onions, sliced
- 1 8-ounce carton dairy sour cream
- 2 tablespoons milk
- 2 tablespoons prepared horseradish
- ½ teaspoon salt
  Dash ground red pepper
  Parsley sprigs (optional)
  Carrot curls (optional)

Break fettuccine into 6-inch pieces. Cook pasta according to package directions; drain. Rinse with cold water; drain again. Remove skin and bones from salmon. Use a fork to coarsely flake; set aside.

In a medium mixing bowl combine cooked fettuccine, chopped eggs, peas, celery, and green onions. In another bowl stir together sour cream, milk, horseradish, salt, and red pepper; pour over fettuccine mixture. Toss to coat. Add salmon; toss gently so as to not break up salmon. Cover and chill in the refrigerator. Garnish with parsley sprigs and carrots curls, if desired. Makes 4 servings.

Per serving: 371 cal., 21 g pro., 28 g carbo., 19 g fat, 172 mg chol., 595 mg sodium. USRDA: 20% vit. A, 10% vit. C, 25% thiamine, 23% riboflavin, 33% niacin, 22% calcium, 13% iron, 34% phosphorus.

AIOLI (GARLIC MAYONNAISE)

  3 **cloves garlic**
  1 **egg**
  2 **tablespoons lemon juice**
  ¼ **teaspoon salt**
Dash pepper
  1 **cup salad oil**

In a blender container or food processor bowl combine garlic, egg, lemon juice, salt, and pepper. Cover; blend or process for 5 seconds.

    With appliance running, add salad oil in a very slow steady stream, blending till smooth and thick. Stop to scrape the sides as necessary. Transfer mixture to a storage container. Cover and chill. Makes about 1 cup.

HERBED MAYONNAISE

Store this homemade mayonnaise for up to one month in a tightly covered jar in the refrigerator—

  ¼ **cup loosely packed watercress leaves**
  ¼ **cup loosely packed parsley sprigs**
  1 **green onion, sliced**
  3 **egg yolks**
  2 **tablespoons lemon juice**
  ½ **teaspoon Dijon-style mustard**
  1 **cup salad oil**

In a blender container or food processor bowl place watercress, parsley, and green onion. Cover; blend or process. Add egg yolks, lemon juice, and mustard; blend or process till smooth.

    With appliance running, add salad oil in a very slow steady stream, blending till smooth and thick. Stop to scrape the sides as necessary. Add pepper to taste. Transfer to a storage container. Cover and store in the refrigerator. Makes 1⅓ cups mayonnaise.

    Per tablespoon: 101 cal., 1 g pro., 0 g carbo., 11 g fat, 36 mg chol., and 5 mg sodium.

GREEK CHICKEN SALAD

When you want to add a new twist to this refreshing chilled salad, serve it in whole wheat pita bread halves with shredded Boston lettuce—

  3 **cups cubed cooked chicken**
  2 **medium cucumbers, peeled, seeded, and chopped (about 2½ cups)**
  1¼ **cups crumbled feta cheese (5 ounces)**
  ⅔ **cup sliced pitted ripe olives**
  ¼ **cup snipped parsley**
  1 **recipe Aioli (see recipe at left) *or* 1 cup mayonnaise plus 3 cloves garlic, minced**
  ½ **cup plain yogurt**
  1 **tablespoon dried oregano, crushed**
Boston lettuce leaves

In a large mixing bowl combine chicken, cucumber, feta cheese, olives, and parsley; set aside.

    For dressing, in a small mixing bowl stir together Aioli (or mayonnaise and garlic), yogurt, and oregano; add to the chicken mixture.

    Toss mixture gently till coated. Cover and chill. Serve on Boston lettuce leaves. Makes 6 servings.

    Per serving: 255 cal., 29 g pro., 8 g carbo., 12 g fat, 119 mg chol., 546 mg sodium. USRDA: 11% vit. A, 24% vit. C, 10% riboflavin, 42% niacin, 19% calcium, 12% iron, 33% phosphorus.

SMOKED TURKEY SANDWICH

Purchase a smoked turkey breast and slice it for sandwiches, or buy smoked presliced turkey at the deli—

  1 **tablespoon Herbed Mayonnaise (see recipe at left)**
  1 **slice dark rye bread**
  ¼ **cup loosely packed watercress leaves**
  3 **ounces thinly sliced smoked turkey breast**
  2 **slices bacon, crisp-cooked and drained**
  2 **teaspoons crumbled blue cheese**

Spread Herbed Mayonnaise over 1 side of rye bread slice. Top bread with watercress leaves, then turkey, bacon, and blue cheese. Serve immediately. Makes 1 serving.

    Per serving: 541 cal., 42 g pro., 19 g carbo., 33 g fat, 138 mg chol., 618 sodium. USRDA: 18% vit. A, 15% vit. C, 19% thiamine, 23% riboflavin, 58% niacin, 11% calcium, 17% iron, 44% phosphorus.

GARLIC CHILI DRESSING

For the roast duck salad you need only half of the dressing recipe. Use the other half on a pasta or tossed green salad. The dressing will keep for up to a week. The tangy chili paste is available in specialty food shops—

  1 **tablespoon salad oil**
  1½ **teaspoons chili paste with garlic *or* ½ to 1 teaspoon crushed red pepper and 1 clove garlic, minced**
  ¼ **cup vinegar**
  ¼ **cup soy sauce**
  2 **tablespoons brown sugar**
  1 **tablespoon sesame oil**

In a small saucepan heat salad oil over medium heat. Add chili paste (or crushed red pepper and garlic) and cook about 1 minute or till fragrant. Remove from the heat. Add vinegar, soy sauce, brown sugar, and sesame oil. Stir to dissolve brown sugar. Cover and chill. Makes about 1 cup.

    Per tablespoon: 25 cal., 27 g pro., 2 g carbo., 2 g fat, 333 mg sodium.

DUCK SALAD

Susan suggests that you roast the duck a day ahead—

- 1 5-pound domestic duckling
- 2 tablespoons dry sherry
- 2 tablespoons soy sauce
- 1 green onion, sliced
- 1 large clove garlic, minced
- ½ teaspoon salt
- 4 teaspoons honey
- 1 tablespoon water
- 1 cup fresh *or* frozen pea pods, cooked, drained, and halved crosswise
- 1 red sweet pepper, cut into strips
- 2 green onions, sliced
- ½ recipe Garlic Chili Dressing (see recipe, page 114)
- ¼ cup whole cashews, toasted

Rinse duck cavity with cold water. Pat dry with paper towels; sprinkle cavity and outside with salt. In a small mixing bowl combine sherry, soy sauce, 1 sliced green onion, garlic, and salt. Pour *1 tablespoon* of the mixture into the duck cavity. Add honey and water to remaining soy mixture.

Skewer duck neck skin to back; tie legs to tail. Twist wing tips under back. Prick skin all over with fork. Liberally brush soy mixture over duck. Place duck, breast side up, on a rack in a large roasting pan. Insert a meat thermometer. Roast in a 325° oven for 1¾ to 2¼ hours, basting with reserved honey-soy mixture every 30 minutes. Duck is done when drumstick moves easily in socket or thermometer registers 185° F. Let duck cool completely.

Remove skin from breast and legs of cooled duck. Trim and discard all fat from skin. Cut skin into ½-inch squares. In a skillet cook and stir duck skin over medium heat about 4 minutes or till crisp. Drain skin thoroughly on paper towels. Remove meat from duck breast and legs. Cut into 1½-inch bias-sliced strips.

To assemble salad, combine duck meat, pea pods, red sweet pepper, and 2 sliced green onions. Shake Garlic Chili Dressing well and pour *half* over salad; toss. Cover salad and chill thoroughly. Before serving, stir in duck skin and toasted cashews. Makes 4 servings.

Per serving: 395 cal., 22 g pro., 21 g carbo., 25 g fat, 64 mg chol., 1,725 mg sodium. USRDA: 15% vit. A, 102% vit. C, 16% thiamine, 16% riboflavin, 22% niacin, 5% calcium, 20% iron, 24% phosphorus.

STRAWBERRY-RHUBARB TART

Diane's Desserts uses only fresh, seasonal fruits. To make it easy for you, our Test Kitchen found that frozen fruits work well, too—

- 3 cups fresh *or* frozen unsweetened sliced rhubarb, thawed
- 3 cups sliced strawberries
- 1 cup sugar
- ¼ cup all-purpose flour
- Dash salt
- Few dashes ground cinnamon
- 1 recipe Pastry Dough (see recipe, page 116)
- ¼ cup ground blanched almonds
- Dash ground cinnamon
- 1 teaspoon sugar

In a large mixing bowl combine rhubarb and strawberries. Stir in ½ cup of sugar. Let stand for 15 minutes. Drain off excess fruit juices.

In a small mixing bowl stir together remaining ½ cup sugar, flour, salt, and a few dashes cinnamon. Add to fruit mixture. Set aside.

Divide Pastry Dough in half. On a lightly floured surface roll *half* of the Pastry Dough into a 10-inch circle. Fit dough into an 8-inch flan pan or spring-form pan, allowing 1½ inches up the sides. Press bottom and sides gently to remove any air bubbles.

Stir together almonds and remaining dash cinnamon. Spread almond mixture over pastry in pan. Turn fruit mixture into pastry-lined pan.

Roll remaining pastry into a ⅛-inch-thick circle. Sprinkle 1 teaspoon sugar over pastry circle. Gently roll sugar into pastry. Cut pastry into long, thin rectangles and alternate across the top of the pie. (Or, cut pastry into ½-inch-wide strips and weave across top for a lattice crust.)

Seal and flute edges of pie. Bake, uncovered, in a 375° oven for 50 to 55 minutes or till done. Serve warm. Makes 8 to 10 servings.

Per serving: 404 cal., 5 g pro., 61 g carbo., 16 g fat, 23 mg chol., 290 mg sodium. USRDA: 80% vit. C, 18% thiamine, 15% riboflavin, 13% niacin, and 13% iron.

PEAR CUSTARD TART

Parts of this delectable dessert can be made ahead. Prepare and freeze the un-baked pastry dough weeks beforehand. You also can marinate the pears three days ahead so they pick up the red color from the wine—

- 1½ **cups water**
-   1 **cup Zinfandel *or* dry red wine**
-   ¼ **cup sugar**
-   1 **thin strip lemon peel (about 4 × 1 inches)**
-   1 **tablespoon lemon juice**
-   2 **to 3 medium pears, peeled and cored**
-   ½ **recipe Pastry Dough (see recipe at right)**
-   1 **recipe Pastry Cream (see recipe at right)**
-   2 **tablespoons currant jelly**

In a large saucepan combine water, wine, sugar, lemon peel, and lemon juice. Cook and stir over medium heat till sugar dissolves. Bring to boiling; add pears. Reduce the heat and simmer, uncovered, for 10 minutes or till pears are tender. Remove from the heat; cool. Cover and chill for several hours or up to 3 days.

On a lightly floured surface roll Pastry Dough into a 10-inch circle. Fit into the bottom and up the sides of an 8-inch pastry ring placed on a greased baking sheet. (Or, fit dough into an 8-inch flan pan or springform pan, allowing 1 inch up sides.)

Press bottom and sides gently to remove air bubbles. Trim and flute edges. Prick bottom and sides with the tines of a fork. Bake in a 450° oven for 10 to 12 minutes or till crust is golden. Cool crust thoroughly on a wire rack.

Fill cooled crust with warm Pastry Cream. Cover surface of cream with clear plastic wrap; chill thoroughly.

To serve, remove pear halves from liquid and thinly slice. Overlap and arrange pear slices in concentric circles over Pastry Cream. Melt currant jelly and brush onto pears. Makes 8 to 10 servings.

Per serving: 342 cal., 4 g pro., 49 g carbo., 13 g fat, 90 mg chol., 209 mg sodium. USRDA: 10% vit. A, and 11% riboflavin.

PASTRY DOUGH

This versatile dough can be made ahead and frozen. Just wrap the prepared crust in a moisture- and vaporproof material, then seal and label. Store pastry in your freezer for up to three months—

- 2 **cups all-purpose flour**
- ½ **teaspoon salt**
- ⅓ **cup unsalted butter**
- ¼ **cup shortening**
- ⅓ **cup ice water**

In a medium mixing bowl stir together flour and salt. Cut in butter and shortening till pieces are the size of small peas. Sprinkle *1 tablespoon* of the water over part of the mixture; gently toss with a fork. Repeat till all is moistened. Form dough into a ball. Use as directed in tarts and dumplings.

PASTRY CREAM

- ½ **cup sugar**
- 2 **tablespoons cornstarch**
- 1½ **cups milk**
- 2 **beaten egg yolks**
- 2 **tablespoons unsalted butter**
- 1 **teaspoon vanilla**

In a heavy medium saucepan combine sugar and cornstarch. Stir in milk. Cook and stir over medium heat till thickened and bubbly; cook and stir for 2 minutes more. Remove from the heat.

Gradually stir about ¾ cup of the hot mixture into egg yolks. Return mixture to pan. Cook and stir for 2 minutes more. Remove from the heat. Stir in butter and vanilla. Use as directed in Pear Custard Tart. Makes 1¾ cups.

APPLE DUMPLINGS

Diane and John prefer Rome Beauty or McCoon apples for their dumplings—

- 1 **recipe Pastry Dough (see recipe at left)**
- 2 **tablespoons chopped dried apricots**
- 2 **tablespoons chopped dried figs**
- 2 **tablespoons raisins**
- 2 **tablespoons chopped walnuts**
- 1 **tablespoon brown sugar**
- 1 **tablespoon butter *or* margarine, melted**
- 4 **small cooking apples (¾ to 1¼ pounds)**
- ¼ **cup maple syrup**

Light cream (optional)

Divide the Pastry Dough into 4 portions. On a floured surface roll *each* portion of dough to ⅛-inch thickness; trim into an 8-inch circle. Reroll the pastry trimmings. With a knife, cut leaves from pastry scraps.

For filling, in a small mixing bowl stir together dried apricots, figs, raisins, walnuts, brown sugar, and melted butter or margarine.

Core apples but do not peel. Place an apple in the center of *each* dough circle. Press *one-fourth* of the filling into the core of *each* apple. Bring dough up around *each* apple to resemble a bundle, pressing edges together at the top to seal. Trim excess dough. Moisten 1 side of pastry leaves with water and attach to the tops of wrapped apples.

Place apples in a greased shallow baking pan. Bake in a 375° oven about 45 minutes or till pastry is golden. Brush dumplings with maple syrup during the last 5 minutes of baking. Remove dumplings from pan immediately. Serve warm with cream, if desired. Makes 4 servings.

Per serving: 434 cal., 5 g pro., 63 g carbo., 20 g fat, 32 mg chol., 261 mg sodium. USRDA: 20% vit. A, 17% thiamine, 10% niacin, 10% iron.

WHOLE WHEAT CRITTERS

Healthful Snacks For Hungry Kids

By
Diana McMillen

Fill your cookie jar with fun! Stir up a batch of Whole Wheat Critters—then let your child cut them into favorite animal shapes. Making and eating these crackers are great ways to beat the after-school blahs.

Whole Wheat Critters

Spread peanut butter or softened cream cheese on the baked crackers for an even better treat—

- 2 **cups whole wheat flour**
- 1 **cup all-purpose flour**
- 1 **teaspoon baking powder**
- ½ **cup butter** *or* **margarine**
- ½ **cup packed brown sugar**
- ⅓ **cup honey**
- 1 **teaspoon vanilla**
- ½ **cup milk**
- 2 **tablespoons granulated sugar**
- ½ **teaspoon ground nutmeg**

Combine flours and baking powder. Beat butter or margarine 30 seconds. Add brown sugar, honey, and vanilla; beat till fluffy. Add dry ingredients and milk alternately to beaten mixture, beating after each addition. Divide in half. Cover; chill several hours or overnight.

On floured surface roll *half* of the dough to ⅛-inch thickness. Using large cutters, cut into desired shapes; reroll as needed. Place on ungreased baking sheets. Using tines of a fork, prick sparingly. Combine granulated sugar and nutmeg; sprinkle over crackers. Repeat with remaining dough. Bake in a 350° oven 12 to 14 minutes. Remove immediately; cool on wire rack. Makes about 36.

Per critter: 83 cal., 1 g pro., 14 g carbo., 3 g fat, 8 mg chol., 42 mg sodium.

Photograph: Ron Crofoot. Food stylist: Judy Tills.

WEEKNIGHT
Gourmet

Herbed mustard, or any mustard on hand, adds flair to seafood. This scallop dish goes together in less than 25 minutes—what a deal!

FANCY MEALS WITH FAST-FOOD EASE

Serve an epicurean delight on a regular weeknight. Yes, it is possible! We've created gourmet dinners that prove you don't have to wait till the weekend for fine food. That's because these recipes are so, so simple—each one stars a ready-to-use ingredient from a can or jar. The result: Elegance in no time at all.

By
Diana McMillen

Photographs: Ron Crofoot
Food stylist: Judy Tills

Scallop Moutarde

- 1 **pound fresh** *or* **frozen sea scallops**
- 2 **cups shredded unpeeled zucchini**
- 2 **tablespoons cooking oil**
- 2 **tablespoons purchased herbed mustard**
- 2 **teaspoons lemon juice**
- 1 **teaspoon cornstarch**
- 3 **tablespoons cashews**

Thaw the scallops. Halve large scallops. In a steamer basket steam zucchini, covered, over boiling water for 2 minutes. Remove from heat; keep warm over hot water.

In a wok heat oil. Add *half* the scallops to wok; stir-fry 2 to 3 minutes. Remove from wok. Repeat with remaining scallops; remove. Combine ¼ cup *water*, mustard, lemon, and cornstarch; add to wok. Cook and stir till bubbly; cook 2 minutes more. Serve scallops with zucchini. Spoon sauce over; sprinkle with cashews. Serves 4.

Per serving: 246 cal., 29 g pro., 9 g carbo., 12 g fat, 60 mg chol., 408 mg sodium. USRDA: 23% vit. C, 12% thiamine, 11% niacin, 16% calcium, 22% iron, 44% phosphorus.

Zesty chutney packs a wallop of spicy fruit flavor. Brush it over broiling chicken for a quick and delicious golden finish.

Luscious fudge sauce from a jar enriches this dessert. What a heavenly way to end a Monday—or any day. Try it this week!

30-Minute Chutney Chicken

- 2 whole large chicken breasts, halved lengthwise
- 4 ounces orzo (¾ cup) or noodles
- 2 tablespoons snipped parsley
- 1 tablespoon cooking oil
- ⅓ cup purchased chutney
- 1 tablespoon dry white wine or water
- 12 ounces fresh or frozen pea pods, cooked

Place chicken, skin side down, on unheated rack of broiler pan. Broil chicken 5 to 6 inches from heat 10 min-

utes. Turn; broil 10 minutes more. Meanwhile, cook orzo according to package directions 5 to 8 minutes. Drain; toss with parsley and oil. Keep warm. Combine chutney and wine; heat through. Brush chicken with chutney mixture; broil 5 minutes. Serve chicken over orzo on pea pods. Spoon remaining chutney over. Serves 4.

Per serving: 452 cal., 45 g pro., 43 g carbo., 9 g fat, 27 mg chol., 133 mg sodium. USRDA: 16% vit. A, 21% vit. C, 36% thiamine, 27% riboflavin, 86% niacin, 27% iron, 51% phosphorus.

Fudge Cream Hearts

- 6 6-inch squares cheesecloth
- 1 8-ounce package cream cheese, cut up
- 2 tablespoons bottled fudge sauce
- ¼ cup sifted powdered sugar
- 1 cup whipping cream

Moisten the cheesecloth squares. Line six ½-cup molds or custard cups with the cheesecloth, overlapping edges. Beat the cheese and fudge sauce with an electric mixer till well combined. Add sugar; beat on high speed till fluffy.

Wash beaters. In another bowl beat cream till soft peaks form; fold into fudge mixture. Spoon into molds. Cover with cheesecloth; quick-chill in freezer 30 to 45 minutes or chill in refrigerator 3 to 24 hours. To serve, spoon additional fudge sauce onto serving plates. Unmold; remove cheesecloth. Place on plates; top with purchased chocolates. Drizzle with sauce. Serves 6.

Per serving: 298 cal., 4 g pro., 10 g carbo., 28 g fat, 86 mg chol., 115 mg sodium. USRDA: 22% vit. A.

FANCY MEALS WITH FAST-FOOD EASE

Bottled barbecue sauce and frozen fruit juice blend for a terrific glaze to brush on lamb chops. Remember this fix-up for other meats, too.

This dish is so simple and it tastes sensational! Cranberry sauce adds the gusto to this four-ingredient, 20-minute culinary delight.

Glazed Lamb Chops

- ½ of a 6-ounce can frozen tangerine *or* orange juice concentrate, thawed
- ⅓ cup bottled barbecue sauce
- 4 lamb sirloin chops, cut ¾ to 1 inch thick (1¼ pounds)
- 1 9-ounce package frozen green beans, cooked and drained

For sauce: In a small saucepan combine the tangerine concentrate and barbecue sauce; heat through. Place chops on an unheated rack of broiler pan. Brush with some sauce. Broil 3 inches from heat for 6 minutes. Turn and brush again with sauce. Broil 4 to 6 minutes more for medium doneness. (Or, grill over *medium* coals for 18 to 22 minutes for medium doneness, turning once.) Serve with green beans. Pass the remaining sauce. Makes 4 servings.

Per serving: 396 cal., 21 g pro., 15 g carbo., 28 g fat, 87 mg chol., 217 mg sodium. USRDA: 16% vit. A, 49% vit. C, 14% thiamine, 16% riboflavin, 24% niacin, 11% iron, 19% phosphorus.

Cranberry-Capped Turkey

- 1 10-ounce package frozen rice and wild rice with green beans and mushrooms
- 2 tablespoons water
- 2 cups cubed smoked fully cooked turkey breast (about 10 ounces)
- ¼ cup whole berry cranberry sauce

In a medium saucepan cook rice according to package directions. Stir in the water and turkey. Heat through, stirring occasionally. Stir in cranberry sauce, heat 1 minute more. Makes 4 servings.

Per serving: 236 cal., 26 g pro., 23 g carbo., 4 g fat, 59 mg chol., 869 mg sodium. USRDA: 45% niacin, 25% phosphorus.

Create a tempting main-dish salad just by uncapping a jar of artichoke hearts. The flavor-packed marinade starts the dressing.

Go ahead, grab a jar of gourmet fruits in brandy; then put it to mouth-watering-good use. Individual fruit trifles show off the spiked fruit.

Antipasto Salad Supper

- 1 6-ounce jar marinated artichoke hearts *or* mushrooms
- 4 cups torn mixed greens
- 2 cups fully cooked Canadian-style bacon *or* ham cut into julienne strips
- 1 cup broken Melba toast
- 1 tablespoon water
- 1 tablespoon lemon juice
- 1 teaspoon sugar

Drain artichokes, reserving ¼ *cup* marinade. Cut any large artichokes into bite-size pieces. In individual bowls or on plates, arrange the greens, Canadian bacon, toast, and artichokes. Stir together reserved marinade, water, lemon juice, and sugar; drizzle over salad. Makes 4 servings.

Per serving: 403 cal., 23 g pro., 21 g carbo., 26 g fat, 59 mg chol., 2,292 mg sodium. USRDA: 32% vit. A, 25% vit. C, 47% thiamine, 13% riboflavin, 22% niacin, 22% iron, 20% phosphorus.

Brandied Fruit Trifle

- 1 8-ounce can pear quarters, cut in half
- 1½ cups purchased fruit in brandy or liqueur (1 12- to 16-ounce jar)
- 1 tablespoon cornstarch
- 3 cups purchased pound cake cut into ½-inch cubes
- 1 4-ounce container frozen whipped dessert topping, thawed

Drain pears, reserving ¼ *cup* syrup. Halve, pit, and quarter any large brandied fruit, if necessary. (Measure ⅓ cup liquid with fruit.) In saucepan combine reserved pear liquid, pears, and brandied fruit with sauce. Combine cornstarch and 1 tablespoon *water;* add to saucepan. Cook till bubbly; cook 2 minutes. Cover; cool.

In individual sherbets layer *half* the cake cubes, *half* the fruit mixture, and *half* the topping. Repeat layers once. Drizzle with melted *raspberry jelly* and garnish with a cookie, if desired. Makes 6 servings.

Per serving: 338 cal., 3 g pro., 49 g carbo., 12 g fat, 38 mg chol., and 32 mg sodium. USRDA: 12% vit. A.

FANCY BREADS...
FAST!

N o time to bake anymore? Explore the growing number of convenience baking products—from packaged biscuit mix to phyllo dough. With a twist of the dough or a sprinkling of flavorful toppers, bread products such as these yield scrumptious results.

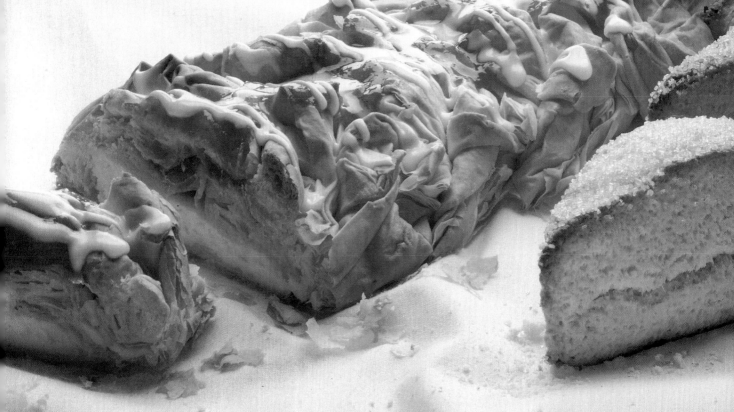

ICED APRICOT BRAID

Thanks to phyllo dough from a box, anyone can make elegant pastry like this coffee cake without compromising one bit of flavor.

PARMESAN PARSLEY KNOTS

Open the tube, shape the dough, coat with a Parmesan mixture, and bake. It's that easy to serve stylish homemade dinner rolls!

PEACH YOGURT SCONES

Stir up just five ingredients—biscuit mix, sugar, an egg, yogurt, and butter or margarine—to create triangular scones. Fifteen minutes later serve these treats hot from the oven.

NUTMEG RAISIN COFFEE RING

In less than 20 minutes, the batter for a breakfast treat is ready for baking. That's because there's no flour to measure and no long rising time.

FANCY BREADS...*FAST!*

Count on convenience from the freezer—loaves of frozen bread dough. Wrap the yeast doughs around a simple filling: sugar, cinnamon, and dried fruit bits. Then, twist together the white and whole wheat doughs to form a two-tone breakfast bread.

FRUIT TWIST BREAD

- 1 16-ounce loaf frozen white bread dough
- 1 16-ounce loaf frozen wheat bread dough
- ¼ cup sugar
- 1 teaspoon cinnamon
- 1 6-ounce package (⅔ cup) dried fruit bits
- 1 beaten egg
- 1 cup sifted powdered sugar
- 1 teaspoon vanilla

Thaw doughs; halve lengthwise. On floured surface roll each portion to form a 12x5½-inch rectangle. Brush with *water*. Combine sugar and cinnamon; sprinkle over rectangles. Sprinkle with fruit. From long side, roll up jelly-roll style; seal. On a greased baking sheet place a wheat and white rope, seam sides down. Twist together. Seal ends; tuck under. Repeat with remaining ropes. Cover; let rise till double. Combine egg and 1 tablespoon *water;* brush loaves. Bake in 350° oven 25 to 30 minutes. Cover with foil after 15 minutes. Cool. Mix powdered sugar, vanilla, and 3 to 4 teaspoons *water;* drizzle over. Makes two, 20 servings each.

Per serving: 162 cal., 5 g pro., 33 g carbo., 2 g fat, 14 mg chol., 239 mg sodium.

PUMPKIN-JAM BREAD PUDDING

Strawberry, boysenberry, or even plum—choose any gourmet jam or preserve that appeals to you—

- 2 **cups dry whole wheat** *or* **white bread cubes**
- ½ **cup chopped pecans**
- ½ **cup jam** *or* **preserves**
- 4 **eggs**
- 1 **14-ounce can** *sweetened condensed* **milk**
- ¾ **cup canned pumpkin**
- 1 **teaspoon pumpkin pie spice**
- 1½ **cups milk**
- **Light cream** *or* **whipped cream (optional)**

Combine bread cubes and pecans; arrange *half* of the mixture in the bottom of a 9x9x2-inch baking dish or baking pan. Spoon jam or preserves in dollops over bread cube mixture. Arrange remaining bread cubes over mixture.

In a medium mixing bowl slightly beat eggs. Stir in condensed milk, pumpkin, and pumpkin pie spice. Gradually stir in milk, mixing well.

Pour egg mixture over bread and jam in the baking dish. Place the baking dish in a large roasting pan. Pour boiling water into roasting pan around dish to a depth of ½ inch. Bake in a 350° oven about 45 minutes or till knife inserted comes out clean. Serve warm with light cream or whipped cream, if desired. Makes 6 servings.

Per serving: 473 cal., 14 g pro., 65 g carbo., 19 g fat, 199 mg chol., 200 mg sodium. USRDA: 51% vit. A, 15% thiamine, 29% riboflavin, 29% calcium, and 32% phosphorus.

Pumpkin-Jam Bread Pudding

BRAN WAFFLES

Bran muffin mix saves you steps in whipping up a batch of flavor-packed waffles. Serve the waffles for breakfast or as a dinner finale topped with whipped cream—

- 1 **9¾-ounce package bran muffin mix**
- 1 **cup milk**
- 1 **slightly beaten egg**
- ⅓ **cup coarsely chopped walnuts**
- 1 **recipe Honeyed Fruit Sauce**

Lightly grease a 7-inch waffle iron, then preheat. Meanwhile, in a medium mixing bowl combine muffin mix, milk, egg, and walnuts. Pour ⅓ to ½ cup batter onto grids of the preheated waffle iron. Close lid quickly; do not open during baking.

Using a fork, carefully remove the baked waffle from the grid. Repeat with the remaining bran batter till all is used. Serve waffles topped with warm Honeyed Fruit Sauce. Makes 4 or 5 (7-inch) waffles.

Honeyed Fruit Sauce: In a small saucepan combine one 10-ounce package *frozen red raspberries,* thawed; ¼ cup *orange juice;* 1 tablespoon *cornstarch;* and 1 tablespoon *honey.* Cook and stir till thickened and bubbly. Cook and stir for 2 minutes more.

Pour the thickened sauce into a sieve over a bowl. Push the sauce through the sieve with the back of a wooden spoon to remove raspberry seeds. Serve sauce over waffles. Makes 1¼ cups sauce.

Per waffle: 464 cal., 10 g pro., 67 g carbo., 18 g fat, 72 mg chol., 501 mg sodium. USRDA: 31% vit. C, 22% thiamine, 20% riboflavin, 13% niacin, 31% calcium, 12% iron, 46% phosphorus.

Bran Waffles

GRANOLA QUICK BREAD

Coconut and lemon peel add a tropical twist to date quick bread. Use a serrated knife to slice this moist loaf—

- 1 17-ounce package date quick bread mix
- 1 cup milk
- 1 beaten egg
- 1 teaspoon finely shredded lemon peel
- ½ cup granola
- ½ cup coconut

Grease and flour a 9x5x3-inch loaf pan or 8x4x2-inch loaf pan; set aside. In a mixing bowl combine bread mix, milk, egg, and lemon peel; stir just till moistened. Fold in granola and coconut.

Turn batter into the prepared loaf pan. Bake in a 350° oven till done. Allow 45 minutes for the 9x5x3-inch pan and about 70 minutes for the 8x4x2-inch pan. Cool for 10 minutes on a wire rack. Remove bread from the pan. Cool thoroughly on a wire rack. Makes 1 loaf—10 servings.

Per serving: 287 cal., 5 g pro., 60 g carbo., 4 g fat, 32 mg chol., 189 mg sodium. USRDA: 18% thiamine, 16% riboflavin, and 13% niacin.

Granola Quick Bread

CRANBERRY-CAPPED TURKEY

Here's the microwave version of the recipe that appears on page 122—

- 1 10-ounce package frozen rice and wild rice with green beans and mushrooms
- 2 cups cubed smoked fully cooked turkey breast (about 10 ounces)
- ¼ cup whole berry cranberry sauce

In a 2-quart nonmetal casserole cook frozen rice and vegetable mixture in the microwave oven according to package directions. Stir in smoked turkey.

Micro-cook, uncovered, on 100% power (HIGH) for 2 to 3 minutes or till the mixture is heated through, stirring once. Stir in cranberry sauce. Cook, uncovered, on high power for 30 seconds more. Makes 4 servings.

Per serving: 236 cal., 26 g pro., 23 g carbo., 4 g fat, 59 mg chol., and 869 mg sodium. USRDA: 45% niacin and 25% phosphorus.

ICED APRICOT BRAID

Serve this attractive twisted coffee bread for breakfast or tea. Choose from apricot, prune, or cherry pastry filling—

- 1 8-ounce package cream cheese, softened
- ⅓ cup sugar
- 1 tablespoon lemon juice
- 10 sheets frozen phyllo dough (17x12-inch rectangles), thawed
- ½ cup butter *or* margarine, melted
- ½ cup apricot, prune, *or* cherry cake and pastry filling
- 1 recipe Powdered Sugar Icing

For filling, in a small mixing bowl combine cream cheese, sugar, and lemon juice; beat till smooth and set aside.

Unfold phyllo dough; cover first with waxed paper, then with a dampened towel. Remove 1 sheet of the phyllo dough; brush lightly with some of the melted butter or margarine. Fold the sheet of phyllo lengthwise into thirds; brush the top with melted butter or margarine.

Place the folded phyllo crosswise at 1 end of a 15x10x1-inch baking pan. Repeat with the remaining phyllo and butter or margarine. Arrange the phyllo strips, overlapping, in the pan to form a 17x15-inch rectangle with edges of phyllo strips overlapping about 2½ inches, and ends of the strips extending over edges of pan.

Spread the cream cheese mixture lengthwise down the center of the arranged phyllo strips in a 12x2½-inch area. Starting at 1 end, fold and twist the phyllo strips at an angle over the filling (see the how-to photo, page 124). Tuck the ends under; brush again with any remaining butter or margarine.

Bake the twisted coffee bread in a 375° oven about 30 minutes or till the bread is golden. Spoon apricot, prune, or cherry filling down the center of the braid. Return the bread to the oven. Bake for 3 to 5 minutes more or till the filling is heated through. Drizzle with Powdered Sugar Icing. Serve warm or cool. Makes 8 servings.

Powdered Sugar Icing: In a small mixing bowl stir together 1 cup *sifted powdered sugar*, ¼ teaspoon *vanilla*, and enough *milk* (about 4 teaspoons) to make the icing of pouring consistency.

Per serving: 400 cal., 5 g pro., 46 g carbo., 23 g fat, 67 mg chol., 626 mg sodium. USRDA: 27% vit. A, 10% thiamine, 10% riboflavin.

PARMESAN PARSLEY KNOTS

These individual rolls are so-o-o-o simple to make and so-o-o-o good to eat!—

- 1 11-ounce package (8) refrigerated breadsticks
- 3 tablespoons grated Parmesan cheese
- 2 teaspoons dried parsley flakes, crushed
- 2 tablespoons milk

Remove breadsticks from package; separate into individual ropes. On a lightly floured surface roll each breadstick into a 12-inch-long rope. Tie each rope in a loose knot, leaving 2 long ends. Tuck the top end of the rope under roll (see how-to photo, page 124). Bring the bottom end up and tuck into the center of the roll.

In a small mixing bowl combine Parmesan cheese and parsley flakes. Brush knots with the milk. Carefully dip each knot into the cheese mixture. Place the knots 2 to 3 inches apart on a greased baking sheet. Bake in a 350° oven about 15 minutes or till golden. Serve warm or cool. Makes 8 knots.

Per knot: 154 cal., 5 g pro., 28 g carbo., 2 g fat, 4 mg chol., and 278 mg sodium.

PEACH YOGURT SCONES

Sink your teeth into this tender version of the British Isles specialty—

- 2½ cups packaged biscuit mix
- ¼ cup sugar
- ½ cup peach *or* apple yogurt
- 1 beaten egg
- 2 tablespoons butter *or* margarine, melted
- Sugar

In a medium mixing bowl combine packaged biscuit mix and ¼ cup sugar. Stir together peach or apple yogurt, beaten egg, and melted butter or margarine. Stir the yogurt mixture into the biscuit mixture, mixing just till the scone dough clings together.

Knead dough gently on a floured surface for 8 to 10 strokes. Pat or roll the scone dough to form a 6-inch circle. Cut the dough into 10 wedges (see how-to photo, page 125).

Sprinkle each of the wedges with some sugar. Place the sugared wedges on an ungreased baking sheet. Bake scones in a 425° oven for 10 to 12 minutes or till golden. Serve the scones warm for breakfast, for brunch, or for afternoon tea. Makes 10 scones.

Per scone: 214 cal., 4 g pro., 34 g carbo., 7 g fat, 33 mg chol., 457 mg sodium. USRDA: 11% thiamine and 11% phosphorus.

NUTMEG RAISIN COFFEE CAKE

Bake your coffee cake in a kugelhopf pan for a shapely difference. Serve with butter and honey—

- 1 16-ounce package hot roll mix
- ¾ teaspoon ground nutmeg
- 1¼ cups milk
- ½ cup butter *or* margarine
- ⅓ cup packed brown sugar
- 2 eggs
- ¾ cup currants *or* raisins
- Sifted powdered sugar

In a large mixer bowl combine hot roll mix yeast packet and *1 cup* of the flour from the hot roll mix. Stir in nutmeg. Set aside.

In a small saucepan heat milk, butter or margarine, and brown sugar just till the mixture is warm (115° to 120°) and butter is almost melted, stirring constantly.

Add warm mixture to the flour mixture; add eggs. Beat with an electric mixer on low speed for ½ minute, scraping the sides of the bowl constantly. Beat mixture for 3 minutes on high speed. Stir in the remaining flour just till combined. Stir in currants or raisins. *Do not overbeat.*

Pour the batter into a greased 10-cup kugelhopf pan or a fluted tube pan (see how-to photo, page 125). Let the batter rise in a warm place till nearly double (about 40 minutes).

Bake in a 350° oven for 35 to 40 minutes or till done. If necessary, cover the coffee cake with foil the last 10 to 15 minutes to prevent overbrowning. Remove from the pan; cool on a wire rack. Sprinkle with powdered sugar to serve. Makes 12 servings.

Per serving: 285 cal., 6 g pro., 40 g carbo., 12 g fat, 69 mg chol., 281 mg sodium. USRDA: 13% thiamine.

DOUBLE WHEAT FOLDOVERS

Wheat berries and raspberry jam nestle inside whole wheat pastry—

- ½ cup cooked wheat berries
- 2 tablespoons raspberry jam
- 1½ cups whole wheat flour
- 1 teaspoon baking powder
- ¼ teaspoon salt
- ½ cup butter *or* margarine
- ½ cup packed brown sugar
- 1 egg
- 1 teaspoon vanilla

For filling, in a small mixing bowl combine cooked wheat berries and jam. Cover and chill in the refrigerator.

For pastry, in a medium mixing bowl stir together whole wheat flour, baking powder, and salt. In a small mixer bowl beat butter or margarine on medium speed of electric mixer for 30 seconds. Add brown sugar and beat till fluffy. Add egg and vanilla; beat well. Add dry ingredients; beat till combined. Cover and chill in the refrigerator for 2 hours.

On a lightly floured surface roll dough ⅛ inch thick. Cut into 2½-inch rounds, dipping cutter into flour between cuts. Place *1 teaspoon* filling atop *each* round. Fold dough in half over filling; seal edges. Bake on an ungreased baking sheet in a 375° oven for 10 to 12 minutes or till done. Cool on a wire rack. Makes 24.

Per serving: 96 cal., 1.6 g pro., 14 g carbo., 4 g fat, 22 mg chol., and 65 mg sodium.

SPANISH PUMPKIN CHICKEN

This southwestern-style dish is good with turkey legs and wings, too—

- 1 2½- to 3-pound broiler-fryer chicken, cut up and skinned
- 2 tablespoons cooking oil
- 1 medium onion, chopped (½ cup)
- ½ cup chopped green pepper
- 1 clove garlic, minced
- 1 tablespoon chili powder
- ¼ teaspoon salt
- ⅛ teaspoon pepper
- ⅛ teaspoon ground cumin
- 3 cups cubed, peeled pumpkin *or* winter squash
- 1 16-ounce can tomatoes, cut up
- 1 4-ounce can diced green chili peppers
- Hot cooked rice

In a 4½-quart Dutch oven brown *half* of the chicken pieces in hot oil; remove and set aside. Brown remaining chicken pieces. Remove chicken and oil, reserving 2 tablespoons oil in pan.

To reserved oil, add onion, green pepper, and garlic. Cook and stir about 2 minutes or till tender. Add chili powder, salt, pepper, and cumin. Cook and stir for 1 minute more.

Add browned chicken, pumpkin or squash, *undrained* tomatoes, and *undrained* chili peppers. Stir gently to combine. Bring to boiling; reduce heat. Cover and simmer for 30 minutes. Uncover and simmer about 15 minutes more or till chicken is done and pumpkin or squash is tender. Serve over hot cooked rice. Makes 6 servings.

Per serving with ½ cup rice: 442 cal., 57 g pro., 22 g carbo., 13 g fat, 198 mg chol., 410 mg sodium. USRDA: 108% vit. A, 83% vit. C, 15% thiamine, 33% riboflavin, 107% niacin, 29% iron, and 54% phosphorus.

BABA AU PEAR

The traditional baba is a spongelike cake soaked in a sugar syrup. In our take-off, tangy apricot-pear syrup seeps into individual angel cupcakes—

- 1 package angel cake mix *or* 1 recipe homemade angel cake
- ⅔ cup apricot nectar
- ⅔ cup water
- 3 tablespoons sugar
- 2 fresh pears, peeled, cored, and sliced, *or* one 16-ounce can sliced pears
- 2 tablespoons cornstarch
- 2 tablespoons water
- 1 tablespoon lemon juice
- ¼ teaspoon almond extract
- Mint leaves (optional)

Prepare angel cake as directed. Fill 12 large (2¾-inch) unlined and ungreased muffin cups, using ⅓ *cup* batter for *each.* Pour remaining batter into an ungreased 9x5x3-inch loaf pan. Bake in a 350° oven till done, 20 minutes for cupcakes and 30 minutes for loaf. Cool (invert loaf to cool).

Meanwhile, for syrup, in a medium saucepan combine apricot nectar, ⅔ cup water, and sugar. Bring to boiling, stirring constantly to dissolve sugar. Add fresh pears. (Do not cook canned pears.) Reduce heat; cover and simmer about 8 minutes or till tender. Remove pears with slotted spoon and set aside.

Carefully remove cupcakes and loaf from pans. Freeze loaf in moisture- and vaporproof-wrap for another use. Poke each cupcake in 6 places with a toothpick. Slowly spoon *1 teaspoon* of the syrup over *each* cupcake.

Drain canned pears, reserving 2 tablespoons juice. Combine cornstarch and 2 tablespoons water or reserved canned pear juice. Add cornstarch mixture to remaining syrup. Cook and stir till thickened and bubbly. Cook and stir for 2 minutes more.

Stir in cooked or canned pears, lemon juice, and almond extract. Heat through or chill for 1 hour. Serve over cupcakes. Garnish with mint leaves, if desired. Makes 12 servings.

Per serving: 178 cal., 3 g pro., 42 g carbo., 78 mg sodium.

FRUIT AND OAT NIBBLE MIX

- 1 cup rolled oats
- 1 cup mixed nuts
- ½ cup coconut
- ¼ cup toasted wheat germ
- ½ cup honey
- 2 tablespoons cooking oil
- ¼ teaspoon ground allspice
- 1 cup dried apricots, snipped
- ½ cup raisins

In a medium mixing bowl stir together oats, nuts, coconut, and wheat germ. Combine honey, oil, and allspice. Drizzle *half* of the honey mixture over oat mixture. Toss. Repeat with remaining honey mixture.

Spread mixture in a 13x9x2-inch baking pan. Bake in a 300° oven for 30 to 40 minutes or till golden, stirring every 15 minutes. Remove from oven. Transfer to another greased pan; cool without stirring.

Break cooled mixture into bite-size pieces. Stir in apricots and raisins. Store mixture in an airtight container. Makes 7 cups.

Per serving: 391 cal., 9 g pro., 58 g carbo., 17 g fat, and 158 mg sodium. USRDA: 40% vit. A, 23% niacin, 12% thiamine, 15% iron, 20% phosphorus.

Fruit and Oat Nibble Mix

NOVEMBER

Better Homes and Gardens.

November 1985
$1.50

HOLIDAY ENTERTAINING
25 Fabulous Recipes
Plus…Menus!

CHRISTMAS MAKE-AHEADS!
Victorian Dolls,
Decorations, and
Stockings

See Our
Home Improvement
Contest WINNERS!
TERRIFIC IDEAS FOR
YOUR House

WINTER BLOOMS TO
BRIGHTEN YOUR
ROOMS

TOFFEE-TOPPED
'STUFFED PUFF'
PAGE 125

HOLIDAY TURKEY, TRIMMED TO SIZE
Turkey Breast Florentine

By Joy Taylor

Turkey for Thanksgiving, of course! And this year you can uphold tradition without going "whole bird." Satisfy a sixsome with this scaled-down-to-size turkey breast—no one will even miss the wishbone!

ERNIE BLOCK. FOOD STYLIST: VICKI JOHNSON

TURKEY BREAST FLORENTINE

- 1 **3-pound turkey breast portion**
- 5 **slices bacon**
- ½ **cup chopped onion**
- 3 **tablespoons all-purpose flour**
- ½ **teaspoon dried tarragon, crushed**
- 1½ **cups milk**
- 1 **10-ounce package frozen chopped spinach, cooked and well drained**
- 1 **2½-ounce jar sliced mushrooms, drained**

Butter *or* margarine, melted

- ⅓ **cup shredded American cheese**

Bone turkey breast. Butterfly turkey by splitting lengthwise about halfway through; spread meat open. At the V formed by the cut, make 2 more lengthwise slits perpendicular to the right and left of the V; spread meat open. Place turkey between plastic wrap. Pound to ½-inch thickness. (Turkey should measure about 11x8 inches.)

Cut up 2 slices bacon. Cook cut-up bacon just till done; drain, reserving drippings. Cook onion in drippings till tender. Blend in flour, tarragon, and dash *pepper*. Add milk. Cook and stir till thickened and bubbly. Remove from heat. Combine ½ *cup* sauce, cooked bacon, spinach, and mushrooms.

Cover and chill remaining sauce. Place turkey skin side down; top with spinach mixture. Roll up. Secure with string. Place on rack in baking pan. Brush turkey with butter. Bake, loosely covered with foil, in a 350° oven 1½ hours. Uncover; remove string. Lay remaining bacon slices over turkey. Bake 30 minutes or till internal temperature is 180°. Meanwhile, stir cheese into remaining sauce; heat through. Serve sauce with turkey. Serves 6.

Per serving: 494 cal., 63 g pro., 9 g carbo., 21 g fat, 156 mg chol., 366 mg sodium. USRDA: 64% vit. A, 16% vit. C, 15% thiamine, 30% riboflavin, 101% niacin, 18% calcium, 18% iron, 61% phosphorus.

HOLIDAY TURKEY, TRIMMED TO SIZE
Turkey Roulade

Tender turkey white meat is always in demand at the dinner table. This year, there will be plenty for holiday feasters when you stuff turkey fillets with fresh vegetables. Pretty to look at, and best of all, this entrée is light and lean.

ERNIE BLOCK. FOOD STYLIST: VICKI JOHNSON

Look for packages labeled turkey breast steaks or tenderloin fillets. To save time and energy on your feast day (or any day!), roll up these bundles a day ahead of time. Then when you're ready to eat, start the cooking process, and enjoy the turkey in less than 30 minutes—

TURKEY ROULADE

- 4 turkey breast tenderloin fillets (about 1 pound)
- 2 carrots, cut into julienne strips
- ½ large green pepper, cut into strips
- 2 tablespoons cooking oil
- ⅔ cup orange juice
- ⅔ cup bottled barbecue sauce

Hot cooked rice

Place turkey fillets between 2 pieces of clear plastic wrap. Pound with a mallet to about ¼-inch thickness. (Turkey portions should each measure about 6 to 8 inches long and 4 inches wide.)

Place several carrot and green pepper strips crosswise on each turkey portion; roll up jelly-roll style from short side. Secure bundles with wooden toothpicks. In a 10-inch skillet brown the turkey bundles in hot cooking oil. Drain off fat. Combine the orange juice and bottled barbecue sauce. Add to the skillet. Bring mixture to boiling; reduce heat. Cover and simmer about 20 minutes or till turkey is tender. Remove picks. Serve with hot cooked rice. Makes 4 servings.

Per serving: 284 cal., 29 g pro., 12 g carbo., 13 g fat, 65 mg chol., 430 mg sodium. USRDA: 86% vit. A, 63% vit. C, 50% niacin, 10% iron, and 26% phosphorus.

133

SUPER STARTERS

Pita Piped with Hummus

Brioche-Chicken Curry Favorites

Pop-the-Cork Pasta Crunch

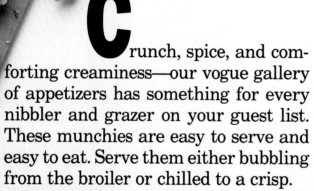

Crunch, spice, and comforting creaminess—our vogue gallery of appetizers has something for every nibbler and grazer on your guest list. These munchies are easy to serve and easy to eat. Serve them either bubbling from the broiler or chilled to a crisp.

Another bonus—you can make and store many of these munchies up to two weeks ahead. Take to the kitchen to prepare the others shortly before you expect to hear the doorbell ring.

Pick and choose from the ideas pictured here to create a get-together spread with your own special style. Or try our tempting menus on *page 138* for combinations that make a meal.

Well-Dressed Crudités

Pizza with Pecan Pizzazz

Photographs: Ernie Block
Food stylist: Vickie Johnson

Smoked Salmon Shells

Here's-to-Bavaria Spread

Spring-Is-Sprung Rolls

Pretzel Twist and Shout

Sesame-Speckled Riblets

Striped Cheese

Bit-o'-Zucchini Bites

Thumbelina Turkey Burgers

Rippled-Beef Skewers

Spice-of-Life Cashews

Drenched Fruit Sticks

Smoothie Sauce for Veggies

HOLIDAY ENTERTAINING
HAPPY ENDINGS

Go ahead, indulge yourself—'tis the season for luscious desserts! Our 1985 collection offers irresistible choices. Can't decide? Make them all.

Toffee-Topped Stuffed Puffs

Warm caramel sauce meets frosty homemade ice cream—an unmatchable combination. You can store the cream puffs and ice cream in the freezer for up to 5 days. The sauce keeps for 1 to 2 days in the refrigerator; warm just before serving. Ready with your spoons?

Cranberry Pear-fect Pastry

Pastry is easy! Especially when you start with frozen puff pastry shells. That's the timesaving secret of our freestanding pie. Another tip—forget those last-minute preparations. Bake several hours before the party and warm your pear-fect dessert just before serving.

136

Kiwi-Orange Custard and Cake

Dazzle your guests without frazzling yourself. The day before the party, plan to bake the cake and cook the pastry cream. When the time is right for dessert, top it all with the kiwi fruit and orange slices.

Salzburger Nöckerl

This Austrian classic (SĂLZ-ber-ger KNÖCK-ehrl) has captured the palates of many. Now it's your turn. When drop-in guests surprise you, take to the kitchen and whip together these lemon-flavored clouds. All you need are eggs, sugar, flour, and lemon.

Chocolate-Mousse Cake

Some people think the only REAL dessert is chocolate. They'll be satisfied when they bite into this one. It's worth every calorie!

137

NO-DINNER DINNERS

Make a Meal of Appetizers and Desserts

If it's fun to make a meal of only appetizers and desserts at a restaurant, it's even better at home where you can plan and prepare it all. These menus without main dishes suit three scenarios: a last-minute gathering, a small planned get-together, and a pull-out-the-stops shindig. Re-create our menus, mix and match them, or devise your very own.

Remember to balance rich, dense, and highly flavored foods with simple, fresh items. Serve hot foods hot, cold foods cold and some room-temperature nibblers such as crackers, nuts, and cheeses. You don't have to do all the work. Make some of the fare and buy the rest to round out the menu and ease your time.

IMPROMPTU INVITE

Pizza with Pecan Pizzazz*
Spice-of-Life Cashews*
Smoothie Sauce for Veggies*
Sesame Crackers
Boursin Cheese
Salzburger Nöckerl*
White Wine and Hot Cider

Friendly Fiesta

Pitas Piped with Hummus *
Smoked Salmon Shells*
Well-Dressed Crudités*
Thumbelina Turkey Burgers*
Soft Cream Cheese Spread
Crisp Breadsticks
Mixed Nuts
Toffee-Topped Stuffed Puffs*
Wine Coolers and
Java Hot Chocolate

HOLIDAY WHIRL

Rippled-Beef Skewers*
Striped Cheese*
Pretzel Twist and Shout*
Pop-the-Cork Pasta Crunch*
Drenched Fruit Sticks*
Spring-Is-Sprung Rolls*
Kiwi-Orange Custard and Cake*
Chocolate-Mousse Cake*
Mulled Cranberry Cider

Get Set for Impromptu Invite

You just invited several friends to come tonight for a casual get-together. Here's the timetable.
● First, make a fast trip to the nearest supermarket!
● Two hours ahead: Prepare Spice-of-Life Cashews and the Smoothie Sauce. Blanch and cool the pea pods and cauliflower. Prepare the Pizza with Pecan Pizzazz; cover and chill till time to bake. Chill the wine.
● One hour ahead: Set out the serving dishes and prepare the buffet table. Set out Spice-of-Life Cashews, crackers, and Boursin cheese.
● A half-hour ahead: Arrange the platter of Smoothie Sauce for Veggies and heat the cider.
● When guests arrive: Bake the Pizza with Pecan Pizzazz.
● Later: Prepare and serve the fluffy Salzburger Nöckerl.

Get Set for Friendly Fiesta

You're hosting friends for fine conversation and good food.
● Up to 5 days before: Make the ice cream and cream puffs for the Toffee-Topped Stuffed Puffs.
● A day ahead: Make and chill Hummus, turkey burgers, caramel sauce, and Well-Dressed Crudités.
● Two hours ahead: Toast pita quarters in the oven; arrange in napkin-lined basket. Arrange serving table.
● One hour ahead: Assemble the Smoked Salmon Shells; cover and chill till time to bake. Set out nibblers.
● A half-hour ahead: Set out the Well-Dressed Crudités in a cabbage bowl and cheese spread. Pipe Hummus onto a serving plate. Prepare Java Hot Chocolate.
● When guests arrive: Warm the turkey burgers; bake the salmon shells.
● Later: Let guests assemble their own cream puffs with caramel sauce.

Get Set for Holiday Whirl

Pull out the stops! It's party time—a festive holiday evening.
● Three days ahead: Make Striped Cheese, Pretzel Twist and Shout, and Pop-the-Cork Pasta Crunch.
● One day ahead: Make Chocolate-Mousse Cake and cake and custard for Kiwi-Orange Custard and Cake.
● Early in the day: Marinate Rippled-Beef Skewers and Drenched Fruit Sticks. Clean the vegetables.
● Two hours ahead: Prepare filling for Spring-Is-Sprung Rolls.
● One hour ahead: Warm the cider. Set out the Striped Cheese, Pretzel Twist and Shout, and Pop-the-Cork Pasta Crunch.
● When guests arrive: Assemble and fry Spring-Is-Sprung Rolls, broil Rippled-Beef Skewers, and serve the Drenched Fruit Sticks.
● Later: Arrange fruit over custard for Kiwi-Orange Custard and Cake. Slice Chocolate-Mousse Cake.

BRIOCHE-CHICKEN CURRY FAVORITES

Team delicate brioche with curried chicken for a bite-size appetizer—

    1 package active dry yeast
    ¼ cup warm water (110° to 115°)
    ½ cup butter *or* margarine
    ¼ cup sugar
    ¼ teaspoon salt
    5 eggs
    3½ cups all-purpose flour
    1 egg yolk
    1 tablespoon water
    1 recipe Curried Chicken Filling
       (see recipe at right)

In a measuring cup soften yeast in ¼ cup warm water. Set aside. In a large mixer bowl beat together butter or margarine, sugar, and salt. Add eggs, *1 cup* of the flour, and yeast mixture. Beat well. Using a spoon, stir in remaining flour till smooth. (Dough will be soft and sticky.) Cover and refrigerate dough overnight.

Stir dough down. Turn out onto a lightly floured surface. Divide dough into quarters; set 1 portion aside. (Keep dough covered when not working with it.) Divide each of the remaining quarters into 16 pieces, making a total of 48 pieces. With floured hands, form each into a ball, tucking under edges. Place balls in greased 1¾-inch muffin pans.

Divide reserved dough into 48 pieces; shape into small balls. With a floured index finger, make an indentation in each ball in muffin pan. Press a small ball into each indentation. Combine egg yolk with 1 tablespoon water; brush over rolls. Cover; let rise till nearly double (40 to 45 minutes). Bake in a 375° oven about 12 minutes or till done.

To serve, pull off top ball of brioche. Using a teaspoon, hollow out bottom, leaving a ½-inch-thick shell. Fill with Curried Chicken Filling. Replace top. Serve immediately. Makes 48.

Note: Brioche can be made ahead and frozen. Thaw at room temperature, covered, for 1 hour before filling. Make the filling the day of the party.

Per filled brioche: 164 cal., 7 g pro., 16 g carbo., 8 g fat, 69 mg chol., 101 mg sodium. USRDA: 10% niacin.

CURRIED CHICKEN FILLING

    2 3-ounce packages cream
       cheese, softened
    ⅔ cup plain yogurt
    4 teaspoons curry powder
    4 teaspoons lemon juice
    ¼ teaspoon salt
    ⅛ teaspoon pepper
    2 cups finely chopped, cooked
       chicken
    ¾ cup raisins, snipped
    ⅔ cup finely chopped almonds,
       toasted
    ½ cup coconut

In a large mixing bowl beat cream cheese till smooth. Add yogurt, curry powder, lemon juice, salt, and pepper. Beat till smooth. Stir in chicken, raisins, almonds, and coconut. Cover and chill. Fill each individual brioche with *1 tablespoon* of the mixture. Makes about 2¾ cups filling.

PIZZA WITH PECAN PIZZAZZ

Keep the slices warm on a hot tray—

    1 8-ounce package (8) refrigerated
       crescent rolls
    1 medium onion, finely chopped
    1 green pepper, finely chopped
    1 red sweet pepper, finely
       chopped
    ½ teaspoon dried rosemary,
       crushed
    1 tablespoon olive oil *or* cooking
       oil
    ¼ cup grated Parmesan cheese
    ½ cup chopped pecans

Unroll crescent rolls. Press perforations together to form four 6x4-inch rectangles. Place rectangles on an ungreased baking sheet. Bake in a 375° oven for 5 minutes.

Meanwhile, in a skillet cook onion, green and red peppers, and rosemary in hot oil till tender. Sprinkle Parmesan over partially baked crusts. Top with vegetable mixture.

Before serving, bake in a 375° oven for 6 to 7 minutes more or till edges are golden. Sprinkle with pecans. Cool for 2 minutes, then cut each rectangle into 4 triangles. Serve warm. Makes 16.

Per serving: 96 cal., 2 g pro., 8 g carbo., 10 g fat, 1 mg chol., 138 mg sodium. USRDA: 10% vit. A, 58% vit. C.

PITA PIPED WITH HUMMUS

Hummus is a Middle Eastern dip made with garbanzo beans, garlic, and tahini (sesame seed paste). Try it with plain tortilla chips, too—

    1 15-ounce can garbanzo beans,
       drained
    ¼ cup tahini *or* 2 tablespoons
       creamy peanut butter with 1
       tablespoon hot water *and* 2
       teaspoons sesame oil
    3 tablespoons lemon juice
    1 tablespoon olive oil *or* salad oil
    3 cloves garlic
    ¼ teaspoon salt
    6 small pita bread rounds
Melted butter *or* margarine
Cherry tomatoes (optional)
Fresh snipped chives (optional)

For hummus, in a blender container or food processor bowl combine garbanzo beans, tahini, lemon juice, olive oil or salad oil, garlic, and salt. Cover; blend or process till smooth. Cover and chill.

Split each pita in half horizontally; cut each half into 6 or 8 wedges. Brush rough side with melted butter or margarine. Place in a single layer, buttered side up, on a baking sheet. Bake in a 350° oven for 8 to 10 minutes or till crisp and slightly brown. Repeat with remaining pita wedges.

To serve, pipe hummus onto a serving plate with a cake decorator's tube, cookie press, or pastry bag fitted with a fluted tip. (Or, place hummus in a serving bowl or on a plate.) Serve with pita wedges. Garnish with tomatoes and chives, if desired. Makes 2 cups dip.

Per tablespoon hummus with 1 wedge of pita bread: 39 cal., 1 g pro., 4 g carbo., 2 g fat, 1 mg chol., 27 mg sodium.

WELL-DRESSED CRUDITÉS

- 1½ cups whole fresh mushrooms (4 ounces)
- 1 9-ounce package frozen artichoke hearts, cooked and drained
- 1 cup broccoli flowerets (4 ounces)
- 1 cup cherry tomatoes
- 1 small cucumber, halved lengthwise and sliced crosswise into ½-inch-thick pieces
- ⅓ cup olive oil *or* salad oil
- ⅓ cup vinegar
- 1 tablespoon Dijon-style mustard
- 1 clove garlic, minced
- 1 teaspoon bouquet garni *or* fines herbes
- 1 head red cabbage (about 2 pounds)

Rinse mushrooms and trim ends. In a large bowl combine mushrooms, artichoke hearts, broccoli flowerets, tomatoes, and cucumber slices. Set aside.

In a small bowl combine olive or salad oil, vinegar, mustard, garlic, and bouquet garni or fines herbes. Pour over vegetables. Toss gently to distribute marinade. Cover and refrigerate for 24 hours, stirring 2 or 3 times.

To serve, slice bottom off cabbage to make it sit flat. Cut cabbage into 6 wedges, cutting to within 1 inch of bottom. Spread out 5 to 7 outer leaves of each wedge. To form a "bowl," cut out and reserve the inside of each wedge (see photo at right). Remove core at base of the bowl.

Cut reserved cabbage sections into 1-inch pieces and toss with marinated vegetables. Using a slotted spoon, transfer *half* of the vegetables to the cabbage bowl. Refill cabbage with vegetables as necessary. Serve with wooden toothpicks. Makes 36 (¼-cup) servings.

Per serving: 32 cal., 1 g pro., 3 g carbo., 2 g fat, 0 mg chol., 17 mg sodium. USRDA: 35% vit. C.

A cabbage bowl is an attractive way to display your crudités.

SMOKED SALMON SHELLS

- ⅓ cup finely chopped water chestnuts
- ⅓ cup mayonnaise *or* salad dressing
- ¼ teaspoon dried dillweed
- 1 3⅔-ounce package sliced smoked red salmon, chopped *or* one 3¼-ounce can smoked salmon, drained
- 2 sticks piecrust mix
- 1 slightly beaten egg yolk
- 1 tablespoon water

For salmon filling, in a small mixing bowl stir together water chestnuts, mayonnaise or salad dressing, and dillweed. Stir in salmon. (If using canned salmon, remove skin and bones, then chop.) Cover and chill for 1 hour.

Prepare piecrust mix according to package directions. Divide dough in half. On a lightly floured surface, roll half into a 16x8-inch rectangle. Place the dough rectangle over a madeleine pan with 2¼x1¼-inch shell molds. Press pastry into shells.

Fill *each* shell with about *1 tablespoon* of the salmon filling. Brush water around outlines of shells. Roll out remaining pastry half and place over the filled madeleine pan. Press and seal around shells with fingers. With a fluted pastry wheel, trim around edge of pan, then cut between the shells.

Before serving, bake in a 450° oven for 15 minutes. Meanwhile, stir together egg yolk and water. Carefully transfer each shell from the madeleine pan to a baking sheet (see photo below). Brush shells with egg mixture. Bake for 8 to 10 minutes more or till golden brown. Serve warm. Makes 12.

To prepare without a madeleine pan: Prepare 1 piecrust stick according to package directions. On a lightly floured surface, roll into a 12x9-inch rectangle. Cut dough into twelve 3-inch squares. Spoon about *1½ teaspoons* of salmon filling on half of *each* square. Brush water around the edge of pastry; fold in half to form a triangle. Press and seal around the edges with the tines of a fork. Beat egg yolk and water together. Brush triangles with egg yolk mixture. Bake in a 400° oven for 8 to 10 minutes or till golden brown.

Microwave reheating directions: Prepare and bake the Smoked Salmon Shells as directed. Cool. Store, covered, in the refrigerator up to 24 hours. To reheat, place shells in a circle on a nonmetal plate. Micro-cook, uncovered, on 100% power (HIGH) for 2 to 3 minutes, giving dish a half-turn once.

Per serving: 186 cal., 4 g pro., 12 g carbo., 14 g fat, 28 mg chol., 643 mg sodium.

Bake the half-baked shells on a baking sheet to finish browning.

PRETZEL TWIST AND SHOUT

1½ to 2½ cups all-purpose flour
1 package active dry yeast
1½ cups milk
¼ cup honey
1 teaspoon salt
2 cups whole wheat flour
1 egg white
1 tablespoon water
2 tablespoons poppy seed,
   sesame seed, *or* grated
   Parmesan cheese
Prepared mustard (optional)

In a large mixer bowl combine *1½ cups* of the all-purpose flour and yeast. In a small saucepan heat milk, honey, and salt till lukewarm (115° to 120°); stir constantly. Add to flour mixture.

Beat with an electric mixer on low speed for 1 minute, scraping sides of bowl constantly. Beat for 3 minutes on high speed. Using a spoon, stir in the whole wheat flour and as much of the remaining all-purpose flour as you can.

Turn onto a lightly floured surface. Knead in enough of the remaining flour to make a moderately stiff dough that is smooth and elastic (6 to 8 minutes). Shape into a ball. Place in a greased bowl. Turn once to grease surface. Cover; let rise in warm place till double (about 45 minutes).

Punch dough down. Turn out onto lightly floured surface. Divide into 4 portions. Cover and let rest for 10 minutes. Refrigerate 3 portions.

Divide 1 dough portion into 9 small pieces. Roll each piece into a rope about 12 inches long. Shape each rope into a circle, overlapping about 4 inches from each end; leave ends free. Take 1 end of dough in each hand and twist at the point where dough overlaps (see photo at right). Carefully lift ends across to opposite edges of the circle. Tuck ends under edge for pretzel shape; moisten and press to seal. Repeat with remaining dough to make 36 pretzels total. Let rise, uncovered, for 20 minutes.

Meanwhile, in a 3-quart Dutch oven bring 2 quarts *water* and 2 tablespoons *salt* to boiling. Lower 4 or 5 pretzels at a time into water; boil for 2 minutes, turning once. Remove from water with slotted spoon. Drain for a few seconds on a wire rack. Place ½ inch apart on a well-greased baking sheet.

Combine egg white and 1 tablespoon water; brush pretzels. Sprinkle with poppy seed, sesame seed, or Parmesan cheese. Bake in a 350° oven for 25 to 30 minutes or till golden brown. Serve with mustard, if desired. Makes 36 pretzels.

Per pretzel: 59 cal., 2 g pro., 11 g carbo., 1 g fat, 1 mg chol., 66 mg sodium.

To shape a pretzel, twist the ends at the point where the dough overlaps.

SPICE-OF-LIFE CASHEWS

2 cups cashews
2 tablespoons butter *or* margarine
½ teaspoon ground cinnamon
½ teaspoon ground allspice

In a large skillet combine cashews, butter or margarine, cinnamon, and allspice. Cook over medium heat, stirring constantly, for 10 to 15 minutes or till nuts are toasted. Spread on a baking sheet or aluminum foil to cool. Cool completely. Makes 2 cups.

Microwave directions: In a 2-quart nonmetal casserole place butter or margarine. Micro-cook, uncovered, on 100% power (HIGH) for 30 to 60 seconds or till melted. Stir in cinnamon and allspice. Add cashews, stirring well to coat the nuts. Cook, uncovered, for 5 to 6 minutes or till nuts are toasted, stirring 3 times. Cool as directed.

Per tablespoon: 55 cal., 2 g pro., 3 g carbo., 5 g fat, 2 mg chol., 10 mg sodium.

BIT-O'-ZUCCHINI BITES

You can also make this quichelike treat in an 8-inch square baking pan—

2 tablespoons chopped onion
1 clove garlic, minced
1 tablespoon butter *or* margarine
1½ cups shredded zucchini (2 small)
3 slightly beaten eggs
1½ cups shredded Monterey Jack cheese (6 ounces)
3 tablespoons cornmeal
¼ teaspoon cumin seed, crushed
¼ teaspoon dried oregano, crushed

In a large skillet cook onion and garlic in butter or margarine till onion is tender but not brown. Add zucchini and cook about 2 minutes or till crisp-tender. Remove from heat.

In a large mixing bowl combine eggs, shredded cheese, cornmeal, cumin, oregano, and zucchini mixture. Spoon a scant *2 tablespoons* of egg mixture into individual greased 1¾-inch muffin pans. Bake in a 325° oven for 15 to 18 minutes or till set. (Or, pour all the batter into a greased 8x8x2-inch baking pan. Bake for 20 to 25 minutes or till set. Cut into bite-size squares.) Remove from pan. Serve warm. Makes about 24 appetizers.

Microwave directions: In a 1½- or 2-quart nonmetal casserole place butter or margarine. Micro-cook, uncovered, on 100% power (HIGH) for 40 to 50 seconds or till melted. Stir in onion and garlic. Cook, covered, for 2 minutes. Stir in zucchini. Cook, covered, for 2 minutes more or till vegetables are crisp-tender, stirring once. Remove from oven; cool for 5 minutes.

Stir beaten eggs into vegetable mixture. Stir in cheese, cornmeal, cumin, and oregano. Spoon mixture into small muffin pans or an 8x8x2-inch baking pan and bake as directed.

Per appetizer: 40 cal., 3 g pro., 1 g carbo., 2 g fat, 31 mg chol., and 51 mg sodium.

HERE'S-TO-BAVARIA SPREAD

Sauerkraut and turkey ham star in this sour cream-frosted spread—

- 1 14-ounce can sauerkraut, well drained and snipped
- 1 cup finely shredded cheddar cheese (4 ounces)
- 1 cup finely chopped turkey ham (5 ounces)
- ½ cup saltine cracker crumbs (14 crackers)
- ½ cup mayonnaise *or* salad dressing
- 2 tablespoons snipped parsley
- 2 tablespoons chopped pimiento
- 1 tablespoon finely chopped onion
- 1 8-ounce carton dairy sour cream
Shredded cheddar cheese (optional)
Chopped pimiento (optional)
Party rye bread

In a large mixing bowl stir together sauerkraut, 1 cup cheese, turkey ham, cracker crumbs, mayonnaise or salad dressing, parsley, pimiento, and onion. Shape into a mound on a dinner plate. Spread sour cream evenly over top and sides. Cover and chill till serving time.

Before serving, garnish with additional shredded cheese and pimiento, if desired. Serve with party rye bread. Makes 3½ cups.

Per tablespoon with 1 slice bread: 54 cal., 2 g pro., 5 g carbo., 3 g fat, 6 mg chol., 118 mg sodium.

THUMBELINA TURKEY BURGERS

- ¼ cup boiling water
- 3 tablespoons brown sugar
- 3 tablespoons lime *or* lemon juice
- 1 medium cucumber, cut into ¼-inch-thick slices
- ½ of a small onion, halved lengthwise and thinly sliced
- 1 red *or* green chili pepper, finely chopped
- 1 pound ground raw turkey
- 4 teaspoons fish sauce *or* soy sauce
- 1 tablespoon red curry paste *or* 1 teaspoon chili powder *and* ½ teaspoon sesame oil *or* salad oil

In a large mixing bowl combine ¼ cup boiling water, brown sugar, and lime or lemon juice. Stir till sugar is dissolved. Add cucumber slices, onion, and red or green chili pepper. Stir to coat. Cover and chill for up to 3 days.

In a medium mixing bowl combine turkey, fish sauce or soy sauce, and red curry paste. Mix well. Shape mixture into 1-inch balls; flatten slightly. Place on a baking sheet. Bake in a 375° oven for 25 to 30 minutes or till golden.

To serve, spear meatballs and/or a cucumber slice on a fondue fork. Dip into sauce. Makes 25 to 30 burgers.

Microwave directions: Make and shape Thumbelina Turkey Burgers as directed. Arrange turkey burgers in an 8x8x2-inch nonmetal baking dish. Micro-cook, covered with waxed paper, on 100% power (HIGH) for 5 to 7 minutes, turning meatballs over and giving dish a half-turn once.

Make-ahead directions: Make and bake Thumbelina Turkey Burgers as directed. To freeze, drain burgers on paper towels. Place on a shallow baking pan and freeze till firm. Wrap cooked burgers in moisture- and vaporproof wrap. Seal, label, and freeze.

Reheating directions: Place frozen burgers on baking sheet; bake in a 375° oven for 15 to 20 minutes or till hot.

Microwave reheating directions: In a 9-inch nonmetal pie plate place *half* of the frozen burgers. Cover loosely with waxed paper. Micro-cook on 100% (HIGH) for 2 to 3 minutes or till heated through, giving dish a half-turn once. Repeat with remaining burgers.

Per burger: 36 cal., 4 g pro., 2 g carbo., 1 g fat, 12 mg chol., 90 mg sodium. USRDA: 12% vit. C.

SESAME-SPECKLED RIBLETS

- 4 pounds meaty pork spareribs, sawed in half across bone
- ½ cup bottled barbecue sauce
- ⅓ cup orange marmalade
- 2 tablespoons toasted sesame seed
Savoy cabbage (optional)

Cut meat into 2-rib portions. In a Dutch oven place ribs; add enough water to cover. Bring to boiling; reduce heat. Cover; simmer for 30 minutes. Drain.

Meanwhile, for sauce, in a small saucepan stir together barbecue sauce and marmalade. Heat and stir just till marmalade is melted.

Place ribs, meaty side up, in a shallow baking pan. Brush generously with sauce. Bake in a 350° oven, uncovered, for 15 minutes. Brush with remaining sauce. Sprinkle with sesame seed. Bake for 10 minutes more. To serve, on a serving plate arrange ribs on savoy cabbage, if desired. Makes about 24.

Per serving: 151 cal., 6 g pro., 3 g carbo., 12 g fat, 27 mg chol., and 54 mg sodium.

DRENCHED FRUIT STICKS

- 1 large apple, cut into thin wedges
- ¾ cup fresh pineapple chunks
- ¾ cup seedless red *or* green grapes
- ¼ cup sweet vermouth
- 1 tablespoon sugar
- 1 tablespoon crème de cassis
- 2 teaspoons lemon juice
- 1 pineapple (optional)

In a medium mixing bowl combine apple wedges, pineapple, and grapes. In small mixing bowl stir together vermouth, sugar, crème de cassis, and lemon juice. Pour vermouth mixture over fruit and toss gently. Cover and chill in the refrigerator for 2 hours.

To serve, place 1 apple wedge, 1 pineapple chunk, and 1 grape on a wooden toothpick. Arrange picks in the outer shell of a pineapple, if desired. Makes 12 to 15 servings.

Per serving: 33 cal., 0 g pro., 7 g carbo., 0 g fat, 0 mg chol., and 1 mg sodium.

STRIPED CHEESE

Make this sophisticated hors d'oeuvre up to four days ahead of the party—

- 1 8-ounce package cream cheese, softened
- ¼ cup butter *or* margarine, softened
- 1 tablespoon milk
- 1 recipe Spinach-Cheese Filling (see recipe below)

French bread slices

Line a 7½x3½x2-inch pan lengthwise with plastic wrap; set side. In a small mixer bowl combine cream cheese and butter or margarine; beat till smooth. Beat in milk.

Spread *one third* of the cheese-butter mixture evenly in the bottom of the pan. Top with *half* of the Spinach-Cheese Filling and spread evenly. Repeat layering, ending with the cheese-butter mixture. Seal top layer to side to completely cover fillings. Cover and refrigerate for several hours or till firm.

Unmold and remove plastic wrap gently. Serve on sliced French bread. Makes 30 servings (2½ cups mixture).

Per serving: 123 cal., 4 g pro., 9 g carbo., 2 g fat, 17 mg chol., 152 mg sodium. USRDA: 11% vit. A.

SPINACH-CHEESE FILLING

- 1 cup lightly packed fresh spinach leaves *or* 1 cup frozen, chopped spinach, partially thawed
- 1 cup lightly packed fresh parsley, stems removed
- ¼ cup chopped pine nuts *or* walnuts
- ¼ cup salad oil
- 1 clove garlic, minced
- 1 teaspoon dried basil, crushed
- 1 cup grated Parmesan cheese

In a blender container or food processor bowl combine spinach, parsley, pine nuts or walnuts, salad oil, garlic, and basil. Cover and blend or process till nearly smooth. (If using a blender, scrape down sides often.) Add Parmesan cheese. Blend or process till combined. Use as filling for Striped Cheese. Makes 1¼ cups.

SPRING-IS-SPRUNG ROLLS

- 4 ounces Chinese cellophane noodles
- ½ pound ground pork
- ¼ pound fresh *or* frozen peeled and deveined shrimp, chopped
- 2 carrots, shredded (1 cup)
- 4 medium green onions, sliced (¼ cup)
- 2 teaspoons finely chopped fresh gingerroot
- 2 cloves garlic, minced
- 1 tablespoon cooking oil (optional)
- 1 tablespoon soy sauce
- 1 teaspoon sesame oil
- 15 *or* 16 spring roll *or* egg roll skins, halved
- 1 tablespoon all-purpose flour
- 1 tablespoon water

Cooking oil for deep-fat frying
Bottled plum sauce (optional)

Soak noodles in cold water for 10 minutes. Drain well. Set aside.

For filling, in a medium skillet cook noodles, pork, shrimp, carrots, green onion, gingerroot, and garlic till meat is no longer pink, adding 1 tablespoon cooking oil, if necessary. Drain off fat. Stir in soy sauce and sesame oil.

Spoon *1 rounded tablespoon* filling along ½ of the width of *each* halved spring roll or egg roll skin. Fold opposite ends to center; starting from long side, roll up spring roll envelope-style. Stir together flour and water; brush mixture on the edges of each spring roll. Press to seal.

Fry rolls, a few at a time, in hot oil (365°) about 1 minute or till golden brown. Drain on paper towels. Serve warm with bottled plum sauce. Makes 30 to 32 appetizers.

Microwave directions: Soak cellophane noodles as directed. Crumble ground pork into a 2-quart nonmetal casserole. Add shrimp, carrots, green onion, gingerroot, garlic, and noodles. Micro-cook, covered, on 100% power (HIGH) for 5 to 6 minutes or till pork is done, stirring twice to break up mixture. Drain. Stir in soy sauce and sesame oil. Continue as directed above.

Make-ahead directions: To freeze, wrap fried spring rolls in moisture- and vaporproof wrap. Seal, label, and freeze for up to 1 week.

Reheating directions: Place frozen rolls on a baking sheet and bake in 350° oven for 20 to 25 minutes or till warm.

Microwave reheating directions: In a nonmetal 12x7½x2-inch baking dish arrange *half* of the frozen spring rolls. Micro-cook, uncovered, on 70% power (MEDIUM-HIGH) for 4 to 6 minutes or till heated through, rearranging rolls once. Repeat with remaining rolls.

Per serving: 102 cal., 5 g pro., 9 g carbo., 5 g fat, 17 mg chol., 147 mg sodium. USRDA: 17% vit. A.

POP-THE-CORK PASTA CRUNCH

- 1 7-ounce package corkscrew macaroni
- ½ cup grated Parmesan cheese
- ½ teaspoon Italian seasoning
- ⅛ teaspoon garlic salt

Cooking oil for deep-fat frying

Cook macaroni according to package directions; drain. Rinse with cold water; drain. Pat moisture from macaroni with paper towels. Stir together Parmesan cheese, Italian seasoning, and garlic salt. Set aside.

In a deep skillet or deep-fat fryer heat 1½ inches of oil to 365°. Fry macaroni, 12 at a time, in hot oil till light brown (1 to 1½ minutes). Stir to separate. Using a slotted spoon, remove from oil. Drain on paper towels.

While macaroni is warm, sprinkle with the cheese mixture. Toss gently to coat. Cool. Makes 10 (½-cup) servings.

Per serving: 134 cal., 4 g pro., 15 g carbo., 6 g fat, 5 mg chol., 61 mg sodium.

RIPPLED-BEEF SKEWERS

- 1 **pound boneless beef sirloin steak**
- 18 **to 20 6-inch bamboo skewers**
- ⅓ **cup soy sauce**
- 2 **green onions, sliced**
- 1 **teaspoon grated gingerroot**
- 1 **teaspoon sesame oil**
Quartered orange slices (optional)
Green onions (optional)

Partially freeze beef. Soak the bamboo skewers in warm water for 20 to 30 minutes. Slice beef across the grain into 4x1x¼-inch strips. Halve each strip crosswise.

For marinade, in a bowl combine soy sauce, green onion, gingerroot, and sesame oil. Place meat strips in a shallow dish; add marinade. Stir to coat. Cover and refrigerate for 15 minutes.

Remove the meat from marinade; thread 2 pieces on each skewer. Broil immediately or cover and refrigerate for several hours.

To broil, place skewers on the unheated rack of a broiler pan or a baking sheet. Broil 6 to 8 inches from heat for 1½ minutes. Turn and broil for 1 to 1½ minutes more or till done. Place an orange triangle on the end of each skewer, if desired. Serve warm. Place on plates with whole green onions, if desired. Makes 18 to 20 appetizers.

Microwave directions: Cut, marinate, and thread the beef on skewers as directed. Place *half* of the skewers on a large nonmetal plate. Micro-cook, uncovered, on 100% power (HIGH) for 3 to 4 minutes or till done, turning pieces over and giving dish a half-turn once. Place an orange triangle on the end of each skewer, if desired. Repeat for remaining skewers.

Per appetizer: 40 cal., 4 g pro., 1 g carbo., 2 g fat, 10 mg chol., and 396 mg sodium.

SMOOTHIE SAUCE FOR VEGGIES

- 1 **8-ounce package cream cheese, softened**
- 1 **cup mayonnaise *or* salad dressing**
- 2 **teaspoons finely shredded lime peel**
- ¼ **cup lime juice**
- 2 **tablespoons Dijon-style mustard**
- 2 **teaspoons prepared horseradish**
- 1 **teaspoon poppy seed**
- ¼ **teaspoon salt**
- 3 **cups cauliflower flowerets**
- 1½ **cups fresh *or* frozen pea pods**

For sauce, in a medium mixing bowl stir together cream cheese and mayonnaise or salad dressing. Stir in lime peel, lime juice, mustard, horseradish, poppy seed, and salt. Cover and chill for several hours.

In a large saucepan place cauliflower in enough boiling water to cover. Cook about 1 minute or till crisp-tender. Drain. Hold cauliflower under cold running water. Drain well. Repeat with fresh pea pods, except cook for 30 seconds. (For frozen pea pods do not cook; hold under warm running water till thawed.) Cover and chill.

Before serving, arrange vegetables on a serving platter with a bowl of sauce. Makes 12 to 16 servings (2⅓ cups sauce.)

Per 2 tablespoons sauce and ¼ cup vegetables: 68 cal., 1 g pro., 1 g carbo., 7 g fat, 11 mg chol., 76 mg sodium.

GOIN' NUTS GINGER DIP

- 1 **cup blanched almonds**
- 1 **8-ounce carton plain yogurt**
- 2 **tablespoons lemon juice**
- 1 **teaspoon sugar**
- ½ **teaspoon grated gingerroot**
- ¼ **teaspoon salt**
- 1 **tablespoon snipped chives**
Crackers

In a shallow baking pan toast almonds in a 350° oven for 5 to 10 minutes or till light brown. Cool.

In a blender container or food processor bowl combine nuts, yogurt, and lemon juice. Cover and blend or process till nearly smooth. Add sugar, gingerroot, and salt. Blend or process till mixed. Stir in chives.

Transfer to a serving bowl; cover and chill till serving time. Serve the chilled dip with crackers (see photo below). Makes 1⅓ cups dip.

Per tablespoon dip: 47 cal., 2 g pro., 2 g carbo., 4 g fat, 1 mg chol., and 31 mg sodium.

Serve Goin' Nuts Ginger Dip with crackers.

GO-FOR-GAZPACHO SHRIMP

A seafood cocktail with the flavors of chilled gazpacho soup—

    4 cups water
    1 tablespoon salt
 1½ pounds fresh *or* frozen peeled
      and deveined shrimp
    3 medium tomatoes, peeled,
      seeded, and chopped
    1 medium red onion, halved length-
      wise and thinly sliced
    1 green pepper, chopped
    ½ cup tomato juice
    2 tablespoons red wine vinegar
    1 tablespoon olive oil *or* salad oil
    2 cloves garlic, minced
    1 tablespoon fresh snipped
      parsley *or* 1 teaspoon dried
      parsley flakes
    ¼ teaspoon dried oregano,
      crushed
    ¼ to ½ teaspoon bottled hot
      pepper sauce
 Escarole leaves (optional)

In a large saucepan combine water and salt. Bring to boiling. Add fresh or frozen shrimp; simmer for 1 to 3 minutes or till shrimp turn pink. Drain.

In a large mixing bowl combine tomatoes, onion, green pepper, tomato juice, vinegar, oil, garlic, parsley, oregano, and hot pepper sauce. Stir in the shrimp. Cover and refrigerate for several hours or till thoroughly chilled.

Before serving, drain the mixture. Serve shrimp and vegetables on lettuce-lined plates, if desired. Makes 8 to 10 (½-cup) appetizer servings.

Per serving: 93 cal., 14 g pro., 5 g carbo., 2 g fat, 110 mg chol., 125 mg sodium. USRDA: 10% vit. A, 54% vit. C, 13% niacin, 13% phosphorus.

A tangy marinade gives this shrimp appetizer its flavor.

WRAP-AND-ROLL GREEN CHILIES

    1 4-ounce can chopped green chili
      peppers, drained
    1 cup shredded Monterey Jack
      cheese (4 ounces)
   30 wonton skins
 Cooking oil for deep-fat frying
    1 recipe Tomato-Coriander Sauce
      (see recipe at right)

In a medium mixing bowl combine chili peppers and cheese. Position wonton skins with 1 point toward you (see photo below). Spoon *1 rounded teaspoon* of filling just off center of *each* skin. Fold bottom point of wonton skin over filling; tuck point under filling. Roll once to cover filling, leaving about 1 inch unrolled at the top of skin. Moisten the right-hand corner of skin with water.

Follow these wrapping steps for a delicious appetizer.

Grasp the right- and left-hand corners of skin; bring these corners toward you below the filling. Overlap the left-hand corner over the right-hand corner; press the wonton skin securely to seal. Fry wontons, a few at a time, in deep hot oil (365°) for 1 to 1½ minutes or till golden. Drain on paper towels.

Serve hot with Tomato-Coriander Sauce. Makes 30 appetizer servings.

Per serving with 2 teaspoons sauce: 61 cal., 2 g pro., 8 g carbo., 2 g fat, 6 mg chol., 100 mg sodium.

Crunchy stuffed wonton skins taste great paired with a sauce.

TOMATO-CORIANDER SAUCE

Make this up to three days ahead and serve warm at the party. Coriander is otherwise known as cilantro—

    1 7½-ounce can tomatoes
    2 tablespoons fresh snipped
      coriander *or* parsley
    1 small green onion, cut up (2
      tablespoons)
    1 tablespoon butter *or* margarine
    2 cloves garlic, minced
    ¼ teaspoon paprika

In a blender container or food processor bowl combine *undrained* tomatoes, coriander or parsley, green onion, butter or margarine, garlic, and paprika. Cover; blend or process till finely chopped.

Serve warm or refrigerate for up to 3 days. Before serving, in a small saucepan bring sauce to boiling, then reduce heat. Simmer, uncovered, for 5 minutes. Makes 1 cup.

TOFFEE-TOPPED STUFFED PUFFS

A recipe special enough for the November cover of our magazine. For smaller servings, give each diner one puff—

- ½ cup water
- ¼ cup butter *or* margarine
- ½ cup all-purpose flour
- ⅛ teaspoon salt
- 2 eggs
- 1 recipe Toasted Butter Pecan Ice Cream (see recipe at right) *or* purchased ice cream
- 1 recipe Caramel Sauce (see recipe at right)

In a medium saucepan combine water and butter or margarine. Bring to boiling. Add flour and salt all at once; stir vigorously. Cook and stir till the mixture forms a ball that doesn't separate. Remove from heat and cool slightly, about 5 minutes.

Add eggs, 1 at a time; beat well after each addition for 1 minute or till smooth. Drop dough by well-rounded teaspoon 2 inches apart onto a greased baking sheet, making 12 puffs total. Bake in a 400° oven about 30 minutes till golden and puffed.

Using a serrated knife, slice off the top *one-third* of each puff. Remove any soft dough inside. Cool slightly. Fill each warm puff with a small scoop of Toasted Butter Pecan Ice Cream. Serve warm Caramel Sauce over each. Makes 12 puffs, 6 servings.

Per serving: 643 cal., 7 g pro., 63 g carbo., 42 g fat, 204 mg chol., 261 mg sodium. USRDA: 33% vit. A, 10% thiamine, 15% riboflavin, 15% calcium, 13% iron, and 14% phosphorus.

TOASTED BUTTER PECAN ICE CREAM

Dig into the toasted nuts and caramelized sugar in this rich ice cream. It could become a regular at your house—

- ½ cup coarsely chopped pecans
- ¼ cup sugar
- 1 tablespoon butter *or* margarine
- 2 cups light cream
- 1 cup packed brown sugar
- 2 teaspoons vanilla
- 2 cups whipping cream

In a heavy 8-inch skillet combine pecans, sugar, and butter or margarine. Stir mixture constantly over medium heat for 6 to 8 minutes or till sugar melts and turns a rich brown color. Remove from heat.

Spread nuts on a buttered baking sheet or foil; separate into clusters. Cool. Break clusters into small chunks.

In a large mixing bowl combine light cream, brown sugar, and vanilla; stir till sugar is dissolved. Stir in the pecan mixture and whipping cream.

Freeze in an ice-cream freezer according to manufacturer's directions. Makes 1½ quarts ice cream.

CARAMEL SAUCE

You can store this sauce for up to two weeks in the refrigerator—

- 1½ cups packed brown sugar
- 1 tablespoon cornstarch
- 1 cup light cream
- 2 tablespoons butter *or* margarine

In a medium saucepan combine brown sugar and cornstarch. Add cream and butter or margarine. Cook and stir till mixture boils. Reduce heat and simmer for 8 to 10 minutes or till mixture thickens, stirring occasionally. Serve warm over puffs. Makes about 1¾ cups.

Microwave directions: In a 4-cup glass measure combine brown sugar and cornstarch. Stir in light cream. Micro-cook, uncovered, on 100% power (HIGH) for 4 to 5 minutes or till mixture thickens, stirring after every minute. Cook for 30 seconds more. Stir in butter or margarine.

SALZBURGER NOCKERL

This egg-rich dessert is not only simple, it's a showstopper! Assemble the ingredients before you serve the entrée. Then, after the main course, beat them together and bake. You'll have just enough time during baking to prepare the dessert coffee. Your dinner guests will never even miss you—

- 6 egg whites
- ½ teaspoon finely shredded lemon peel
- 1 tablespoon lemon juice
- ½ teaspoon vanilla
- ¼ cup sugar
- 4 egg yolks
- 1 tablespoon all-purpose flour
- Powdered sugar (optional)

Generously butter a 12x7½x2-inch baking dish or 2-quart oval baking dish; set aside.

In a large mixer bowl combine egg whites, lemon peel, lemon juice, and vanilla. Beat with an electric mixer on medium speed till soft peaks form (tips curl). Gradually add sugar, beating on high speed till stiff peaks form (tips stand straight).

In a small mixer bowl beat egg yolks with an electric mixer on high speed about 5 minutes or till thick and lemon colored; fold in flour.

Fold some of the beaten egg white mixture into yolk mixture. Gently fold egg yolk mixture into the remaining stiff-beaten egg whites. Spoon egg mixture into baking dish, forming 5 or 6 even mounds.

Bake in a 375° oven for 10 to 12 minutes or till outside is a golden brown and a knife inserted in the center comes out clean. Sift powdered sugar lightly over top, if desired. Serve immediately. Makes 5 or 6 servings.

Note: Separate the cold eggs, then bring them to room temperature to obtain the best volume. Beat the egg whites and yolks well to ensure a light, fluffy texture.

Per serving: 112 cal., 7 g pro., 12 g carbo., 4 g fat, 202 mg chol., 65 mg sodium. USRDA: 10% riboflavin.

CRANBERRY PEAR-FECT PASTRY

Frozen patty shells are "as easy as pie" to prepare—

1 **10-ounce package frozen patty shells**
1 **cup cranberries**
⅓ **cup water**
½ **cup sugar**
1 **tablespoon cornstarch**
½ **teaspoon ground cinnamon**
2 **cups peeled, cored, and sliced pears (3 pears)**
½ **cup chopped walnuts**
1 **egg yolk**
1 **tablespoon water**
Sweetened whipped cream (optional)

Thaw patty shells according to package directions. On a lightly floured surface stack 3 patties, 1 on top of another. Roll into a 12-inch circle. Trim to make a 10-inch circle. Reserve, wrap, and chill pastry trimmings.

Place circle on a baking sheet. Cover with clear plastic wrap. Roll remaining patty shells into a 12-inch circle; do not trim. Place over smaller circle. Cover all with plastic wrap. Chill pastry in the refrigerator for 1 to 4 hours.

Meanwhile, in a medium saucepan combine cranberries and water. Bring to boiling; reduce heat. Simmer, uncovered, for 3 minutes. Stir together sugar, cornstarch, and cinnamon. Add to hot cranberries; stir constantly till mixture is thickened and bubbly. Cook and stir for 2 minutes more. Remove from heat; cover the surface with clear plastic wrap and cool.

Remove plastic wrap from pastry; set aside top layer. Gently stir pears and walnuts into cooled cranberry mixture. Place cranberry mixture on bottom pastry, leaving a 1-inch border. Beat together the egg yolk and water; brush onto border.

Set larger circle over cranberry filling, pressing edges to seal. Fold top edge under smaller circle and seal. Flute edge, if desired. Brush top of pastry with additional egg yolk mixture.

Using a paring knife, carve a 5-inch-long pear shape in the center of the pie, leaving the pear shape attached at ¼-inch intervals. Carve decorative leaves out of the reserved pastry trimmings and place on top of pastry.

Bake in a 425° oven for 20 minutes. Brush edges with remaining egg yolk mixture. Bake for 3 to 5 minutes more or till pastry is golden. Serve with whipped cream, if desired.

To reheat cooled pastry, place in a 350° oven, uncovered, for 15 to 20 minutes or till warm. Makes 6 to 8 servings.

Per serving: 439 cal., 6 g pro., 52 g carbo., 25 g fat, 42 mg chol., 251 mg sodium. USRDA: 17% thiamine.

CHOCOLATE-MOUSSE CAKE

Make this dessert one day ahead and store it in the refrigerator. Before serving, pipe Chocolate Whipped Cream on the top and add hazelnuts. Slice the cake thinly to serve—

1 **cup whole hazelnuts (4 ounces)**
3 **tablespoons butter** *or* **margarine, melted**
2 **8-ounce packages (16 squares) semisweet chocolate, cut up**
1 **cup whipping cream**
6 **eggs**
1 **teaspoon vanilla**
⅓ **cup all-purpose flour**
¼ **cup sugar**
1 **recipe Chocolate Whipped Cream (see recipe at right)**
Shelled whole hazelnuts (optional)

Grease a 9-inch springform pan. In a blender container or food processor bowl coarsely grind 1 cup hazelnuts to make 1¼ cups. Stir together hazelnuts and melted butter or margarine. Press onto bottom and 1½ inches up sides of prepared pan.

In a medium saucepan combine cut-up chocolate and ½ *cup* of the whipping cream; stir over low heat till chocolate is melted. Remove from heat. (Or, place cut-up chocolate and cream in a 2-cup glass measure. Micro-cook, uncovered, on 100% power (HIGH) for 3 minutes or till chocolate is melted. Stir after 2 minutes.)

In a mixer bowl beat eggs and vanilla with an electric mixer on low speed till well mixed. Add flour and sugar; beat on high speed for 10 minutes or till thick and lemon colored.

In a small mixer bowl beat the remaining ½ cup whipping cream just till soft peaks form. Stir about *one-fourth* of the egg mixture into chocolate mixture. Fold remaining egg mixture into chocolate mixture; fold in whipped cream. Turn into prepared pan.

Bake in a 325° oven for 30 to 35 minutes or till puffed on the outer *one-third* of the top. The center will be slightly soft. Cool for 20 minutes in pan on wire rack. Remove pan sides. Cool for 3 to 4 hours. Serve at room temperature or chilled. Garnish with Chocolate Whipped Cream and whole hazelnuts, if desired. Makes 16 to 20 servings.

Per serving: 341 cal., 6 g pro., 24 g carbo., 27 g fat, 126 mg chol., 58 mg sodium. USRDA: 12% vit. A and 13% phosphorus.

CHOCOLATE WHIPPED CREAM

Next time you need a whipped topping, make it chocolate. Use this quick and easy topping to dress up a buttery pound cake, or dollop it on your favorite chocolate pudding—

½ **cup whipping cream**
½ **ounce (½ square) semisweet chocolate**

In a small saucepan combine whipping cream and chocolate. Stir over low heat till chocolate is melted. Remove from heat and stir till no chocolate specks remain. Pour into a small mixer bowl; cover and chill.

Before serving, beat chilled cream mixture with an electric mixer till stiff peaks form (tips stand straight).

Per tablespoon: 31 cal., 0 g pro., 1 g carbo., 3 g fat, 10 mg chol., and 2 mg sodium.

KIWI-ORANGE CUSTARD AND CAKE

This lovely dessert takes advantage of the season's best fruits: oranges and kiwi fruit. The next time you make it, experiment with different fruits and create a new arrangement—

- 1 recipe Flan Sponge (see recipe at right)
- 1 recipe Pastry Cream (see recipe at right)
- 1 kiwi fruit
- 2 medium oranges
- 2 tablespoons orange liqueur
- 2 tablespoons orange marmalade *or* apricot jam
- 1 teaspoon water

Orange peel knot (optional)
Candied kumquat flower (optional)

Prepare Flan Sponge and Pastry Cream as directed.

Peel and thinly slice kiwi fruit. Set aside. Peel oranges, removing white membrane. Slice thinly; discard seeds.

To serve, sprinkle orange liqueur over cooled Flan Sponge. Spread with Pastry Cream. Overlap oranges around rim of cake to form a circle. Arrange a circle of kiwi in the center.

In a small saucepan combine orange marmalade or apricot jam and water. Heat and stir over low heat till jam is melted; cool slightly. Brush melted jam over fruit. Garnish with an orange peel knot and candied kumquat flower, if desired. Cover and chill dessert till serving time for up to 8 hours. Makes 12 servings.

Per serving: 237 cal., 5 g pro., 40 g carbo., 6 g fat, 138 mg chol., 130 mg sodium. USRDA: 9% vit. A, 31% vit. C, 11% riboflavin, 11% phosphorus.

FLAN SPONGE

This firm, yet tender cake can be made ahead and frozen. Use this recipe for other desserts, too—

- 1 cup all-purpose flour
- 1 teaspoon baking powder
- ¼ teaspoon salt
- 2 eggs
- 1 cup sugar
- ½ cup milk
- 2 tablespoons butter *or* margarine

Grease a 10-inch springform or cake pan. In a medium mixing bowl stir together flour, baking powder, and salt. Set aside.

In a small mixer bowl beat eggs with an electric mixer on high speed for 4 minutes or till thick and lemon colored. Gradually add sugar, beating on medium speed for 4 to 5 minutes.

Fold flour mixture into egg mixture; stir just till blended. In a small saucepan heat milk with butter or margarine till butter is melted; stir into batter and mix well.

Pour batter into prepared pan, spreading evenly. Bake in a 350° oven for 20 to 25 minutes or till cake tests done when a wooden toothpick inserted in center comes out clean.

Cool in pan on wire rack for 10 minutes. Remove from pan and cool thoroughly on wire rack. Use for Kiwi-Orange Custard and Cake. Makes 1 cake, 12 servings.

Per serving: 137 cal., 3 g pro., 25 g carbo., 3 g fat, 48 mg chol., and 67 mg sodium.

PASTRY CREAM

This versatile cream can be used with many desserts. Try it in a tart with a fruit topping—

- ⅓ cup sugar
- 3 tablespoons all-purpose flour
- ¼ teaspoon salt
- 1½ cups milk
- 4 slightly beaten egg yolks

In a medium saucepan combine sugar, flour, and salt. Slowly add milk, stirring to combine. Cook and stir over medium heat till thickened and bubbly. Cook and stir for 1 minute more.

Slowly stir about *half* of the hot mixture into beaten yolks. Return all to the saucepan. Cook and stir for 2 minutes more. Cover surface with waxed paper or clear plastic wrap. Cool. (Do not stir during cooling so the mixture will not separate.) Use for Kiwi-Orange Custard and Cake. Makes 1⅔ cups.

Microwave directions: In a 1-quart nonmetal casserole stir together sugar, flour, and salt. Slowly add milk, stirring to combine. Micro-cook, uncovered, on 100% power (HIGH) for 4 to 6 minutes or till thickened and bubbly, stirring after every minute.

Stir about *half* of the hot mixture into beaten yolks. Return all to the casserole. Cook, uncovered, for 30 to 60 seconds or till edges are bubbly, stirring after every 30 seconds. Cook for 30 seconds more. Cover the surface with waxed paper or clear plastic wrap. Cool without stirring.

Per serving: 66 cal., 2 g pro., 8 g carbo., 3 g fat, 88 mg chol., and 63 mg sodium.

DECEMBER

HOLIDAY CONTEST RECIPE

WINNERS!

35 FAMILY FAVORITE RECIPES

My winning recipe was passed down from my great-grandmother. . . .

Each guest who attends my annual Christmas open house gets a package of this fudge. . . .

On Christmas Eve the whole family lends a hand in preparing the Christmas morning treat. . . .

This recipe has become our own family tradition. . . .

Letter after letter, entries in our Holiday Recipe Contest proved that traditions are built on family recipes. Last winter, thousands of you answered our call to share cherished favorites with us. The *Better Homes and Gardens* staff tackled the task of choosing 35 winners.

So, with a roll of the drum, here they are! Fit a few of these prizewinners into your holiday cooking schedule—they're sure to become a tradition in your home.

Produced by Diana McMillen
Food photographs: William K. Sladcik
Food stylist: Fran Paulson

MAIN DISHES

PEPPERED CHUTNEY ROAST
Betty Sue Smith
Colorado Springs, Colo.

Everyone is a winner with this dressed-up beef tenderloin topped with a glossy chutney glaze.

Clayre M. Heaslip
Redlands, Calif.

$1,000 WINNER
CHICKEN BREAST À L'ORANGE

Clayre trimmed the holiday bird down to size with flair and imagination. Now the star of the meal is her rice-stuffed chicken.

$500 WINNERS

BASIL-STUFFED LAMB ROAST

Denise L. Stetson
Wyoming, R.I.

Savory and succulent—this holiday roast shows off fresh lamb. Spinach, onion, and herbs flavor the stuffing.

COQ AU VIN ROSETTES

David D. Williams
Des Moines, Iowa

Creamy circles of pasta became a new tradition for the Williams family. Chicken and mushrooms spiral in bundles.

ORANGE-GLAZED TURKEY

Mary Lynn Brown
Upland, Calif.

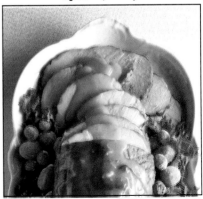

A yule-worthy entrée that's a perfect fit for today's small family. It starts with a rolled boneless turkey roast.

151

APPETIZERS AND BEVERAGES

Marilyn Mueller
Fayetteville, Ark.

$1,000 WINNER / CRANBERRY CHEESECAKE SHAKE

Everyone loves cheesecake—and this liquid version will satisfy cheesecake addicts everywhere. So thick and so luscious, it's flavored with cranberries!

$500 WINNERS

GRANDMA'S SALAMI PIE	SHOYSTER COCKTAIL	RASPBERRY PUNCH	CHEESEBALL WITH EVERYTHING
Rose Strohmaier *Port Murray, N.J.*	Anthony Lamar Bierly *Winona, Minn.*	Connie Reese *San Francisco, Calif.*	Bonnie Jean Edwards *Fargo, N. Dak.*

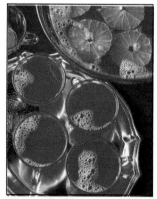

Grandma craves it—pastry, cheese, salami—and your party guests will, too.

Shrimp and oysters swim in a zesty cocktail sauce. The appetizer is delish!

Cheers! To Connie and all of you and yours during this holiday season.

It's full of everything that a cheeseball should have—cheeses, herbs, and more!

FOOD GIFTS

Deborah Jordan
Tacoma, Wash.

$1,000 WINNER / CHOCLAVA

A chocolate lover's version of baklava—a classic Greek pastry. Debbie
entices quite a following of Choclava enthusiasts with her winning recipe.

$500 WINNERS

TARRAGON-WINE MUSTARD SAUCE	MORNING GLORIOUS MUFFINS	BAKED CRANBERRY SAUCE	GINGERED HOLIDAY CHUTNEY
Linda Slater *Arvada, Colo.*	**Michele Oneil** *Boylston, Mass.*	**Joan L. Fosnight** *Elm Grove, Wis.*	**Margery Mulkey** *Boise, Idaho*

Present the special sauce in a hand-labeled jar with a tag that says to chill.

Tuck some warm-from-the-oven muffins in an open box or basket for delivery.

As a gift, offer the sauce in a covered sauce bowl that's topped with a ribbon.

For an extra-memorable gift, include a ham with this winning chutney.

SIDE DISHES

HOLIDAY CONTEST RECIPE

$1,000 WINNER / LEMON-PARSLEY STUFFING

With your glorious holiday bird, try this sophisticated and simple, winning stuffing recipe. It's fresh and lemony—a blue-ribbon best.

$500 WINNERS

BROCCOLI AND CRAB BISQUE
Pamela Wilde
Salt Lake City, Utah

The creamy seafood soup makes a dazzling first course or sandwich companion.

CURRIED RICE RING
Florence Bienenfeld
Marina Del Rey, Calif.

Fill the flavorful spiced rice ring with your choice of mixed vegetables.

BLACK-EYED PEA CASSEROLE
Jo Hackler
Pittsburg, Tex.

A New Year's Day tradition for the Hacklers, this recipe is said to bring good luck.

FINLAND CASSEROLE
Carole F. Rautio
Galloway, Ohio

Carole cooks this vegetable combination for her Finnish husband, Nils.

COOKIES AND CANDIES

Kate Beckman
Chino, Calif.

$1,000 WINNER / NEW ZEALAND HOLLY COOKIES

Kate's great-grandmother (whose family came from New Zealand) made these raspberry-filled cookies every year. Kate now carries on the tradition.

$500 WINNERS

HONEY-FILLED NUGGETS	HOLIDAY CHOCOLATE FANS	CRUNCHY NUT FUDGE	MOCHA NUT DIVINITY
Audrey Bledsoe	Virginia E. Mampre	Mildred Ringler	D. R. Sarkisian
Smyrna, Ga.	*Houston, Tex.*	*Virginia Beach, Va.*	*Inman, S.C.*

A fancy filling of nuts, honey, and cherries packs each of the cookies.

Surprise! These chocolaty cookies start with delicate phyllo dough.

Sugared peanuts fill this fudge. Serve the leftover peanuts as an added treat.

Instant Swiss coffee powder makes a delightful difference in creamy, rich divinity.

HOMEMADE BAKED GOODS

Linda Ann Rohr
Stamford, Conn.

$1,000 WINNER / NUTCRACKER SWEET TART

Here's a delightful title for an extraordinary dessert. Linda serves her
four-star tart to holiday tree trimmers. Swirls of sauce bedeck the pastry.

$500 WINNERS

CRANBERRY PUMPKIN RING	CHRISTMAS TREE TREATS	FUDGY FRUITCAKE DROPS	WHEATEN APPLE RING
Elizabeth Domkowski *Knoxville, Tenn.*	Joy D. Miller *Accord, N.Y.*	Samuel Mancuso *East Meadow, N.Y.*	Jackie Kunovic *Canfield, Ohio*

Distinctive—cranberry and pumpkin in a spiral coffee bread.

The tender bread with sausage filling is a favorite with Joy's children.

These cookies offer you double the chocolate: semisweet pieces and cocoa.

Nutritious and delicious— the wheat bread touts apples, raisins, and nuts.

JUNIOR DIVISION

Kathy Resler (10)
Goshen, Ind.

$1,000 WINNER / WHOLE WHEAT CARROT-BANANA BREAD

Kathy's nutrition-conscious family curb sweets during the holidays—but
not great-tasting treats. This wholesome quick bread is just one example.

$500 WINNERS

PEANUT DATE BALLS	ANISE COOKIES	CAROB PEANUT CLUSTERS	SANTA'S ELVES' HOLIDAY TREAT
Dean Consylman (aged 8) *Noblesville, Ind.*	Eve Shore (aged 10) *Williamsburg, Iowa*	Genny Darais (aged 13) *Orem, Utah*	Teddi Schuster (aged 12) *St. John, Wash.*

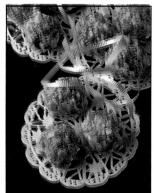

Dean created this special treat while experimenting in the kitchen.

Eve's cookie recipe was passed down from her great-grandmother.

Genny and her grandmother invented this nutty candy recipe.

Her mom inspired Teddi to make this top-notch dessert recipe.

CHICKEN BREAST À L'ORANGE

```
 2  tablespoons apple juice
 2  tablespoons apricot brandy
Dash ground allspice
Dash ground cinnamon
Dash ground cloves
 ½  cup chopped mixed dried fruit
 ⅓  cup chopped onion
 1  tablespoon butter or margarine
 ¼  teaspoon poultry seasoning
 ½  cup cooked brown rice
 4  whole chicken breasts, skinned,
    boned, and halved lengthwise
 1  recipe Orange Sauce (see recipe
    at right)
 ¼  cup snipped parsley
 3  tablespoons sliced almonds,
    toasted
```

In a small mixing bowl combine apple juice, brandy, allspice, cinnamon, and cloves. Add mixed dried fruit; let stand 2 hours.

In a small saucepan cook onion in butter or margarine till onion is tender but not brown. Stir in poultry seasoning, ¼ teaspoon *salt*, and dash *pepper*. Remove from heat; stir in cooked rice. Drain fruit, reserving liquid. Add fruit to rice mixture.

Place each chicken breast half between 2 pieces of clear plastic wrap. With a meat mallet, pound each piece to ¼-inch thickness. Remove the plastic wrap. Place about *2 tablespoons* rice mixture in the center of *each* chicken piece; fold in sides and roll chicken around rice, forming a bundle. Place, seam side down, in a 12x7½x2-inch baking dish. (At this point, chicken may be covered and chilled till needed.)

Prepare Orange Sauce; pour over chicken. Cover with foil. Bake, covered, in a 350° oven for 30 to 40 minutes or till chicken is tender. Sprinkle with parsley and almonds. Makes 8 servings.

Orange Sauce: In a small saucepan melt 2 tablespoons *butter* or *margarine.* Stir in 2 tablespoons all-purpose *flour,* 1½ teaspoons ground *cinnamon,* ¾ teaspoon finely shredded *orange peel,* and several dashes bottled *hot pepper sauce.* Add 1¼ cups *orange juice* and the reserved liquid from dried fruit. Cook and stir till thickened and bubbly.

Per serving: 277 cal., 30 g pro., 17 g carbo., 9 g fat, 14 mg chol., 157 mg sodium. USRDA: 21% vit. A, 39% vit. C, 10% thiamine, 16% riboflavin, 57% niacin, 4% calcium, 14% iron, 33% phosphorus.

PEPPERED CHUTNEY ROAST

```
 ¾  cup unsweetened pineapple juice
 ½  cup steak sauce
 ⅓  cup Worcestershire sauce
 ⅓  cup port wine
 ¼  cup lemon juice
 2  teaspoons seasoned salt
 1  teaspoon pepper
 1  teaspoon lemon-pepper
    seasoning
 1  teaspoon dry mustard
 1  3- to 4-pound beef tenderloin
 2  teaspoons cracked pepper
 3  or 4 slices bacon
 ⅓  cup chutney
Hot cooked brussels sprouts
    (optional)
```

For marinade, stir together the first 9 ingredients. Place meat in a large plastic bag; set in a baking dish. Pour marinade over meat; close bag. Refrigerate several hours or overnight, turning meat occasionally to distribute marinade. Drain, reserving marinade.

Rub beef tenderloin with cracked pepper. Place meat on a rack in a shallow roasting pan. Arrange bacon slices over tenderloin. Roast, uncovered, in a 425° oven for 30 to 45 minutes or till meat thermometer registers 135°. Baste tenderloin twice during roasting with the reserved marinade.

Spoon chutney over meat. Bake for 5 to 10 minutes more or till thermometer registers 140°. Transfer meat to a serving platter. Let stand for 15 minutes before slicing. Serve with brussels sprouts, if desired. Serves 12 to 16.

Per serving: 234 cal., 18 g pro., 10 g carbo., 12 g fat, 51 mg chol., 644 mg sodium. USRDA: 19% riboflavin, 12% niacin, 15% phosphorus.

BASIL-STUFFED LAMB ROAST

```
 ¾  cup chopped onion
 ⅓  cup chopped celery
 2  cloves garlic, minced
 ¼  cup olive oil or cooking oil
 2  beaten eggs
 1  10-ounce package frozen
    chopped spinach, thawed
 ¼  cup snipped parsley
 3  tablespoons fresh snipped basil
    or 1 tablespoon dried basil,
    crushed
 ¼  teaspoon dried marjoram,
    crushed
 6  cups unseasoned croutons
 ¼  cup grated Parmesan cheese
 1  5- to 7-pound leg of lamb, boned
    and butterflied
 1  teaspoon dried rosemary,
    crushed
Apple peel rosettes (optional)
Sprigs of fresh mint (optional)
Sprigs of fresh marjoram (optional)
```

For stuffing, in a small saucepan cook onion, celery, and garlic in hot oil till tender but not brown. In a large bowl combine eggs, spinach, parsley, basil, marjoram, and ¼ teaspoon *pepper;* add onion mixture. Stir in croutons and cheese. Drizzle with ½ cup *water* to moisten, tossing lightly. Set aside.

Remove fell (pinkish-red, paper-thin layer) from surface of meat. Pound meat to an even thickness. Sprinkle with rosemary. Spread stuffing over roast. Roll up; tie securely.

Place roast, seam side down, on a rack in a shallow roasting pan. Insert a meat thermometer into the thickest portion of meat. Roast, uncovered, in a 325° oven for 1½ to 2 hours or till thermometer registers 150°. Let stand for 15 minutes before carving. Remove strings; garnish with apple peel rosettes and sprigs of mint and marjoram, if desired. Serves 12.

Per serving: 467 cal., 32 g pro., 10 g carbo., 32 g fat, 158 mg chol., 218 mg sodium. USRDA: 43% vit. A, 17% vit. C, 23% thiamine, 28% riboflavin, 44% niacin, 20% iron, 32% phosphorus.

COQ AU VIN ROSETTES

Start this tradition in your family: The lucky diner who discovers the whole almond in the Christmas entrée opens the first holiday gift—

- 4 **medium chicken breasts, skinned and boned**
- 1 **medium onion, finely chopped**
- 8 **ounces fresh mushrooms, sliced**
- ¼ **cup butter *or* margarine**
- ¾ **cup dry white wine**
- ½ **teaspoon dried tarragon, crushed**
- ½ **teaspoon salt**
- ½ **teaspoon white pepper**
- 8 **lasagna noodles, cooked and drained**
- 1 **8-ounce package cream cheese, cut up**
- ½ **cup light cream *or* milk**
- ½ **cup dairy sour cream**
- 1½ **cups shredded Gruyère cheese (6 ounces)**
- 1 **cup shredded Muenster cheese (4 ounces)**
- 1 **whole almond**
- 3 **tablespoons slivered almonds, toasted**

Snipped parsley

Cut chicken into 1-inch pieces. In a 10-inch skillet cook onion and mushrooms in butter or margarine till tender but not brown. Add chicken, wine, tarragon, salt, and pepper. Bring to boiling; reduce heat. Cover and simmer for 8 to 10 minutes or till chicken is tender.

Meanwhile, halve lasagna noodles lengthwise. Curl each into a 2½-inch-diameter ring and place in a 13x9x2-inch baking dish. Using a slotted spoon, spoon chicken-mushroom mixture into center of lasagna rings.

To broth in the skillet add cream cheese, light cream or milk, sour cream, *half* of the Gruyère, and *half* of the Muenster cheese. Cook and stir till cheeses are melted (do not boil); pour over lasagna rings. Insert a whole almond in one of the rings. Sprinkle remaining cheeses and slivered almonds over rings. Bake, covered, in a 325° oven for 35 minutes. Garnish with parsley. Spoon sauce over when served. Makes 8 servings.

Per serving: 661 cal., 45 g pro., 27 g carbo., 40 g fat, 195 mg chol., 500 mg sodium. USRDA: 30% vit. A, 17% thiamine, 41% riboflavin, 65% niacin, 35% calcium, 18% iron, 61% phosphorus.

ORANGE-GLAZED TURKEY

- 1 **4- to 6-pound frozen boneless turkey roast**
- ¾ **cup butter *or* margarine, melted**
- 6 **small oranges**
- ¼ **cup water**
- 2 **tablespoons all-purpose flour**
- ¼ **teaspoon ground nutmeg**
- 2 **tablespoons orange liqueur**

Sugar-coated cranberries and kumquats (optional)
Curly endive (optional)
Cranberry-orange relish (optional)

Thaw turkey. Place turkey roast on a rack in a shallow roasting pan. Brush with some of the butter or margarine. Roast according to package directions. Finely shred the peel of 1 orange to obtain *1 tablespoon* peel; set aside. Juice all of the oranges (should have about 2 cups juice). Stir together the remaining melted butter and orange juice. Baste turkey with orange juice mixture frequently during the last 30 minutes of roasting. Remove turkey to meat platter; cover to keep warm.

Combine pan juices and remaining orange juice mixture; add water if necessary to make 2 cups. Set aside. In saucepan combine water and flour; add orange juice mixture, orange peel, and nutmeg. Cook and stir till thickened and bubbly; cook and stir 2 minutes more. Stir in orange liqueur. Spoon some sauce over turkey; pass remaining. Surround turkey with sugar-coated cranberries and kumquats or endive, if desired. Serve with cranberry-orange relish, if desired. Makes 12 to 16 servings.

Per serving: 436 cal., 32 g pro., 6 g carbo., 30 g fat, 170 mg chol., 277 mg sodium. USRDA: 15% vit. A, 36% vit. C, 14% riboflavin, 37% niacin, 13% iron, 38% phosphorus.

CRANBERRY CHEESECAKE SHAKE

- 1 **egg**
- 1 **3-ounce package cream cheese, softened**
- ½ **cup milk**
- 2 **cups vanilla ice cream**
- 1 **8-ounce can jellied cranberry sauce**
- 1 **cup cranberries**

Place egg in a blender container. Cover and blend 15 to 30 seconds. Add cream cheese and milk. Cover and blend till well combined. Add ice cream, cranberry sauce, and cranberries. Cover and blend till well combined. Stop and scrape down sides, if necessary. Serve immediately or cover and chill till needed. Makes 4 (8-ounce) servings.

Per serving: 342 cal., 8 g pro., 40 g carbo., 18 g fat, 118 mg chol., 127 mg sodium. USRDA: 17% vit. A, 17% riboflavin, 16% calcium, 16% phosphorus.

GRANDMA'S SALAMI PIE

3½ cups all-purpose flour
½ teaspoon salt
1 cup shortening
2 tablespoons cooking oil
⅓ to ½ cup cold water
12 ounces salami, diced (2½ cups)
3 cups shredded Swiss cheese
(12 ounces)
5 hard-cooked eggs, sliced
1 cup grated Romano cheese
4 beaten eggs
½ teaspoon pepper

In a mixing bowl combine flour and salt. Cut in shortening till size of small peas. Stir in oil. Sprinkle 1 or 2 tablespoons water over flour mixture; gently toss with a fork. Repeat till all is moistened. Form dough into a ball.

On a lightly floured surface roll out *two-thirds* of the dough to form a 16x12-inch rectangle. Press into bottom and up sides of a 13x9x2-inch baking pan. Layer in pan in order: salami, Swiss cheese, hard-cooked eggs, and Romano cheese. Combine eggs and pepper; pour into pan.

On a lightly floured surface roll remaining dough to a 14x10-inch rectangle. Prick well with a fork. Place over filling in pan. Seal top and bottom crust edges together by rolling edges toward center. Flute edges. Bake in a 375° oven about 65 minutes or till golden. Cool 45 minutes. Cut into small rectangles to serve. Serves 28 to 32.

Per serving: 270 cal., 11 g pro., 13 g carbo., 19 g fat, 106 mg chol., 343 mg sodium. USRDA: 11% thiamine, 12% riboflavin, 17% calcium, and 18% phosphorus.

SHOYSTER COCKTAIL

12 fresh *or* frozen medium shrimp,
cooked and shelled, *or* one
6-ounce package frozen cooked
shrimp, thawed
12 fresh shucked oysters,
halved
1 cup cocktail sauce
1 medium avocado, seeded,
peeled, and chopped
1 small tomato, seeded and
chopped (½ cup)
1 small onion, finely chopped
¼ cup lime juice
2 tablespoons snipped parsley
1 medium red *or* green chili
pepper, seeded and chopped
½ teaspoon bottled hot pepper
sauce
1 clove garlic, minced
Leaf lettuce
Assorted crackers
Lemon wedges

Cut shrimp into bite-size pieces, if necessary. In a medium mixing bowl stir together shrimp, oysters, cocktail sauce, chopped avocado, chopped tomato, chopped onion, lime juice, snipped parsley, red or green chili pepper, bottled hot pepper sauce, and minced garlic. Cover and chill shrimp mixture for several hours.

To serve, spoon mixture onto individual lettuce-lined dishes. Serve with assorted crackers and lemon wedges. Makes 4 to 6 servings.

Per serving: 247 cal., 14 g pro., 28 g carbo., 10 g fat, 78 mg chol., 999 mg sodium. USRDA: 35% vit. A, 153% vit. C, 14% thiamine, 15% riboflavin, 20% niacin, 21% iron, 19% phosphorus.

CHEESE BALL WITH EVERYTHING

2 cups shredded Swiss cheese
(8 ounces)
2 cups shredded cheddar cheese
(8 ounces)
1 8-ounce package cream cheese,
softened
½ cup dairy sour cream
½ cup finely chopped onion
1 2-ounce jar diced pimiento
2 tablespoons sweet pickle relish
10 slices bacon, crisp-cooked,
drained, and crumbled
½ cup finely chopped pecans
Dash salt
Dash pepper
¼ cup snipped parsley
1 tablespoon poppy seed
Assorted crackers

Let Swiss and cheddar cheeses come to room temperature. In a large mixer bowl beat together cream cheese and sour cream till fluffy. Beat in Swiss cheese, cheddar cheese, onion, *undrained* pimiento, pickle relish, *half* of the bacon, *half* of the pecans, salt, and pepper. Cover and chill till firm. Shape into 1 large or 2 small balls; place on waxed paper.

In a small bowl combine remaining bacon, remaining pecans, parsley, and poppy seed. Turn mixture out onto a clean sheet of waxed paper. Roll the cheese ball in seed mixture to coat. Wrap and chill.

Let stand 30 minutes at room temperature before serving. Serve with assorted crackers. Makes 2 small or 1 large cheese ball.

Per tablespoon: 60 cal., 3 g pro., 1 g carbo., 5 g fat, 13 mg chol., and 78 mg sodium.

RASPBERRY PUNCH

6 to 8 tangerines (3 to 4
  pounds)
2 or 3 lemons
4 32-ounce bottles cranberry-
  raspberry drink, chilled
1 28-ounce bottle club soda,
  chilled
Peeled, sliced tangerines

Squeeze juice from tangerines (should
have about 2⅔ cups juice). Squeeze
juice from lemons (should have about
⅔ cup juice). In a large punch bowl stir
together tangerine juice, lemon juice,
cranberry-raspberry drink, and club
soda. Garnish with peeled, sliced tangerines. Makes 48 (4-ounce) servings.

Raspberry Wine Punch: Prepare
Raspberry Punch as directed *except* add
one 750-milliliter bottle *dry white wine*
and 1 cup *orange liqueur.* Serves 60.

Per serving: 61 cal., 0 g pro., 16 g
carbo., 0 g fat, 0 mg chol., 1 mg sodium.
USRDA: 31% vit. C.

CHOCLAVA

1 1-pound package frozen phyllo
  dough (about 22 sheets)
1 pound walnuts, finely chopped
1 6-ounce package semisweet
  chocolate pieces, finely chopped
¾ cup sugar
1½ teaspoons ground cinnamon
1¼ cups butter *or* margarine, melted
¾ cup orange juice
½ cup sugar
½ cup honey
2 tablespoons lemon juice
2 squares (2 ounces) semisweet
  chocolate

Thaw phyllo dough according to package directions. Combine walnuts, finely
chopped chocolate, ¾ cup sugar, and
cinnamon; set aside.

Brush the bottom of a 15x11x2-
inch baking pan with some of the melted butter or margarine. Layer *8* of the
phyllo sheets in the pan, brushing each
sheet with butter. Sprinkle about *2
cups* of the nut mixture over phyllo in
pan. Top with another *4* sheets of the
phyllo, brushing each with more of the
melted butter. Sprinkle with *2* cups of
the nut mixture and top with *4* more
phyllo sheets, brushing each sheet with
butter. Top with remaining nut mixture and the remaining phyllo sheets,
brushing each sheet with butter. Drizzle remaining butter over top layer. Using a sharp knife, cut into diamond- or
triangle-shape pieces, cutting to but not
through the bottom layer. Bake in a
325° oven for 1 hour.

Immediately finish cutting the dia-
monds or triangles. Meanwhile, in a
medium saucepan stir together orange
juice, ½ cup sugar, honey, lemon juice,
and ½ cup *water.* Bring to boiling; reduce heat. Simmer for 20 minutes.
Pour over warm dessert in pan. Cool
completely.

In a small saucepan combine chocolate squares and 2 tablespoons *water;*
stir over low heat till smooth. Drizzle
over dessert. Package in airtight containers. Makes about 60 pieces.

Directions to pack with gift: Store
in refrigerator.

Per serving: 153 cal., 2 g pro., 15 g
carbo., 10 g fat, 12 mg chol., and 83 mg
sodium.

TARRAGON-WINE MUSTARD SAUCE

½ cup Dijon-style mustard
⅓ cup olive oil *or* cooking oil
¼ cup white vinegar
¼ cup dry white wine
2 tablespoons dry mustard
1 teaspoon dried basil, crushed
1 teaspoon dried tarragon,
  crushed

In a small bowl stir together all of the
ingredients. Transfer to small attractive jars. Seal and label. Makes about
1⅓ cups mustard mixture.

Directions to pack with gift: Serve
sauce with chilled meats, or as a sauce
on vegetables, or as a basting mixture
for cooking meats.

Per tablespoon: 10 cal., 0 g pro., 1 g
carbo., 1 g fat, 0 mg chol., 78 mg sodium.

MORNING GLORIOUS MUFFINS

2 cups all-purpose flour
1¼ cups sugar
2 teaspoons baking soda
2 teaspoons ground cinnamon
½ teaspoon salt
1½ cups finely shredded carrot
1½ cups peeled and shredded apple
  (1 large)
¾ cup coconut
½ cup snipped pitted dates
½ cup chopped pecans
3 beaten eggs
1 cup cooking oil
½ teaspoon vanilla

In a mixing bowl combine flour, sugar,
soda, cinnamon, and salt. In another
bowl combine carrot, apple, coconut,
dates, and pecans. Stir in beaten eggs,
oil, and vanilla. Add to dry ingredients,
stirring till moistened.

Grease muffin pans or line with
paper-bake cups. Spoon batter into prepared muffin pans. Bake in a 375° oven
for 18 to 20 minutes or till done. Remove from pans; cool on wire racks.
Package muffins for giving as desired.
Makes about 24.

Directions to pack with gift: Serve
muffins with whipped cream cheese.

Per muffin: 207 cal., 2 g pro., 23 g
carbo., 12 g fat, 30 mg chol., 141 mg
sodium. USRDA: 16% vit. A.

BAKED CRANBERRY SAUCE

- 1 **pound cranberries (5 cups)**
- 1 **12-ounce jar (1 cup) orange marmalade**
- 1 **cup chopped pecans**
- 1 **cup coconut**
- ¾ **cup sugar**
- ½ **cup water**

Stir together all ingredients. Spread in a 13x9x2-inch baking dish. Bake, uncovered, in a 350° oven about 30 minutes. Transfer to small attractive jars. Seal and label. Makes about 4 cups.

Directions to pack with gift: Store in refrigerator. Serve warm or chilled over fruit, ice cream, and other desserts or as meat accompaniment.

Per tablespoon: 61 cal., 10 g carbo., 3 g fat, 0 mg chol., 1 mg sodium.

GINGERED HOLIDAY CHUTNEY

You can skip the canning procedure, and instead store the jars of chutney in the refrigerator—

- 2 **cups packed brown sugar**
- ¾ **cup vinegar**
- ½ **teaspoon salt**
- ¼ **teaspoon ground cinnamon**
- ¼ **teaspoon ground red pepper**
- 1 **lime**
- 1 **lemon**
- 1 **pound fresh Anjou pears, peeled, cored, and coarsely chopped (about 3 cups)**
- 1 **cup chopped green pepper**
- 1 **cup chopped sweet red pepper**
- 1 **cup chopped onion**
- 1 **tablespoon chopped candied ginger**
- 1 **cup light raisins**

In a saucepan combine brown sugar, vinegar, salt, cinnamon, and ground red pepper. Bring to boiling; reduce heat. Simmer, uncovered, for 10 minutes. Finely shred peel from lime and lemon; squeeze juice from each.

In a large mixing bowl combine lime and lemon peel and juices, pears, green and red pepper, onion, and ginger. Add raisins, mixing gently. Add mixture to hot syrup. Bring to boiling; reduce heat. Simmer, uncovered, about 1 hour or till thick.

Ladle chutney at once into hot, clean pint jars, leaving a ¼-inch headspace. Wipe jar rims; adjust lids. Process in boiling water bath for 15 minutes (start timing when water boils). (Or, cover and chill chutney.) Makes 2 pints.

Directions to pack with gift: Serve as an accompaniment to cooked ham, poultry, or other meat. (If chutney isn't processed in water bath, be sure to include a note about refrigerating.)

Per tablespoon: 42 cal., 0 g pro., 11 g carbo., 0 g fat, 21 mg chol., 87 mg sodium. USRDA: 18% vit. C.

LEMON-PARSLEY STUFFING

- 10 **cups dry bread cubes (about 14 slices of bread)**
- 1 **cup finely chopped onion**
- 1 **cup snipped parsley**
- 4 **teaspoons finely shredded lemon peel**
- 2 **teaspoons dried marjoram, crushed**
- 1 **teaspoon dried thyme, crushed**
- ½ **teaspoon salt**
- ½ **teaspoon pepper**
- 2 **cloves garlic, minced**
- 2 **slightly beaten eggs**
- 1 **cup butter *or* margarine, melted**
- ⅓ **cup water**
- ¼ **cup lemon juice**

In a large mixing bowl combine bread cubes, onion, parsley, lemon peel, marjoram, thyme, salt, pepper, and garlic. Mix well. Combine eggs, melted butter or margarine, water, and lemon juice; toss with bread mixture.

Use mixture to stuff one 10- to 12-pound turkey, or two 3-pound whole broiler-fryer chickens. (Or, spoon stuffing into a 2-quart casserole. Bake, uncovered, in a 325° oven for 30 to 40 minutes.) Makes about 7 cups stuffing.

Per ½-cup serving: 193 cal., 3 g pro., 13 g carbo., 15 g fat, 77 mg chol., 357 mg sodium. USRDA: 20% vit. A and 17% vit. C.

CURRIED RICE RING

- 2½ **cups water**
- 1¼ **cups brown rice**
- ⅓ **cup dry white wine**
- 1 **teaspoon instant chicken bouillon granules**
- ¼ **teaspoon ground coriander**
- ⅛ **teaspoon pepper**
- 1 **cup sliced fresh mushrooms**
- ¼ **cup chopped onion**
- 1½ **teaspoons curry powder**
- 1 **tablespoon cooking oil**
- ¼ **cup slivered almonds *or* chopped pecans**
- ¼ **cup raisins**
- 2 **tablespoons frozen apple juice concentrate, thawed**
- 1 **tablespoon honey**
- **Hot cooked mixed vegetables**

In a medium saucepan combine water, *uncooked* rice, wine, bouillon granules, coriander, and pepper. Bring to boiling; reduce heat. Cover and simmer about 50 minutes or till rice is tender. Drain any remaining liquid.

In a small saucepan cook mushrooms, onion, and curry powder in hot oil till onion is tender but not brown, stirring occasionally. If necessary, cook over low heat till most of the mushroom liquid has evaporated.

In a bowl combine rice mixture, mushroom mixture, almonds or pecans, raisins, apple juice concentrate, and honey; mix well. Pack mixture into a well-oiled 4-cup ring mold. (To make ahead: Cover and refrigerate rice ring up to 24 hours. To reheat; bake, covered, in a 350° oven for 40 to 45 minutes or till heated through.) To serve, unmold onto a serving plate. Fill center with cooked vegetables. Serves 8.

Per serving: 244 cal., 5 g pro., 47 g carbo., 4 g fat, 0 mg chol., 89 mg sodium. USRDA: 34% vit. A, 12% thiamine, 12% niacin, 14% phosphorus and 11% iron.

BLACK-EYED PEA CASSEROLE

1 10-ounce package frozen
  black-eyed peas
½ cup chopped green *or* sweet red
  pepper
½ cup chopped celery
¼ cup chopped onion
1 clove garlic, minced
1 teaspoon instant chicken
  bouillon granules
2 cups cooked rice
1 4½-ounce can deviled ham
1 teaspoon butter *or* margarine
4 firm medium tomatoes, sliced
¼ cup seasoned fine dry bread
  crumbs
2 tablespoons grated Parmesan
  cheese
⅛ teaspoon ground red pepper
2 tablespoons cooking oil
Celery tops (optional)

In large saucepan combine black-eyed peas, green or red pepper, celery, onion, garlic, bouillon granules, and 2 cups *water*. Bring to boiling; reduce heat. Cover and simmer about 40 minutes or till peas are very tender. Uncover and simmer 20 minutes more. Stir in cooked rice, deviled ham, butter or margarine, and ⅛ teaspoon *pepper*.

Meanwhile, coat tomato slices with mixture of bread crumbs, Parmesan cheese, and ground red pepper. In large skillet cook tomato slices in hot oil till light brown on both sides. Arrange in ring on platter. Top with pea-rice mixture. Garnish with celery tops, if desired. Makes 6 servings.

Per serving: 306 cal., 11 g pro., 36 g carbo., 13 g fat, 18 mg chol., 691 mg sodium. USRDA: 19% vit. A, 71% vit. C, 27% thiamine, 13% niacin, 18% iron, 18% phosphorus.

FINLAND CASSEROLE

3 medium turnips, peeled and
  thinly sliced (2½ cups)
2 medium zucchini, thinly sliced
  (2 cups)
1 large onion, thinly sliced and
  separated into rings
2 large tomatoes, seeded and
  chopped (2¼ cups)
1 cup cauliflower flowerets
1 cup broccoli flowerets
8 tablespoons butter *or* margarine,
  melted
1 tablespoon dry white wine
1½ teaspoons Worcestershire sauce
½ teaspoon garlic powder
½ teaspoon salt
½ teaspoon pepper
¾ cup crushed rich round crackers
  (about 20 crackers)
1 cup shredded cheddar cheese
  (4 ounces)

In a medium saucepan cook turnips, covered, in a small amount of boiling salted water for 4 minutes; add zucchini and onion. Continue cooking for 3 minutes more; drain.

In a large mixing bowl combine cooked turnips, zucchini, onion, tomatoes, cauliflower, broccoli, *6 tablespoons* of the butter or margarine, wine, Worcestershire sauce, garlic powder, salt, and pepper.

Transfer to a 12x7½x2-inch baking dish. Toss crackers with remaining butter; sprinkle over vegetables. Bake in a 350° oven for 40 minutes. Sprinkle with cheese and bake about 5 minutes more or till cheese is melted. Serve with a slotted spoon. Serves 8 to 10.

Per serving: 239 cal., 7 g pro., 15 g carbo., 18 g fat, 50 mg chol., 494 mg sodium. USRDA: 34% vit. A, 101% vit. C, 13% riboflavin, 18% calcium, 15% phosphorus.

NEW ZEALAND HOLLY COOKIES

2 cups all-purpose flour
1 cup sugar
1 teaspoon ground cinnamon
¾ teaspoon baking powder
½ cup butter *or* margarine
1 slightly beaten egg
¼ cup milk
⅔ cup raspberry jam
2 cups sifted powdered sugar
½ teaspoon vanilla
2 to 3 tablespoons milk
Red cinnamon candies
Green food coloring

In a medium mixing bowl combine flour, sugar, cinnamon, baking powder, and ¼ teaspoon *salt*. Cut in butter or margarine till pieces are the size of small peas. Make a well in the center. Combine egg and ¼ cup milk; add all at once to dry mixture. Stir till moistened.

On a lightly floured surface, roll dough to ⅛-inch thickness. Cut into 2-inch circles or flowers with cookie cutter. Place on an ungreased cookie sheet. Bake in a 375° oven for 8 to 10 minutes or till light brown on the bottom. Cool on a wire rack. Place about ½ teaspoon raspberry jam on the bottom of 1 cookie round; top with another round. Repeat with remaining cookies.

In a small mixing bowl stir together powdered sugar, vanilla, and enough milk to make of glazing consistency. Spread top of each cookie with some of the glaze. For holly berries, while icing is still wet, drop 2 or 3 cinnamon candies on each cookie. Allow icing to dry. Using a small paintbrush, paint several holly leaves and a stem on each cookie with the green food coloring. Makes 54.

Per cookie: 76 cal., 1 g pro., 14 g carbo., 2 g fat, 10 mg chol., and 38 mg sodium.

BROCCOLI AND CRAB BISQUE

- 1 **cup sliced leeks**
- 1 **cup sliced fresh mushrooms**
- 1 **cup fresh *or* frozen (thawed and drained) chopped broccoli**
- 1 **clove garlic, minced**
- ¼ **cup butter *or* margarine**
- ¼ **cup all-purpose flour**
- ¼ **teaspoon dried thyme, crushed**
- ⅛ **teaspoon pepper**
- 1 **small bay leaf**
- 3 **cups chicken broth**
- 1 **cup light cream**
- ¾ **cup shredded Jarlsberg *or* Swiss cheese (3 ounces)**
- 1 **6-ounce package frozen crabmeat, thawed and drained**

In a 3-quart saucepan cook leeks, mushrooms, broccoli, and garlic in butter or margarine till crisp-tender. Stir in flour, thyme, pepper, bay leaf, and ⅛ teaspoon *salt*. Add chicken broth and cream all at once. Cook and stir till thickened and bubbly. Cook and stir 1 minute more. Add cheese. Stir till cheese is melted. Add crabmeat; heat through. Makes 6 to 8 servings.

Per serving: 290 cal., 15 g pro., 11 g carbo., 22 g fat, 93 mg chol., 719 mg sodium. USRDA: 42% vit. A, 46% vit. C, 10% thiamine, 17% riboflavin, 16% niacin, 22% calcium, 21% phosphorus.

HONEY-FILLED NUGGETS

- 2 **cups all-purpose flour**
- ¼ **cup sugar**
- 1 **cup butter *or* margarine**
- 1 **teaspoon vanilla**
- ¼ **cup finely chopped walnuts**
- 2 **tablespoons coconut**
- 2 **tablespoons finely chopped candied cherries**
- 2 **tablespoons finely chopped raisins**
- 2 **tablespoons honey**
- ½ **cup flaked coconut**
- ½ **cup finely chopped walnuts**

In a medium mixing bowl stir together flour and sugar. Cut in butter or margarine till pieces are the size of small peas. Stir together vanilla and ¼ cup *ice water*. Sprinkle over flour mixture; mix with hands. Form dough into a ball. Cover and chill for 2 hours.

In a small mixing bowl combine ¼ cup chopped nuts, 2 tablespoons coconut, cherries, raisins, and honey.

Shape chilled dough into ¾-inch balls. Press a deep indentation into each ball. Fill each with about ¼ *teaspoon* honey mixture; pinch dough around filling.

Combine ½ cup coconut and ½ cup finely chopped nuts. Roll balls of dough in nut mixture. Place on a greased cookie sheet. Bake in a 325° oven for 20 minutes. Remove from cookie sheet. Cool on a wire rack. Makes 80.

Per cookie: 49 cal., 1 g pro., 5 g carbo., 3 g fat, 7 mg chol., 28 mg sodium.

HOLIDAY CHOCOLATE FANS

- 1 **1-pound package frozen phyllo dough (about 22 sheets)**
- 1 **cup butter *or* margarine, melted**
- 1 **12-ounce package semisweet chocolate pieces**
- 2 **tablespoons shortening**
- 2 **teaspoons finely shredded orange peel**
- 1 **teaspoon ground cinnamon**
- ½ **teaspoon ground nutmeg**
- 1 **cup coconut *or* finely chopped pistachios, pecans, *or* walnuts**

Thaw phyllo dough according to package directions. Leaving phyllo dough in paper wrapper, cut rolled dough crosswise into 5 portions. Rewrap 4 of the portions in damp towels. Unroll 1 portion of the phyllo, discarding paper wrapper. Halve crosswise.

Take 1 sheet of phyllo dough; brush with melted butter. Top with a second sheet; brush with butter. Repeat with a third sheet. Fold the stack of sheets into ¾-inch folds, starting at a short end and forming an accordion. Pinch together the folds at 1 end; spread folds apart at the other end, forming a fan shape.

Place fans on an ungreased baking sheet. Repeat stacking and folding with remainder of first portion of phyllo. Bake 6 fans at a time in a 375° oven about 5 minutes or till golden brown. Remove to a wire rack; cool. Repeat with remaining 4 portions of phyllo, 1 portion at a time, keeping remainder wrapped till used.

Melt chocolate over low heat; stir in shortening, orange peel, cinnamon, and nutmeg. Dip the wide end of each fan (about ¼ inch) into chocolate mixture; dip into coconut or nuts. Place on a rack to harden chocolate mixture. Makes 65 fans.

Per fan: 88 cal., 1 g pro., 10 g carbo., 5 g fat, 8 mg chol., 108 mg sodium.

CRUNCHY NUT FUDGE

- 1 **egg white**
- ½ **teaspoon water**
- ¼ **cup sugar**
- ¼ **teaspoon ground cinnamon**
- 1½ **cups dry roasted peanuts**
- 2 **cups sugar**
- ½ **cup butter *or* margarine**
- ½ **cup evaporated milk**
- 1 **teaspoon vanilla**

Beat egg white and water till foamy. Combine ¼ cup sugar and cinnamon. Stir sugar-cinnamon mixture and peanuts into egg white mixture. Spread peanut mixture evenly in a buttered 13x9x2-inch baking pan; bake in a 325° oven for 15 minutes. Turn peanut mixture over; bake about 15 minutes more or till brown. Cool in pan. Chop *half* the peanut mixture. Store remaining peanut mixture in an airtight container.

For fudge, butter the sides of a 1½-quart saucepan. In saucepan combine 2 cups sugar, butter or margarine, and evaporated milk. Cook and stir over medium heat till sugar dissolves and mixture comes to boiling. Continue cooking to 236° (soft-ball stage), stirring only as necessary to prevent sticking (mixture should boil gently over entire surface). Immediately remove from heat. Cool without stirring to lukewarm (110°), about 1 hour.

Butter an 8x8x2-inch pan; set aside. Add vanilla and chopped peanut mixture to fudge. Beat vigorously for 7 to 10 minutes or till fudge becomes very thick and just loses its gloss. *Immediately* spread into prepared pan. Score into squares while warm; cut when firm. Makes 48 pieces (1½ pounds).

Per piece: 83 cal., 1 g pro., 10 g carbo., 4 g fat, 7 mg chol., 46 mg sodium.

NUTCRACKER SWEET TART

3⅓ cups all-purpose flour
¼ cup sugar
1 cup butter *or* margarine
2 slightly beaten egg yolks
1 cup sugar
⅓ cup honey
3½ cups chopped pistachio nuts
(about 1 pound)
1 cup milk
¼ cup butter *or* margarine
⅓ cup seedless raspberry jam
2 tablespoons crème de cassis
¼ cup finely chopped pistachio
nuts (about 1 ounce)

Stir together flour and ¼ cup sugar; cut in 1 cup butter or margarine till pieces are the size of small peas. Add egg yolks and ⅓ cup *water;* toss with a fork till moistened. Form into a ball; wrap and chill.

In a saucepan combine 1 cup sugar, honey, and ½ cup *water.* Bring to boiling, stirring till sugar is dissolved. Reduce heat to low; boil gently about 25 minutes or till caramel colored. Stir in 3½ cups nuts, milk, and ¼ cup butter or margarine. Return to boiling; boil over low heat for 15 minutes more.

On a lightly floured surface roll *one-fourth* of chilled dough to an 11-inch circle; fit into a 9-inch flan pan, quiche dish, or cake pan; pour *half* of the nut mixture into crust. Roll out another *one-fourth* of the dough into an 11-inch circle; cut slits. Place over nut mixture. Trim dough ½ inch beyond edge of pan. Fold extra dough over the top; flute edges, sealing well. Repeat for remaining dough and nut mixture.

Bake in a 425° oven for 30 to 35 minutes. Cool. Invert onto a serving platter. In a small saucepan combine jam and crème de cassis; heat till jam is melted. Spoon over tart in a spiral fashion. Garnish edges of tart with ¼ cup nuts. Chill. (Or, wrap tart in moisture- and vaporproof wrap. Seal, label, and freeze. To serve; thaw, then spoon melted jam over tart.) Makes 2 tarts, 8 to 12 servings each.

Per serving: 517 cal., 9 g pro., 54 g carbo., 31 g fat, 78 mg chol., 186 mg sodium. USRDA: 15% vit. A, 24% thiamine, 12% riboflavin, 17% iron, and 19% phosphorus.

CRANBERRY PUMPKIN RING

1¾ to 2¼ cups unbleached *or*
all-purpose flour
1 package active dry yeast
½ cup milk
⅓ cup sugar
¼ cup butter *or* margarine
1 teaspoon ground cinnamon
½ teaspoon ground nutmeg
¼ teaspoon ground cloves
1 egg
½ cup canned pumpkin
1¼ cups whole wheat flour
1¼ cups cranberries
⅓ cup sugar
1 teaspoon finely shredded orange
peel
½ teaspoon ground cinnamon
2 tablespoons butter *or* margarine
1 cup sifted powdered sugar
4 teaspoons milk
¼ teaspoon orange extract

In a mixer bowl combine ½ *cup* flour and yeast. In a saucepan heat ½ cup milk, ⅓ cup sugar, ¼ cup butter or margarine, 1 teaspoon cinnamon, nutmeg, cloves, and ¾ teaspoon *salt* till warm (115° to 120°). Add to flour mixture. Beat with an electric mixer on low speed ½ minute, scraping sides of bowl. Add egg and pumpkin. Beat 3 minutes on high speed. Using a spoon, stir in whole wheat flour and as much of the unbleached flour as you can.

Turn out onto a floured surface. Knead in enough remaining flour to make a moderately stiff dough that is smooth and elastic (6 to 8 minutes total). Shape into a ball. Place in a greased bowl; turn once. Cover; let rise in a warm place till nearly double (about 1 hour).

In a saucepan combine cranberries, ⅓ cup sugar, orange peel, ½ teaspoon cinnamon, and 1 tablespoon *water.* Cook and stir over medium heat till berries pop. Transfer mixture to a bowl; cover and chill.

Punch dough down; let rest 10 minutes. On a lightly floured surface roll dough to a 15x10-inch rectangle. Spread with 2 tablespoons softened butter and then with cranberry filling. Starting at long side, roll up jelly-roll style. Seal seam. Shape into a ring; pinch ends together. Place ring on a greased baking sheet. With kitchen shears, make short cuts from outer edge toward center at 1-inch intervals. Let rise till nearly double (about 30 minutes). Bake in a 375° oven for 25 to 30 minutes, covering with foil the last 10 minutes to prevent overbrowning. Cool on wire rack.

Combine powdered sugar, 4 teaspoons milk, and orange extract; drizzle over ring. (Or, omit glaze. Cool completely; wrap, label, and freeze up to 2 months.) Makes 1 ring, 15 servings.

Per serving: 206 cal., 4 g pro., 36 g carbo., 6 g fat, 32 mg chol., 173 mg sodium. USRDA: 15% vit. A and 11% thiamine.

MOCHA NUT DIVINITY

2½ cups sugar
½ cup light corn syrup
¼ cup instant Swiss-style coffee
powder
2 egg whites
1 cup chopped pecans

In a saucepan combine sugar, corn syrup, coffee powder, and ½ cup *water.* Cook over medium-high heat to boiling, 5 to 7 minutes, stirring constantly with a wooden spoon to dissolve sugar. Cook over medium heat, without stirring, till thermometer registers 260° (about 15 minutes). Remove from heat.

In a large mixer bowl immediately beat egg whites with an electric mixer on medium speed till stiff peaks form (tips stand straight). *Gradually* pour hot mixture in a thin stream over egg whites, beating on high speed and scraping the sides of the bowl occasionally, about 3 minutes. Continue beating on high speed till candy starts to lose its gloss, about 6 to 7 minutes. Fold in nuts. Quickly drop onto a baking sheet lined with waxed paper. Makes about 40 pieces (1¼ pounds).

Per piece: 86 cal., 1 g pro., 17 g carbo., 2 g fat, 0 mg chol., 13 mg sodium.

December

CHRISTMAS TREE TREATS

- ½ pound bulk pork sausage
- 1 small apple, cored and finely chopped
- ⅓ cup raisins
- 2 cups all-purpose flour
- 1 cup whole wheat flour
- 1 tablespoon baking powder
- 1 teaspoon ground cinnamon
- ½ teaspoon ground nutmeg
- ½ cup butter or margarine
- 3 eggs
- ½ cup milk
- 2 tablespoons honey
- 1 slightly beaten egg white
- 2 tablespoons honey
- Chopped candied cherries

For filling, in a skillet cook sausage over medium heat till brown; drain. Add apple and raisins. Cook and stir till apples are tender. Set aside.

In a medium mixing bowl combine all-purpose flour, whole wheat flour, baking powder, cinnamon, nutmeg, and ½ teaspoon *salt*. Cut in butter or margarine till pieces are the size of small peas. In a small bowl beat together 3 eggs, milk, and 2 tablespoons honey. Add to the flour mixture. Stir till well combined.

Turn dough out onto a lightly floured surface. Roll out *half* of the dough to ⅛-inch thickness. Use a 4-inch tree-shape cookie cutter to cut 18 trees. Place trees on a greased baking sheet. Combine egg white and 2 tablespoons honey. Brush trees with egg white mixture. Place *1 rounded tablespoon* filling on center of each tree.

Roll and cut remaining dough as directed above; brush with egg white mixture. Place remaining 18 trees, egg white side down, over filling. Seal edges with tines of fork. Brush remaining egg white mixture over each tree. Decorate with cherries. Bake in a 425° oven for 8 to 10 minutes or till light brown. Serve warm or cooled. Makes 18 trees.

Per tree: 232 cal., 5 g pro., 24 g carbo., 13 g fat, 67 mg chol., 287 mg sodium. USRDA: 13% thiamine.

FUDGY FRUITCAKE DROPS

- ¼ cup butter or margarine
- ½ cup sugar
- 1 egg
- ½ cup grape jelly
- 1 teaspoon vanilla
- 1 cup all-purpose flour
- ¼ cup unsweetened cocoa powder
- 2 teaspoons baking powder
- 2 cups chopped walnuts (8 ounces)
- 1½ cups raisins (8 ounces)
- 1 6-ounce package (1 cup) semisweet chocolate pieces
- Powdered sugar (optional)

In a large mixer bowl beat butter or margarine for 30 seconds; add sugar. Beat till fluffy. Add egg, jelly, and vanilla; beat till well combined. Stir together flour, cocoa powder, and baking powder. Stir flour mixture into beaten mixture. Stir in nuts, raisins, and chocolate pieces. Drop by rounded teaspoonfuls onto greased and floured cookie sheets. Bake in a 350° oven about 10 minutes or till just set. Cool 1 minute. Remove to wire rack; cool. If desired, sift powdered sugar over cooled cookies. Makes about 50 cookies.

Per serving: 92 cal., 1 g pro., 12 g carbo., 5 g fat, 8 mg chol., 28 mg sodium.

WHEATEN APPLE RING

- 3 medium apples, peeled, cored, and finely chopped (¾ pound)
- 1 cup coarsely chopped walnuts
- ⅔ cup raisins
- 2 tablespoons molasses
- 4 to 4½ cups all-purpose flour
- 1 package active dry yeast
- 1 teaspoon ground cinnamon
- ⅓ cup shortening
- 3 tablespoons molasses
- ¾ cup whole wheat flour
- ¼ cup wheat germ
- 1 beaten egg
- 1 recipe Cinnamon-Apple Glaze (at right)
- 1 recipe Caramelized Apple Slices (at right)

In a medium mixing bowl combine apples, walnuts, raisins, and 2 tablespoons molasses. Cover and set aside. In a large mixer bowl stir together *1 cup* of all-purpose flour, yeast, and cinnamon.

In a small saucepan heat shortening, 3 tablespoons molasses, 1 cup *water*, and ½ teaspoon *salt* just till warm (115° to 120°) and shortening is almost melted; stir constantly. Add to flour mixture. Beat with an electric mixer on low speed ½ minute, scraping sides of bowl. Beat 3 minutes on high speed. Using a spoon, stir in whole wheat flour, wheat germ, apple mixture, and as much remaining all-purpose flour as you can.

Turn out onto a lightly floured surface. Knead in enough remaining all-purpose flour to make a moderately soft dough that is well combined and elastic (3 to 5 minutes total). Shape into a ball. Place in a greased bowl; turn once. Cover; let rise in a warm place till nearly double (about 1½ hours).

Punch down; turn dough out onto a lightly floured surface. Divide in half. Cover and let rest 10 minutes. Lightly grease 2 baking sheets. Roll each half of dough into a 15x8-inch rectangle. Starting from the long side, roll up dough, jelly-roll style. Place, seam side down, on baking sheet. Bring ends together to form a ring. Pinch ends to seal. Cut dough into 1-inch sections, cutting from the outside to 1-inch from the center. Cover; let rise till nearly double (30 to 40 minutes).

Combine egg and 1 tablespoon *water;* brush over dough. Bake in a 375° oven for 25 to 30 minutes or till done, covering with foil after 15 minutes if necessary to prevent overbrowning. Remove from pans; drizzle immediately with Cinnamon-Apple Glaze. Garnish with Caramelized Apple Slices. Serve warm or cooled. (Or, omit glaze. Cool completely. Wrap each ring separately, label, and freeze for up to 2 months.) Makes 2 rings, 15 servings each.

Cinnamon-Apple Glaze: In a small mixing bowl stir together 1½ cups sifted *powdered sugar*, 2 tablespoons *apple juice*, and ⅛ teaspoon ground *cinnamon*. Mix well.

Caramelized Apple Slices: Peel, core, and slice 1 medium *apple* into 12 wedges. In a heavy 8-inch skillet heat ¼ cup *sugar* over medium heat for 5 to 7 minutes, stirring constantly, or till sugar melts and turns light brown. Stir in 1 tablespoon *butter* or *margarine*. Add apple wedges; cook over medium-low heat about 5 minutes, stirring occasionally or till apples are nearly tender.

Per serving: 167 cal., 3 g pro., 28 g carbo., 5 g fat, 8 mg chol, 40 mg sodium. USRDA: 11% thiamine.

WHOLE WHEAT CARROT-BANANA BREAD

- ½ cup butter *or* margarine
- 1 cup packed brown sugar
- 2 eggs
- 1 cup all-purpose flour
- 1 cup whole wheat flour
- 1 teaspoon baking soda
- ½ teaspoon baking powder
- ½ teaspoon ground cinnamon
- 1 cup ripe, mashed banana
- 1 cup finely shredded carrots
- ½ cup chopped walnuts

In a mixer bowl beat butter or margarine for 30 seconds. Add sugar; beat till fluffy. Beat in eggs.

In a mixing bowl stir together all-purpose flour, whole wheat flour, baking soda, baking powder, cinnamon, and ½ teaspoon *salt*. Add dry ingredients and banana alternately to beaten mixture, beating after each addition. Fold in carrots and nuts. Pour into 2 greased 7½ x3¾ x2-inch loaf pans. Bake in a 350° oven for 40 to 50 minutes. Makes 2 loaves, 15 servings each.

Per serving: 109 cal., 2 g pro., 15 g carbo., 5 g fat, 26 mg chol., 123 mg sodium. USRDA: 12% vit. A.

PEANUT DATE BALLS

- 1 8-ounce package pitted dates, chopped
- ¼ cup butter *or* margarine
- ¼ cup orange juice
- 1 beaten egg
- 1 tablespoon milk
- ⅓ cup chopped peanuts
- ½ teaspoon vanilla
- 2 cups flaked whole grain corn cereal
- ½ cup finely chopped peanuts

In a 2-quart saucepan combine dates, butter or margarine, and orange juice.

Cook and stir over medium heat till butter is melted and mixture is well combined. Stir together egg and milk. Stir egg mixture into date mixture. Cook and stir over medium heat for 1 to 2 minutes or till very thick. Remove from heat; add ⅓ cup chopped peanuts and vanilla. Stir till mixture is smooth. Stir in cereal. Form into ¾-inch balls; roll in ½ cup finely chopped peanuts. Chill till firm. Makes 42 date balls.

Per date ball: 49 cal., 1 g pro., 6 g carbo., 3 g fat, 9 mg chol., 39 mg sodium.

SANTA'S ELVES' HOLIDAY TREAT

- 2 cups vanilla wafer crumbs
- ½ cup butter *or* margarine, melted
- 2 cups sifted powdered sugar
- 1 8-ounce package cream cheese, softened
- 1 cup butter *or* margarine, softened
- 2 eggs
- 4 medium bananas, sliced
- 1 cup coconut
- 1 8-ounce carton frozen whipped dessert topping, thawed
- 1 cup chopped walnuts
- Small candy canes (optional)
- Banana slices (optional)

Stir together crumbs and melted butter or margarine; press into the bottom of a 13x9x2-inch pan. In a mixer bowl beat powdered sugar, cream cheese, and 1 cup butter or margarine till smooth. Add eggs; beat till fluffy. Spread over crumb mixture in pan.

Arrange banana slices over top; sprinkle with coconut. Spread dessert topping over; sprinkle with nuts. Cover; chill several hours. Cut into squares. Garnish each serving with a candy cane and additional banana slices, if desired. Makes 12 servings.

Per serving: 619 cal., 46 g carbo., 48 g fat, 6 g pro. 139 mg chol., 372 mg sodium. USRDA: 29% vit. A.

ANISE COOKIES

- 2 eggs
- 1 cup sugar
- ¾ teaspoon anise extract
- 1 cup all-purpose flour

In a small mixer bowl beat eggs with an electric mixer on high speed about 4 minutes or till light. Gradually add sugar, beating on high speed about 10 minutes or till thick. Add anise extract. Add flour and beat on low speed till well combined.

Drop the dough from rounded teaspoons onto greased cookie sheets. Loosely cover with waxed paper. Let stand overnight to dry (about 12 hours). Bake in a 350° oven for 10 to 12 minutes. Remove to a wire rack; cool. Makes about 60 cookies.

Note: For the best flavor, store cookies in an airtight container for a few days.

Per cookie: 23 cal., 0 g pro., 5 g carbo., 0 g fat, 8 mg chol., 2 mg sodium.

CAROB PEANUT CLUSTERS

- 1 cup quick-cooking rolled oats
- ½ cup peanuts
- 1 cup sugar
- 3 tablespoons carob powder
- ⅓ cup evaporated milk
- ¼ cup butter *or* margarine
- ¼ cup peanut butter

To toast oats, place oats in a layer in a 15x10x1-inch baking pan. Bake in a 350° oven for 15 to 20 minutes or till toasted, stirring occasionally. In a mixing bowl combine toasted oats and peanuts. Set aside.

In a saucepan stir together sugar and carob powder; stir in milk and butter or margarine. Bring to a full rolling boil over medium heat. Boil gently for 1 minute, stirring constantly. Remove from heat. Stir in peanut butter. Pour mixture over oats and peanuts in mixing bowl. Let cool slightly. Drop by teaspoonfuls onto waxed paper. Chill. Makes 36 clusters.

Per piece: 69 cal., 1 g pro., 9 g carbo., 4 g fat, 5 mg chol., 38 mg sodium.

A SPLENDID FEAST

Gracious southern hosts lavish their guests with homespun hospitality and fine cuisine, especially at Christmastime. Lush, productive land bears a cornucopia of fresh foods—the basis for age-old culinary customs throughout the southern states. Let the traditional southern foods pictured here be a part of your Christmas festivities, too. Prepare the entire menu or select just a few dishes to add a regional touch to your own holiday celebration.

● *Ambrosia* (*center*), layered fruit that you can assemble ahead, is a traditional dessert, but also makes an ideal refresher after the first course.

● *Ham and Rice Dressing* in a golden roasted turkey debuts as the main course. *Creamy Gravy* (*back right*), seasoned with sage, is easy to make. *Nutty Brussels Sprouts* (*around turkey*) uses peanuts, a traditional and favored southern crop.

● *Colonial Baked Apples* (*bottom right*) are a dazzling side dish. Score the peeled apples with fork tines, fill with whipped sweet potatoes, and bake.

● (*Left*) Pumpkin Tarts, Mini-Chocolate Bourbon Bites, and *Lane Cake Squares* served on a tray would make any southern cook proud.

Rice, a staple ingredient today, came to the South by accident. In the late 1600s a ship carrying rice from Madagascar to England was blown off course and landed in South Carolina in need of repairs. The captain, so pleased by the southern hospitality, gave the colonists some of his cargo. Eventually the colonists worked the abundant rivers and streams into waterways needed for growing this new agricultural product.

SOUTHWESTERN CELEBRATION

FESTIVE PARTY FOODS AND GIFTS

● What lies hidden under the Christmas tree *this* year? Surprise a little one with a cheerful catnap sack (*left*). Constructed from a variety of multicolor patches and lovable pieced and embroidered cats, the sack is a masterful piece of patchwork and a gift you'll enjoy making. The matching pillow zips on and off the sack, providing a comfortable headrest for overnights or afternoon siestas.

● Stitch cat pillows in tambour work (*left*) using wool yarns in bright colors. The patterns are easy to fill in and fun to do. Festive candle holders and hand-carved Mexican animals are from the Folk Art International Gallery of San Francisco.

Treats for your piñata party
(left): *Applicious Slush* (*back*),
Tortilla Torte (*left*), and *Stuff-a-Puffs* with *Holiday Guacamole* and
Pepita Turkey Salad fillings (*right*).
(*Above*): *Peanut Butter Animals*
(*back*), *Pronto Pralines* (*center*),
Piñata Cookies (*front*), and
Pineapple Granola (*right*).

To teach the kids about the
celebrations and customs of
our various cultures, let them take
part in a festive holiday piñata
party. Craft the papier-mâché
piñata around a balloon, then
paint and decorate with colored
tissue paper, paper cones, foil,
and bows. Fill with candies and
watch the fun.

171

SOUTHERN HOSPITALITY
GRACIOUS HOLIDAY ENTERTAINING

● Family members will discover special moments when all are drawn together at Christmas.

● This year, decorate for a Christmas feast, southern style (*opposite*). Exquisitely stitched place mats mark the seats of honored guests. With game birds and lacy pierced-paper trees dotting the table, Hutschenreuther's "Comtesse" china continues the opulent effect. "Fountainbleu" crystal by J. G. Durand. "Royal Grandeur" gold flatware by Oneida. Brass candlesticks from Mottahedeh.

● Set the mood for an elegant Southern dinner with bowls of *Crimson Bisque*, a rich tomatoey broth. A splash of sherry gives extra pizzazz, and green onion and lemon peel garnishes add color to each serving. *Beaten Biscuits*, a classic regional bread, are a welcome partner to this simple yet tasty beginning course.

The pierced and painted screen creates a stunning backdrop. Panels are adapted from our wreath's design to frame and hinge as you like.

CRIMSON BISQUE

    3 cups tomato juice
    1 10¾-ounce can condensed
      chicken broth
    2 tablespoons brown sugar
    1 teaspoon Worcestershire sauce
    ¼ teaspoon celery salt
    ⅛ teaspoon onion powder
    ¼ cup dry sherry
Green onion brushes (optional)
Lemon peel strips (optional)

In a 3-quart saucepan stir together tomato juice, chicken broth, brown sugar, Worcestershire sauce, celery salt, and onion powder. Bring to boiling; remove from heat. Stir in sherry. Spoon into individual soup bowls. Garnish with green onion brushes and lemon peel strips, if desired. Makes 6 to 8 servings.

Per serving: 72 cal., 3 g pro., 12 g carbo., 1 g fat, 0 mg chol., 586 mg sodium. USRDA: 20% vit. A, 33% vit. C, 10% niacin.

AMBROSIA

    6 to 8 oranges
    ⅓ cup sifted powdered sugar
    ½ cup coconut
Fresh cranberries (optional)
Lime slices, halved (optional)

Peel and section oranges over a bowl to catch juices. Add sugar to orange sections in bowl; toss to coat. Cover and refrigerate.

Just before serving, layer orange sections and *1 tablespoon* of the coconut in goblets. Garnish with cranberries and lime slices, if desired. Serve chilled. Makes 8 servings.

Per serving: 70 cal., 1 g pro., 15 g carbo., 1 g fat, 0 mg chol., 2 mg sodium. USRDA: 75% vit. C.

BEATEN BISCUITS

    2 cups all-purpose flour
    1 teaspoon sugar
    ½ teaspoon baking powder
    ½ teaspoon salt
    ¼ cup lard *or* shortening
    ⅓ cup milk
    ¼ cup cold water

In a mixing bowl stir together flour, sugar, baking powder, and salt. Cut in lard or shortening till mixture resembles coarse crumbs. Stir together milk and water. Add milk mixture, *1 tablespoon* at a time, to flour mixture till dough sticks together. The dough should be stiff.

Turn dough out onto a lightly floured surface. Beat dough vigorously with the flat side of a wooden spoon or a metal mallet for 15 minutes, turning and folding dough frequently. On a lightly floured surface roll dough to about ⅜-inch thickness. Cut dough with a floured 2-inch biscuit cutter. Dip cutter in flour between cuts.

Place biscuits on an ungreased baking sheet. Prick the top of each biscuit 3 times the with tines of a fork. Bake in a 425° oven for 18 to 20 minutes or till biscuits are light brown. Makes 16 to 18 biscuits.

Per biscuit: 90 cal., 2 g pro., 12 g carbo., 4 g fat, 4 mg chol., 80 mg sodium.

CREAMY GRAVY

Roast turkey
Hot drippings from roast turkey
    ¼ cup all-purpose flour
    1¼ teaspoons dried sage, crushed
    ⅛ teaspoon ground red pepper
Milk *or* light cream

Remove roast turkey to a serving platter; keep warm. Leaving crusty bits in the roasting pan, pour pan drippings into a large measuring cup. Skim off fat from drippings. Return ¼ cup of the fat to the roasting pan; discard any remaining fat. Stir flour, sage, and red pepper into roasting pan with fat. Cook and stir over medium heat till bubbly. Remove from heat.

Add enough milk or cream to the drippings in the measuring cup to equal 2¾ cups total liquid. Stir liquid into flour mixture in pan. Cook and stir till thickened and bubbly. Cook and stir 1 minute more. Makes 2 cups gravy.

Per 2 tablespoons: 82 cal., 1 g pro., 2 g carbo., 8 g fat, 17 mg chol., and 5 mg sodium.

HAM AND RICE DRESSING

    1 pound fresh chestnuts
    1 cup chopped onion
    ½ cup chopped celery
    ½ green pepper, chopped
    2 tablespoons cooking oil
    3½ cups turkey *or* chicken broth
    2 cups chopped fully cooked ham
    1 cup long grain rice
    ½ to 1 teaspoon pepper
    ½ teaspoon salt
    ⅛ teaspoon ground red pepper
    2 beaten eggs

Cut an X in the flat side of each chestnut with a sharp knife. Roast on a baking sheet in a 350° oven for 20 to 25 minutes; cool. Peel and coarsely chop.

In a 3-quart saucepan cook onion, celery, and green pepper in hot oil till tender but not brown. Add chestnuts, *3 cups* broth, ham, *uncooked* rice, pepper, salt, and red pepper. Bring to boiling; reduce heat. Cover; simmer for 30 minutes. Remove from heat. Combine remaining broth and eggs; stir into ham-rice mixture. Use to stuff an uncooked 10- to 12-pound turkey. Makes 6 cups.

Per ½-cup serving: 198 cal., 9 g pro., 20 g carbo., 10 g fat, 63 mg chol., 579 mg sodium. USRDA: 16% vit. C, 14% thiamine, 10% niacin, 10% phosphorus.

COLONIAL BAKED APPLES

- 3 **medium sweet potatoes** *or* **one 18-ounce can vacuum-packed sweet potatoes**
- ½ **teaspoon finely shredded orange peel**
- 2 **tablespoons orange juice**
- 1 **tablespoon brown sugar**
- 1 **tablespoon butter** *or* **margarine**
- ¼ **teaspoon salt**
- ¼ **teaspoon ground nutmeg**
- 1 **beaten egg**
- 2 **tablespoons milk**
- 8 **large cooking apples, peeled and cored**
- ½ **cup corn syrup**
- 2 **tablespoons lemon juice**

If using fresh sweet potatoes, cook, covered, in enough boiling salted water to cover for 25 to 35 minutes or till tender. Drain; peel and cut up. Mash cooked or canned sweet potatoes with an electric mixer on low speed till smooth. (Should have about 1¾ cups mashed potatoes.) Add orange peel, orange juice, brown sugar, butter or margarine, salt, and nutmeg. Add egg and milk; set aside.

Remove a slice from the top of each apple. Score apples by going around the outside surface in a diagonal pattern with the tines of a fork. Using a pastry bag fitted with a star tip, fill apples with sweet potato mixture.

Place apples in a 12x7½x2-inch baking dish. Stir together corn syrup and lemon juice; pour over apples. Bake, uncovered, in a 325° oven about 45 minutes or till tender, basting several times with the corn syrup mixture. Serve immediately. Makes 8 servings.

Per serving: 232 cal., 2 g pro., 52 g carbo., 3 g fat, 37 mg chol., 116 mg sodium. USRDA: 111% vit. A, 36% vit. C, 10% iron.

NUTTY BRUSSELS SPROUTS

- 3 **pints brussels sprouts** *or* **two 16-ounce packages frozen brussels sprouts**
- 2 **tablespoons butter** *or* **margarine**
- ¼ **cup coarsely chopped peanuts**

Trim stems from brussels sprouts. Remove wilted leaves; wash. Cut large sprouts in half lengthwise. Cook the sprouts, covered, in a small amount of boiling salted water for 10 to 15 minutes or till crisp-tender. (If using frozen, cook according to package directions.) Drain. Add butter or margarine; toss gently. Place brussels sprouts around turkey or in a serving bowl. Sprinkle with chopped peanuts. Season to taste with salt and pepper. Serves 8.

Per serving: 120 cal., 6 g pro., 12 g carbo., 7 g fat, 12 mg chol., 70 mg sodium. USRDA: 20% vit. A, 206% vit. C, 11% thiamine, 10% riboflavin, 11% phosphorus.

PUMPKIN TARTS

Piecrust mix for single-crust pie
- 1 **slightly beaten egg**
- 1 **cup canned pumpkin**
- ⅓ **cup sugar**
- ½ **teaspoon pumpkin pie spice**
- ½ **cup milk**
- ½ **cup prepared mincemeat**

Sweetened whipped cream (optional)
Pecan halves (optional)

Prepare piecrust mix according to package directions; roll out to slightly less than ⅛ inch thick. Cut into twelve 4-inch circles. Gently press circles into ungreased 2¾-inch muffin tins, forming ruffles around the edges. *Do not* prick pastry.

In a medium mixing bowl combine egg, pumpkin, sugar, and spice; mix well. Stir in milk. Place about *1 teaspoon* of the mincemeat in each tart shell; top with about *2 tablespoons* of the pumpkin mixture.

Bake pumpkin tarts in a 375° oven for 25 to 30 minutes or till a knife inserted off-center comes out clean. Cool on a wire rack. Cover and chill to store.

Just before serving, dollop each tart with whipped cream and a pecan half, if desired. Makes 12 tarts.

Per tart: 137 cal., 2 g pro., 17 g carbo., 7 g fat, 23 mg chol., 100 mg sodium. USRDA: 25% vit. A.

MINI CHOCOLATE BOURBON BITES

- ½ **cup butter** *or* **margarine**
- ½ **cup packed brown sugar**
- ¼ **cup bourbon**
- 1 **cup all-purpose flour**
- 3 **tablespoons unsweetened cocoa powder**
- ½ **cup miniature semisweet chocolate pieces**
- 1 **slightly beaten egg white**
- 1 **cup finely chopped pecans**

In a large mixer bowl beat butter or margarine and sugar with an electric mixer on medium speed till fluffy. Add bourbon; beat well. Gradually add flour and cocoa powder, beating till well combined. Stir in chocolate pieces. Chill 2 hours or till firm enough to handle.

Shape dough into 1-inch balls. Roll in egg white, then in pecans. Place on a lightly greased baking sheet. Bake in a 350° oven about 12 minutes or till edges are firm. (The center will still be soft.) Cool on baking sheet 1 minute. Transfer to wire racks; cool. Makes about 30.

Per cookie: 104 cal., 1 g pro., 9 g carbo., 7 g fat, 9 mg chol., 40 mg sodium.

LANE CAKE SQUARES

This version of Lane Cake Squares is slightly different from the traditional cake that uses a white frosting—

- 1 1-layer-size white cake mix
- 1 egg yolk
- ⅓ cup sugar
- ⅓ cup evaporated milk
- 2 tablespoons butter *or* margarine
- ¼ cup flaked coconut
- ¼ cup raisins, finely chopped
- ¼ cup chopped pecans
- ¼ cup chopped maraschino cherries

The day before serving, prepare cake mix according to package directions. Spread batter in a greased and floured 8x8x2-inch cake pan. Bake in a 350° oven for 20 to 25 minutes or till done. Cool 10 minutes; invert on wire rack. Invert again; cool completely. Wrap and store.

In a saucepan beat egg yolk slightly. Stir in sugar, milk, and butter or margarine. Cook and stir over medium heat for 2 to 3 minutes or till bubbly. Cook and stir 1 minute more. Stir in coconut, raisins, and pecans. Cool. Dry chopped cherries with paper towels; stir into mixture in saucepan.

Unwrap cake; trim off edges with a wet serrated knife. Spread coconut mixture over cake. Cut cake into 16 square pieces. Makes 16 servings.

Per serving: 251 cal., 3 g pro., 37 g carbo., 11 g fat, 23 mg chol., 164 mg sodium.

APPLICIOUS SLUSH

- 1 16-ounce can applesauce, chilled
- 1 8-ounce carton vanilla yogurt
- 1 6-ounce can frozen apple juice concentrate
- 1 tablespoon sugar
- 10 ice cubes

In a blender container combine all ingredients *except* ice. With blender running, add the ice cubes, 1 at a time, through opening in lid, blending till slushy. Spoon into glasses. Serves 10.

Per serving: 61 cal., 1 g pro., 14 g carbo., 0 g fat, 2 mg chol., 13 mg sodium.

TORTILLA TORTE

Great to make ahead for entertaining—

- 1 8-ounce package cream cheese, softened
- 3 tablespoons chopped, canned green chili peppers, drained
- 1 4½-ounce can deviled ham
- ½ cup dairy sour cream
- ¼ cup taco sauce
- Several drops bottled hot pepper sauce
- 12 6-inch flour tortillas
- Chopped pitted ripe olives
- Shredded cheddar cheese

In a mixer bowl beat cream cheese with an electric mixer for 30 seconds. Set aside *1 tablespoon* chopped green chili peppers. Add remaining chili peppers, deviled ham, sour cream, *2 tablespoons* taco sauce, and hot pepper sauce to cream cheese. Beat till well combined; cover and chill.

Reserve *1 tablespoon* of the cream cheese mixture. Place 1 tortilla on a serving platter; spread with *3 tablespoons* of the cream cheese mixture. Repeat with remaining tortillas and cream cheese mixture, stacking tortillas one on top of another. Cover and chill 4 hours or overnight.

Before serving, spread reserved cream cheese mixture over the top of the stacked tortillas; top with remaining taco sauce. Sprinkle with olives, cheddar cheese, and reserved green chili peppers. Cut into wedges to serve. Serves 16.

Per serving: 185 cal., 5 g pro., 14 g carbo., 12 g fat, 27 mg chol., 205 mg sodium.

STUFF-A-PUFF

- ¾ cup all-purpose flour
- ¼ cup cornmeal
- ½ teaspoon dried oregano, crushed
- ¼ teaspoon salt
- 1 cup water
- ½ cup butter *or* margarine
- 4 eggs
- Cornmeal
- 1 recipe Holiday Guacamole
- 1 recipe Pepita Turkey Salad

In a small mixing bowl stir together flour, ¼ cup cornmeal, oregano, and salt; set aside.

In a 2-quart saucepan combine water and butter or margarine; cook and stir till mixture boils. Add flour mixture all at once; stir vigorously. Cook and stir till mixture forms a ball that doesn't separate. Remove from heat; cool 5 minutes. Add eggs, 1 at a time, beating after each till smooth. Drop batter by teaspoonfuls onto a greased baking sheet. Sprinkle with cornmeal.

Bake in a 400° oven about 25 minutes or till golden brown. Remove from oven; cut off tops and remove any soft dough. Cool. Fill with about *2 tablespoons* of desired filling. Makes 24.

Per puff with 2 tablespoons Holiday Guacamole: 109 cal., 2 g pro., 6 g carbo., 9 g fat, 59 mg chol., and 87 mg sodium.

Per puff with 2 tablespoons Pepita Turkey Salad: 174 cal., 6 g pro., 5 g carbo., 15 g fat, 111 mg chol., 149 mg sodium.

Holiday Guacamole: Stir together one 6-ounce container frozen *avocado dip,* thawed; ¼ cup coarsely chopped *pitted ripe olives;* and 1 large *tomato,* peeled, seeded, and chopped. Cover and chill thoroughly. Makes 1¼ cups.

Pepita Turkey Salad: Stir together ½ cup *mayonnaise* or *salad dressing* and ½ to 1 teaspoon ground *cumin.* Add two 2½- *or* 3-ounce packages thinly sliced *smoked turkey,* chopped; 2 hard-cooked *eggs,* chopped; and ¼ cup *pumpkin seed,* toasted. Cover and chill thoroughly. Sprinkle with *pumpkin seed* before serving. Makes 1⅔ cups.

PEANUT BUTTER ANIMALS

2 cups all-purpose flour
1½ teaspoons baking powder
¾ cup sugar
¾ cup creamy peanut butter
½ cup shortening
1 egg
⅓ cup milk
1 teaspoon vanilla
Milk (optional)
½ cup chopped peanuts (optional)

In a small mixing bowl stir together flour and baking powder. In a large mixer bowl beat sugar, peanut butter, and shortening with an electric mixer on medium speed till fluffy. Add egg, milk, and vanilla; beat well. Add flour mixture, beating till smooth. Divide dough in half; wrap and chill for 1 hour.

On a lightly floured surface, roll out dough, half at a time, to ⅛-inch thickness. Cut dough into desired animal shapes with floured cookie cutters. Transfer to ungreased cookie sheets. Brush with milk and sprinkle with chopped peanuts, if desired. Bake in a 375° oven for 8 to 10 minutes. Cool on a wire rack. Makes about 48 cookies.

Per cookie: 78 cal., 2 g pro., 8 g carbo., 3 g fat, 6 mg chol., 37 mg sodium.

PRONTO PRALINES

1 4-serving-size package *regular* vanilla pudding mix
1 cup packed brown sugar
½ cup sugar
1 5⅓-ounce can (⅔ cup) evaporated milk
1 teaspoon vanilla
2 cups coarsely chopped pecans

In a saucepan combine pudding mix, brown sugar, and sugar; stir in evaporated milk. Bring mixture to a full boil, stirring constantly. Boil for 5 minutes, stirring occasionally to prevent scorching. Remove saucepan from heat; add vanilla. Beat mixture for 3 minutes; *do not overbeat.* (The mixture should be shiny when dropped, not dull and thick.) Stir in pecans. Drop by tablespoonfuls onto waxed paper. Let stand at room temperature for 1 hour to harden. Makes 24 pralines.

Per praline: 139 cal., 1 g pro., 19 g carbo., 7 g fat, 2 mg chol., 32 mg sodium.

PIÑATA COOKIES

¾ cup butter *or* margarine
½ cup sugar
1 egg
1 teaspoon vanilla
1¾ cups all-purpose flour
Small gumdrops *or* chocolate-coated malted milk balls
1 cup sifted powdered sugar
¼ teaspoon vanilla
4 to 5 teaspoons milk
Colored sugar *or* colored candy sprinkles

In a large mixer bowl beat butter or margarine with an electric mixer for 30 seconds. Add sugar; beat till fluffy. Add egg and 1 teaspoon vanilla; beat well. Add flour, beating till well combined. Cover and chill for 1 hour.

Shape *1 level tablespoon* of dough around a gumdrop or malted milk ball to form a ball. Place on ungreased cookie sheets. Bake in a 350° oven 15 to 18 minutes or till edges are golden. Cool.

For frosting, in a small mixing bowl stir together powdered sugar, ¼ teaspoon vanilla, and enough milk to make of dipping consistency. Dip tops of cookies in the frosting; sprinkle with colored sugar or candy sprinkles. Makes 36 cookies.

Per cookie: 95 cal., 1 g pro., 16 g carbo., 4 g fat, 11 mg chol., and 46 mg sodium.

PINEAPPLE GRANOLA

½ cup pineapple preserves
2 tablespoons butter *or* margarine
1 cup regular rolled oats
1 cup unsweetened coconut chips
1 cup dried banana chips

In a medium saucepan combine pineapple preserves and butter or margarine. Cook and stir constantly till butter is melted. Remove pan from heat. Stir in rolled oats, coconut chips, and banana chips. Spread mixture into a greased 13x9x2-inch baking pan.

Bake in a 325° oven about 30 minutes or till light brown, stirring occasionally. Transfer mixture to a large piece of foil or baking sheet; cool. Store in an airtight container. Makes 5 cups.

Per ½-cup serving: 253 cal., 2 g pro., 38 g carbo., 12 g fat, 7 mg chol., and 31 mg sodium.

HOT AND SPICY CRANBERRY DIP

Remember this quick dish for drop-in guests. The flavor is both tangy and sweet—

1 16-ounce can jellied cranberry sauce
3 tablespoons prepared horseradish
2 tablespoons honey
1 tablespoon lemon juice
1 tablespoon Worcestershire sauce
1 clove garlic, minced
½ teaspoon ground red pepper
Orange pieces
Pineapple tidbits
Vienna sausages, sliced

In a medium saucepan combine cranberry sauce, horseradish, honey, lemon juice, Worcestershire sauce, garlic, and red pepper. Bring mixture to boiling; reduce heat. Cover and simmer for 5 minutes. Serve warm with orange pieces, pineapple tidbits, and Vienna sausages. Makes 1½ cups dip.

Per 1 tablespoon serving, dip only: 35 cal., 0.07 g pro., 9 g carbo., 0.04 g fat, 11 mg sodium.

PRIZE TESTED RECIPES

Note: Our Prize Tested Recipes are the winners from a monthly recipe contest sponsored by *Better Homes and Gardens®* magazine, where cooks at home have a chance to show their culinary creativity.

Each month readers send in entries for two predetermined categories. After testing each recipe, our editors select winners for both categories. The magazine features the winning recipes, awarding $100 to the lucky contributors. Here, in chronological order, are the prizewinning recipes from 1985.

SAVORY MUSHROOM SAUTÉ

This tasty side dish topped the Micro-Cooked Vegetable category. It's also an excellent accompaniment to poultry—

- 2 tablespoons butter *or* margarine
- 2 tablespoons dry sherry
- 1 tablespoon lime juice
- 1 tablespoon minced dried onion
- 1 teaspoon fines herbes, crushed
- ¼ teaspoon garlic salt
- 1 pound fresh mushrooms, halved (5½ cups)

In a 2-quart nonmetal casserole stir together butter or margarine, sherry, lime juice, minced dried onion, fines herbes, and garlic salt. Micro-cook, uncovered, on 100% power (HIGH) for 1 minute, stirring once. Stir in mushrooms. Cook, covered, for 6 to 8 minutes or till mushrooms are tender, stirring twice. Serve with beef. Serves 4 or 5.

PASTRY-WRAPPED SALMON RING

This eye-catching recipe from the Canned Fish Entrées category is perfect for special family dinners—

- 1 15½-ounce can pink salmon
- 1½ cups soft bread crumbs (2 slices)
- 2 beaten eggs
- ½ cup finely chopped celery
- 2 tablespoons finely chopped green pepper
- 2 tablespoons finely chopped onion
- 1 tablespoon lemon juice
- 1 8-ounce package (8) refrigerated crescent rolls
Dairy sour cream (optional)
Snipped chives (optional)
Tomato wedges (optional)
Celery leaves (optional)

Generously grease a 5-cup ovenproof ring mold. Set aside. In a mixing bowl drain and flake salmon, removing and discarding skin and bones. Add bread crumbs, eggs, celery, green pepper, onion, and lemon juice; mix well. Separate crescent rolls into triangles. Arrange triangles in ring mold, alternating points and wide ends of triangles so dough drapes over the center and outer edges of the mold. Pat the dough lightly to line the mold, sealing edges as much as possible. Pack the salmon mixture into the dough-lined mold. Turn the ends of dough over the salmon to cover. Press to seal.

Bake in a 375° oven for 30 minutes. Loosen edges. Invert salmon ring onto a serving platter. Serve with sour cream and chives, if desired. Garnish platter with tomato wedges and celery leaves, if desired. Makes 4 to 6 servings.

BARLEY OVEN PILAF

Our February winner in the Rice and Grain Side Dishes category was this impressive grain dish. It's versatile enough to serve with chicken, beef, or pork—

- 3 cups water
- 1 cup quick-cooking barley
- ½ teaspoon salt (optional)
- 1 cup finely chopped onion
- ½ cup shredded carrot
- ½ cup chopped green onion
- 2 tablespoons cooking oil
- ¼ cup toasted wheat germ
- ¼ teaspoon garlic powder
- 2 tablespoons snipped parsley

In a medium saucepan bring water to boiling. Add barley and salt, if desired. Return to boiling. Reduce heat. Cover and simmer for 12 to 15 minutes or till barley is tender. *Do not drain.*

Meanwhile, in a small saucepan cook onion, carrot, and green onion in cooking oil till tender. In a greased 1½-quart casserole combine the *undrained* barley, vegetable mixture, wheat germ, and garlic powder.

Bake, uncovered, in a 350° oven for 25 to 30 minutes or till light brown. Fluff with a fork to serve. Sprinkle with parsley. Makes 8 servings.

CARAMEL PECAN CHEESECAKE

Caramel topping and sour cream combine to make the quick and tasty topper for the nutty cheesecake that won our Favorite Cheesecake category. It's simple, yet sensational—

- 1 cup graham cracker crumbs
- ¾ cup ground pecans
- ¼ cup sugar
- ¼ cup butter *or* margarine, melted
- 12 ounces cream cheese, softened
- ½ cup caramel topping
- 3 eggs
- 2 tablespoons milk
- ½ cup dairy sour cream
- ¼ cup caramel topping

Pecan halves

In a mixing bowl combine graham cracker crumbs, ground pecans, sugar, and butter or margarine. Pat mixture onto the bottom and 1½ inches up sides of an 8-inch springform pan. Set aside.

In large mixer bowl beat cream cheese till fluffy. Gradually beat in ½ cup caramel topping. Add eggs and milk. Beat just till blended. Turn mixture into prepared crust. Bake in a 350° oven for 40 to 45 minutes or till center is set. Cool in pan for 15 minutes.

For topping, combine sour cream and ¼ cup caramel topping. Spoon atop cheesecake. Loosen sides of cheesecake from pan with spatula. Cool for 30 minutes more; remove sides of pan. Cool, then cover and chill. Garnish with pecan halves. Makes 10 to 12 servings.

TROPICAL FRUIT BARS

You'll understand why these bars were the star of the Best-Ever Bar Cookies category. Moist and oh-so-tangy, they make the perfect after-school or after-work snack—

- 1 cup boiling water
- ½ cup finely snipped dried apricots *or* papaya
- 1 cup all-purpose flour
- ½ teaspoon baking powder
- ¼ teaspoon baking soda
- ¼ cup butter *or* margarine
- ½ cup packed brown sugar
- 1 egg
- ½ teaspoon finely shredded lime peel
- 1 tablespoon lime juice
- ½ cup milk
- ½ cup finely chopped walnuts
- 1 recipe Lime Frosting

Pour boiling water over dried fruit. Let stand 5 minutes. Drain and set aside.

Stir together flour, baking powder, and soda. In a small mixer bowl beat butter or margarine for 30 seconds. Add brown sugar. Beat till fluffy. Add egg, lime peel, and lime juice. Beat well. Add dry ingredients and milk alternately to beaten mixture. Fold in fruit and walnuts. Spread batter evenly in a greased 12x7½x2-inch baking pan.

Bake in a 350° oven for 20 to 25 minutes or till done. Cool on a wire rack. Frost with Lime Frosting. Cut into bars to serve. Makes 28.

Lime Frosting: In a small mixer bowl beat together 1½ cups sifted *powdered sugar,* 1 tablespoon softened *butter* or *margarine,* ¼ teaspoon finely shredded *lime peel* (optional), and 1 tablespoon *lime juice.* Add enough *milk* (about 1 tablespoon) to make of spreading consistency.

HERITAGE HAM PASTRIES

You can make this Ham Main Dish winner year-round. Just substitute finely shredded carrot for the winter squash during the summer months—

- 2 eggs
- ⅓ cup milk
- 1½ cups soft whole wheat bread crumbs (2 slices)
- 1 cup finely chopped celery
- 1 cup peeled and shredded butternut squash
- ½ cup finely chopped onion
- 1 teaspoon prepared horseradish
- 1 teaspoon soy sauce
- ¼ teaspoon pepper
- ¾ pound ground fully cooked ham
- 1 10-ounce package (6) frozen patty shells, thawed

Milk *or* beaten egg

In a mixing bowl combine 2 eggs and ⅓ cup milk. Stir in bread crumbs, celery, squash, onion, horseradish, soy sauce, and pepper. Stir in ground ham. Divide meat mixture into 6 portions. Shape into patties about 3½ inches in diameter. Place on a greased baking sheet.

On a floured surface, roll each patty shell into a 6-inch circle. Drape 1 pastry circle over each ham patty. Lightly flute edges. If desired, use a sharp knife to lightly score a design in the top of each pastry. Brush each with milk or beaten egg. Bake in a 400° oven about 20 minutes or till golden brown. Serve immediately. Makes 6 servings.

EASTER FRUIT-AND-NUT BREAD

This lemony fruit-and-nut braid topped our Spring Breads category—

- 3 to 3½ cups all-purpose flour
- 1 package active dry yeast
- ½ cup milk
- ¼ cup sugar
- ¼ cup butter *or* margarine
- ¼ cup water
- ¾ teaspoon grated lemon peel
- ½ teaspoon salt
- 2 egg yolks
- 2 eggs
- 1 cup ground walnuts
- ⅓ cup sugar
- 2 egg whites
- ½ teaspoon lemon juice
- 1 tablespoon water
- ⅓ cup currant jelly
- ¾ cup chopped pitted dates

In a large mixer bowl combine *1½ cups* of the flour and yeast. In a small saucepan heat milk, ¼ cup sugar, butter or margarine, ¼ cup water, lemon peel, and salt just till warm (115° to 120°), stirring constantly. Add to flour mixture. Add egg yolks and *1* of the whole eggs. Beat with an electric mixer on low speed for ½ minute, scraping sides of bowl. Beat for 3 minutes on high speed. Using a spoon, stir in as much of the remaining flour as you can.

Turn out onto a floured surface. Knead in enough remaining flour to make a moderately soft dough. Shape into a ball. Place in a greased bowl. Turn once. Cover and let rise till double. Punch down. Let rest for 10 minutes. Divide dough into 6 portions.

For filling, in a small bowl combine walnuts, ⅓ cup sugar, egg whites, and lemon juice. Set aside. Beat together remaining whole egg and 1 tablespoon water. Set aside.

Roll each dough portion into a 10x4-inch rectangle. Spread *1 tablespoon* of jelly down center third of a rectangle. Spread *2 tablespoons* dates and *3 tablespoons* walnut mixture over dates. Overlap long sides of dough over filling. Brush edges with egg mixture. Seal. Repeat with remaining dough, jelly, dates, and filling to make 6 ropes.

Place 3 ropes, seam side down, on a baking sheet. Braid and seal ends. Repeat with remaining 3 ropes. Brush braids with egg mixture. Cover and let rise till nearly double. Brush with egg mixture again. Bake in a 350° oven for 30 to 35 minutes. Cover the last 15 minutes. Remove from baking sheet and cool. Makes 2 braids.

PEPPY AVOCADO-STUFFED EGGS

Avocados and horseradish mustard give this winning Egg Entreé its pep—

- 4 hard-cooked eggs
- 1 avocado
- Lemon juice
- 2 teaspoons prepared horseradish mustard
- 1 teaspoon lemon juice
- 1 teaspoon salt
- 1 tablespoon finely chopped onion
- 2 tablespoons butter *or* margarine
- 2 tablespoons all-purpose flour
- 1 teaspoon instant chicken bouillon granules
- 1 teaspoon dried parsley flakes
- ½ cup milk
- ½ cup water
- ¼ cup chopped fully cooked ham

Peel eggs and halve lengthwise. Remove the yolks. Set yolks and whites aside. Halve avocado lengthwise. Rub lemon juice over cut edges. Peel and mash 1 half in a mixing bowl. Store the remaining half for another use. Add egg yolks, horseradish mustard, 1 teaspoon lemon juice, and salt to the mashed avocado. Mix well.

Spoon the avocado mixture into the halved egg whites. Arrange stuffed egg whites in 2 individual casseroles.

For sauce, in a small saucepan cook onion in butter or margarine till tender but not brown. Stir in flour, bouillon granules, and parsley. Combine milk and water. Add all at once to flour mixture. Cook and stir till thickened and bubbly.

Pour *half* of the sauce over each casserole. Top each with *half* of the ham. Bake, uncovered, in a 325° oven about 15 minutes or till heated through. Makes 2 main-dish servings.

SHREDDED POTATO AND HAM PIE

This meat-and-potato pie took top honors in our Main-Dish Pies category. For a light supper, serve it with a small dinner salad and bread—

- 4 slightly beaten eggs
- 1 cup frozen mixed peas and carrots
- 1 cup chopped cooked ham, beef, *or* chicken
- 1 cup shredded cheddar cheese (4 ounces)
- ½ cup milk
- ¼ teaspoon dried minced onion
- 2 medium potatoes, peeled and shredded (about 2 cups)
- ½ cup shredded cheddar cheese (2 ounces)

For filling, in a mixing bowl combine eggs, vegetables, meat, 1 cup cheddar cheese, milk, and onion. Set aside.

Combine shredded potatoes and ½ cup cheese. Press onto bottom and up sides of an ungreased 9-inch pie plate. Pour filling into potato-lined pie plate. Bake in a 350° oven for 45 to 50 minutes or till the center is set. Let stand for 5 to 10 minutes before serving. Makes 6 servings.

PASTA VERDE

Pasta Ideas, one of the categories for May, gave us this quick variation on popular pesto—

- 6 slices bacon
- 10 ounces spaghetti *or* other pasta
- 1 10-ounce package frozen chopped spinach
- 2 cloves garlic, minced
- ⅛ teaspoon pepper
- ½ cup cream-style cottage cheese
- ⅓ cup grated Parmesan cheese

In an 8-inch skillet cook bacon till crisp. Drain, reserving *2 tablespoons* drippings. Crumble bacon and set aside.

Cook pasta in a large amount of boiling salted water for 10 to 12 minutes till tender but firm.

Meanwhile, in a medium saucepan cook spinach according to package directions. Place the *undrained* spinach, reserved bacon drippings, garlic, and pepper in a blender container or food processor bowl. Cover and blend or process till smooth. Add cottage cheese. Cover and blend or process till smooth.

Drain pasta. Turn pasta out onto a large platter. Pour spinach mixture over pasta and toss. Sprinkle each serving with some of the bacon and Parmesan cheese. Serve immediately. Makes 10 to 12 side-dish servings.

LINGUINE WITH SAUSAGE AND LEEKS

The Sausage and Frank Ideas category winner stole the show with this easy, quick-to-fix dinnertime dish. Serve it with a bottle of your favorite red wine—

- 1 pound bulk pork sausage
- 2 leeks, thinly sliced
- ¾ cup light cream
- 6 ounces linguine *or* spaghetti

Grated Parmesan *or* Romano cheese

In a 10-inch skillet cook pork sausage and leeks till meat is brown and leeks are tender. Drain off fat.

Add the light cream to the sausage mixture. Cook and stir till the mixture is heated through.

Meanwhile, cook the linguine or spaghetti according to package directions. Drain thoroughly.

Place drained linguine or spaghetti on a heated serving platter. Top with the cooked sausage and leek mixture. Sprinkle each serving with some of the grated Parmesan or Romano cheese. Makes 4 servings.

MARINATED MUSHROOM SALAD

This fancy salad placed first in the Make-Ahead Salads category. It's perfect for a summer luncheon—

- 1 pound fresh mushrooms, sliced (6 cups)
- 2 tablespoons finely chopped onion
- 2 tablespoons lemon juice
- 2 teaspoons sugar
- ¼ teaspoon pepper
- ⅓ cup whipping cream
- ¼ cup dairy sour cream
- ¼ teaspoon salt
- ¼ teaspoon dry mustard

Romaine lettuce
Tomato wedges
Coarsely ground pepper

In a medium mixing bowl toss together mushrooms, onion, lemon juice, sugar, and ¼ teaspoon pepper. Chill at least 30 minutes but not more than 4 hours.

In a small mixer bowl beat whipping cream with an electric mixer. Stir together sour cream, salt, and dry mustard. Fold in whipped cream. Stir into mushroom mixture.

Line 6 salad plates with romaine lettuce. Spoon mixture onto the plates. Garnish each serving with tomato wedges and coarsely ground pepper. Makes 6 servings.

CORN AND RICE SALAD

Planning a picnic? Toss together this Corn Side Dishes winner and top it with cheese just before serving it with grilled burgers—

- 1 16-ounce can whole kernel corn, drained
- 2 cups cooked rice
- ¼ cup chopped sweet red *or* green pepper
- ¼ cup sliced green onion
- ¼ cup chopped pitted ripe olives
- 3 tablespoons olive oil *or* cooking oil
- 3 tablespoons white wine vinegar
- 2 tablespoons soy sauce
- 2 tablespoons snipped parsley *or* 1 tablespoon dried parsley flakes
- ½ teaspoon Dijon-style mustard
- ¼ teaspoon garlic powder
- 8 cherry tomatoes, sliced (1½ cups)
- 1 tablespoon grated Parmesan cheese

In a medium bowl combine corn, rice, red or green pepper, onion, and olives.

In a screw-top jar combine oil, vinegar, soy sauce, parsley, mustard, and garlic powder. Cover and shake to mix. Pour over corn mixture. Cover and chill several hours or overnight.*

To serve, stir in tomatoes. Top with Parmesan cheese. Makes 8 servings.

Note: If using olive oil in dressing, let salad stand at room temperature for 20 minutes before serving.

CHICKEN CANNELLONI

We suggest doubling this Low-Calorie Poultry Dish. Serve half now and freeze the rest for later—

- ¾ cup thinly sliced celery
- ½ cup thinly sliced carrot
- ½ cup sliced fresh mushrooms
- 1 small onion, sliced
- 1 clove garlic, minced
- 1 tablespoon cooking oil
- 1 8-ounce can tomato sauce
- 1 7½-ounce can tomatoes, cut up
- 1 teaspoon Italian seasoning
- ¾ teaspoon sugar
- 3 medium chicken breasts (about 2¼ pounds total), skinned, boned, and halved lengthwise
- ½ cup ricotta cheese
- 3 tablespoons grated Parmesan cheese
- 1 tablespoon chopped green onion
- ½ teaspoon Italian seasoning
- Dash pepper
- 2 ounces mozzarella cheese, cut into thin strips

For sauce, in large saucepan cook celery, carrot, mushrooms, onion, and garlic in hot cooking oil till onion is tender but not brown. Stir in tomato sauce, *undrained* tomatoes, 1 teaspoon Italian seasoning, and sugar. Bring to boiling. Reduce heat. Cook, uncovered, over low heat for 20 minutes.

Meanwhile, pound chicken breasts between 2 pieces of plastic wrap to ¼-inch thickness. Stir together ricotta cheese, Parmesan cheese, green onion, ½ teaspoon Italian seasoning, and pepper. Place about *1½ tablespoons* of the cheese mixture on each chicken piece. Roll up jelly-roll style.

Arrange rolls, seam side down, in an 8x8x2-inch baking dish. Pour sauce over chicken rolls. Bake rolls, covered, in a 375° oven for 25 to 30 minutes or till tender. Place mozzarella cheese strips in a lattice design on rolls. Bake for 3 to 5 minutes more or till cheese is melted. Makes 6 servings.

STRAWBERRY ICE

This fruity ice took top honors in our Light Desserts category for August. It's easy to make with or without an ice-cream freezer—

- ¾ cup sugar
- 1 cup water
- 4 cups fresh *or* frozen strawberries *or* raspberries
- 2 cups pink lemonade
- 2 cups raspberry-cranberry juice drink

In a small saucepan combine sugar and water. Cook over medium heat till boiling. Boil gently for 10 minutes. Cool.

Meanwhile, in a blender container or food processor bowl add strawberries or raspberries. Cover and blend or process till smooth. Strain through a sieve to remove seeds. Stir together cooled sugar syrup, blended berries, lemonade, and cranberry drink. Pour into a 13x9x2-inch pan.

Freeze till almost firm. Break frozen mixture into chunks. Turn into a large mixer bowl and beat till nearly smooth. Return mixture to pan and freeze till firm. (Or, freeze in an ice-cream freezer following manufacturer's instructions.) Makes 8 to 10 cups.

CANTONESE BEEF STIR-FRY WITH HOISIN SAUCE

Cashews add the crunch to this Stir-Fried Beef Suppers winner—

1 pound boneless beef sirloin
¼ cup soy sauce
2 tablespoons cream sherry
2 tablespoons hoisin sauce
2 teaspoons sugar
¾ teaspoon chili paste
¾ teaspoon sesame oil
⅛ teaspoon whole anise
½ cup water
1 tablespoon cornstarch
3 tablespoons cooking oil
4 cups broccoli flowerets
3 medium carrots, thinly
　 bias-sliced
8 ounces fresh pea pods
½ cup sliced green onion
½ cup cashews
Hot cooked rice

Partially freeze beef. Thinly bias-slice across the grain into bite-size pieces. In a small bowl combine soy sauce, sherry, hoisin sauce, sugar, chili paste, sesame oil, and anise. Add beef. Stir to coat. Cover. Chill for 2 to 3 hours. Stir occasionally. Mix water and cornstarch.

Drain beef, reserving marinade. Preheat a wok or large skillet over high heat. Add *1 tablespoon* oil to wok. Add broccoli and carrots. Stir-fry for 4 minutes. Add pea pods and green onion. Stir-fry 2 minutes more. Remove vegetables from wok.

Add *1 tablespoon* oil. Stir-fry *half* of the beef at a time for 2 to 3 minutes or till done, adding more oil as necessary. Return all beef to wok and push it up sides of wok.

Stir cornstarch mixture. Add to wok with reserved marinade. Cook and stir till thickened and bubbly. Cook and stir for 2 minutes more. Return vegetables to wok. Add cashews. Cook and stir about 1 minute more or till mixture is heated through. Serve with hot cooked rice. Makes 6 servings.

TURKEY RED REUBEN

This take-along Brown-Bagger Sandwiches winner is the perfect way to start off lunches for a new school year. Be sure to tuck an ice pack into the lunch box to keep the sandwich cool—

1 tablespoon mayonnaise *or*
　 salad dressing
2 slices rye bread
2 ounces thinly sliced cooked
　 turkey breast
⅓ cup canned shredded sweet-
　 sour red cabbage, drained
1½ ounces sliced Monterey Jack
　 cheese

Spread mayonnaise or salad dressing on one side of both slices of bread. Place sliced turkey on the mayonnaise-side of *one* bread slice. Top with cabbage. Place sliced cheese on the cabbage, then top with remaining slice of bread, mayonnaise side down. Wrap and chill till serving time. Makes 1 serving.

BRATWURST-SPLIT PEA STEW

We give you both the conventional cooking method and crockery cooker method for this Whole-Meal Soups and Stews first-place finisher—

1 11½-ounce can condensed split
　 pea soup
1¼ cups water
1 10-ounce package frozen corn
1 10-ounce package frozen peas
　 and carrots
1½ cups chopped, peeled potatoes
　 (2 medium)
1 cup chopped tomato (1 medium)
½ cup chopped celery
¼ cup chopped green pepper
½ pound smoked sausage links,
　 thinly sliced
1½ teaspoons dried dillweed
1½ teaspoons onion powder
1½ teaspoons chili powder
Salt
Pepper

In a large kettle or Dutch oven combine pea soup, water, corn, peas and carrots, potatoes, tomato, celery, green pepper, bratwurst, dillweed, onion powder, and chili powder. Cover and cook over medium-low heat about 10 minutes or till vegetables are thawed and mixture boils. Simmer, covered, for 25 to 30 minutes more or till vegetables are tender. Season to taste with salt and pepper. Makes 6 to 8 servings.

Crockery cooker method: In a 3½- or 4-quart electric slow crockery cooker combine all ingredients. Stir to mix well. Cover and cook on LOW setting for 10 to 11 hours or till vegetables are tender. Season to taste with salt and pepper.

CARAMEL-PEAR PUDDING CAKE

This yummy cake was adapted from a pineapple-upside-down cake recipe. It's a favorite with our taste panelists, who rated this Pear Desserts category recipe a real winner—

- 1 cup all-purpose flour
- ⅔ cup sugar
- 1½ teaspoons baking powder
- ½ teaspoon ground cinnamon
- ¼ teaspoon salt
- Dash ground cloves
- ½ cup milk
- 4 medium pears, peeled and cut into ½-inch pieces (about 2 cups), *or* one 16-ounce can pears, drained and chopped
- ½ cup chopped pecans
- ¾ cup packed brown sugar
- ¾ cup boiling water
- ¼ cup butter *or* margarine
- Ice cream *or* whipped cream

In a large mixing bowl stir together flour, sugar, baking powder, cinnamon, salt, and cloves. Add milk, then beat till smooth. Stir in pears and pecans. Turn into an ungreased 2-quart casserole.

In another mixing bowl combine brown sugar, boiling water, and butter or margarine. Pour brown sugar mixture evenly over batter.

Bake in a 375° oven about 45 minutes or till done. Serve cake warm with ice cream or whipped cream. Serves 8.

RASPBERRY CHICKEN

You'll find this Special Chicken Entrées winner easy to make, yet sophisticated enough for a special occasion—

- 2 large chicken breasts, skinned, boned, and halved lengthwise (1½ pounds total)
- Salt
- 2 tablespoons butter *or* margarine
- ¼ cup finely chopped onion
- 3 tablespoons raspberry jelly
- 3 tablespoons wine vinegar
- ¼ cup whipping cream
- Steamed fresh vegetables (optional)

Sprinkle chicken with salt. In a 10-inch skillet melt butter or margarine. Add chicken pieces. Cook over medium heat for 5 minutes. Turn chicken and add onion around the edges of the skillet. Cook about 5 minutes more or till chicken is tender and golden, and onion is tender. Transfer chicken to a serving platter. Keep warm.

For sauce, add jelly and vinegar to skillet. Cook and stir, scraping up bits in the pan. Bring to full boil. Boil about 1 minute or till slightly reduced. Stir in whipping cream and return to boiling. Pour sauce over chicken. If desired, serve with steamed fresh vegetables. Makes 4 servings.

TURKEY CHILI WITH PASTA

The winner of our November category, Chili Recipes, is an unusual Cincinnati-style chili, served over hot vermicelli. Ground turkey and unsweetened cocoa powder make it special—

- 2 pounds ground turkey
- 1 large onion, chopped
- 3 cloves garlic, minced
- 1 tablespoon cooking oil (optional)
- 2 16-ounce cans tomatoes, cut up
- ¼ cup unsweetened cocoa powder
- 2 tablespoons chili powder
- 1 teaspoon salt
- 1 teaspoon crushed red pepper
- 1 teaspoon dried oregano, crushed
- 1 teaspoon ground cumin
- 1 16-ounce can kidney beans
- ½ cup water
- 4 cups hot cooked vermicelli (8 ounces)
- 1 cup shredded cheddar cheese (4 ounces)
- ½ cup oyster crackers

In a Dutch oven cook turkey, onion, and garlic till turkey is brown and onion is tender. (Add oil, if necessary.) Stir in *undrained* tomatoes, cocoa powder, chili powder, salt, red pepper, oregano, and cumin. Bring mixture to boiling. Reduce heat. Simmer, covered, for 1 hour, stirring occasionally.

Add *undrained* kidney beans and water to turkey mixture. Return to boiling. Reduce heat. Simmer, covered, for 30 minutes more.

Serve in bowls over hot cooked vermicelli. Sprinkle with cheddar cheese. Top with oyster crackers. Serves 8.

ITALIAN CHEESE TWISTS

These rolls boast not one, not two, but three kinds of herbs. The combination gives this Fast Bread category winner its Italian flavor—

- ¼ cup butter *or* margarine, softened
- ¼ teaspoon basil, crushed
- ¼ teaspoon oregano, crushed
- ¼ teaspoon marjoram, crushed
- ¼ teaspoon garlic powder
- 1 16-ounce loaf frozen bread dough, thawed
- ¾ cup shredded mozzarella cheese (3 ounces)
- 1 slightly beaten egg
- 1 tablespoon water
- 2 tablespoons sesame seed

In a small bowl combine butter or margarine, basil, oregano, marjoram, and garlic powder. Set aside.

On a lightly floured surface roll bread dough into a 12-inch square. Spread the butter-herb mixture evenly over dough. Sprinkle with mozzarella cheese. Fold dough into thirds.

With a sharp knife, cut the folded dough crosswise into twenty-four ½-inch strips. Twist each strip twice and pinch ends to seal. Place about 2 inches apart on a greased baking sheet. Cover and let rise in a warm place till almost double (about 30 minutes).

Beat together the egg and water. Brush over each twist. Sprinkle with sesame seed. Bake in a 375° oven for 10 to 12 minutes or till golden. Cool on a wire rack. Makes 24 twists.

LAYERED TACO BEAN DIP

Try this Holiday Dips and Spreads category winner. It's festive enough for a party and easy enough for every day. Your guests will love the blend of hot spiciness and cool creaminess—

- 2 10½-ounce cans bean dip
- 1 1¼-ounce package taco seasoning mix
- 6 green onions, finely chopped
- 1 cup mayonnaise *or* salad dressing
- 1 cup dairy sour cream
- 1 2¼-ounce can sliced olives, drained

Corn chips

In a large mixing bowl combine the bean dip and the taco seasoning mix. Spread the bean mixture on a 10-inch tray or in a 10-inch pie plate.

Sprinkle the finely chopped onions over the bean mixture. In a small bowl stir together the mayonnaise or salad dressing and sour cream. Spread mayonnaise mixture over onions.

Top with the sliced olives. Chill. Serve with corn chips. Makes 2½ cups.

COCOA-RUM PUDDING

A true top-notch recipe, this Fancy Chocolate Desserts winner features a warm bread pudding capped with a mouthwatering rum hard sauce—

- 2 cups French bread cubes
- 2 cups milk
- 1 cup sugar
- ½ cup unsweetened cocoa powder
- ½ teaspoon ground cinnamon
- 2 slightly beaten eggs
- ½ cup raisins
- 1 tablespoon butter *or* margarine, melted
- 2 teaspoons vanilla
- 1 recipe Sweet Rum Hard Sauce

Place bread cubes in a large bowl. Add milk and let stand about 10 minutes.

In a small bowl stir together sugar, cocoa powder, and cinnamon. In another bowl combine eggs, raisins, butter or margarine, and vanilla. Add sugar mixture. Mix well. Stir into bread mixture.

Pour bread mixture into an ungreased 10x6x2-inch baking dish. Bake in a 375° oven for 40 to 45 minutes or till a knife inserted near center comes out clean. Serve warm with Sweet Rum Hard Sauce. Makes 6 to 8 servings.

Sweet Rum Hard Sauce: In a small mixer bowl beat together 1 cup sifted *powdered sugar* and ½ cup *butter* or *margarine*. Add 1 tablespoon *rum* or ½ teaspoon *rum extract*. Beat till fluffy. Cover and chill. Makes ¾ cup.

Turkey Roasting Guide

I t's turkey time again! Roast your bird to succulent perfection using these cooking times and tips.

THAWING THE TURKEY

Refrigerator thawing: Leave the original wrap on the frozen bird; place the bird on a tray. Refrigerate 3 to 4 days, about 24 hours for each 5 pounds.

Cold-water thawing: Place the frozen turkey in its original wrap in a sink filled with cold water. Change water every 30 minutes. Allow 30 minutes thawing time for each pound of turkey.

BEFORE ROASTING

After thawing: Unwrap, free legs and tail, then remove giblets and neck piece from the cavities. Rinse bird; pat dry. *Don't stuff bird till you cook it.*

To stuff the turkey: Spoon some stuffing loosely into neck cavity; pull neck skin over stuffing and fasten the skin securely to back of bird with a skewer. Place turkey, neck side down, in large bowl. Lightly spoon stuffing into the body cavity; do not pack the stuffing or the mixture will not cook properly. If turkey has a band of skin across its tail, tuck drumsticks under the band. Otherwise, securely tie legs to tail. Twist wing tips under the back.

ROASTING THE TURKEY

Open roasting pan directions: Place bird, breast side up, on rack in shallow roasting pan. Brush with cooking oil. Insert meat thermometer in center of inside thigh muscle, making sure that the bulb does not touch a bone. Cover turkey loosely with a foil "cap" that barely touches bird. Press foil lightly at ends of drumsticks and neck. Roast in 325° oven. Baste occasionally with drippings or oil. Remove foil last 30 minutes for final browning.

Covered roasting pan directions: Place turkey, breast side up, on a rack in roasting pan; brush with cooking oil. Insert meat thermometer. Do not add water. Roast, covered with vent open, in 325° oven 20 to 25 minutes per pound. Uncover; drain, reserving pan juices. Raise the oven temperature to 475°. Continue roasting for 20 minutes more or till turkey is brown.

For a foil-wrapped turkey: Wrap the turkey, breast side up, in a piece of greased, heavy foil. Place in large shallow roasting pan. Insert meat thermometer in the thigh muscle through the foil. Place pan in a 450° oven. Roast turkey till done. Open the foil for the last 20 to 30 minutes of cooking time.

For frozen prestuffed turkey: Remove wrap from the frozen turkey. Do not thaw turkey. Place the frozen turkey on a rack in a shallow roasting pan; brush bird with cooking oil, butter, or margarine. Place in a 325° oven. Baste turkey occasionally with pan drippings or oil. Cover entire turkey loosely with foil to prevent overbrowning, if necessary. After 3 hours, insert meat thermometer in center of inside thigh muscle. Roast till done.

Testing doneness: For the above methods, roast the turkey till the meat thermometer registers 180° to 185° or till the thickest part of the drumstick is soft and the drumstick twists in the socket. Make sure the turkey juices are no longer pink when skin is pricked with a long-tined fork. Remove the turkey from oven; loosely cover with foil. Let the turkey stand for 15 minutes before slicing. If the bird is stuffed, the temperature of the stuffing should read 165° to be sufficiently cooked.

TURKEY ROASTING TIMES

Because birds differ in size, shape, and tenderness, use these roasting times as a general guide.

Type of Turkey	Ready-to-Cook Weight	Oven Temp.	Guide to Roasting Time
Stuffed Whole Turkey	6–8 lb.	325°	3–3½ hr.
	8–12 lb.	325°	3½–4½ hr.
	12–16 lb.	325°	4–5 hr.
	16–20 lb.	325°	4½–5½ hr.
	20–24 lb.	325°	5–6½ hr.
Foil-Wrapped Turkey (unstuffed)	8–10 lb.	450°	1¼–1¾ hr.
	10–12 lb.	450°	1¾–2¼ hr.
	12–16 lb.	450°	2¼–3 hr.
	16–20 lb.	450°	3–3½ hr.
	20–24 lb.	450°	3½–4½ hr.
Frozen Prestuffed Turkey	7–9 lb.	325°	5–5½ hr.
	9–11 lb.	325°	5½–6 hr.
	11–14 lb.	325°	6–6½ hr.
	14–16 lb.	325°	6½–7 hr.
Turkey Breast and Portions	2–4 lb.	325°	1½–2 hr.
	3–5 lb.	325°	1½–2½ hr.
	5–7 lb.	325°	2–2½ hr.

Servings: For turkey weighing 12 lb. or less, allow 1 lb. per serving; over 12 lb. allow ¾ lb. per serving. For boneless turkey breast, allow 4 oz. per serving.

Turkey breast and breast portions: Place thawed turkey, skin side up, on a rack in a shallow roasting pan. Insert a meat thermometer. Brush turkey breast or breast portion with oil, butter, or margarine. Roast, uncovered, in a 325° oven. Baste occasionally with oil. Cover turkey loosely with foil to prevent overbrowning. Roast till internal temperature registers 170° (do not overcook). Let turkey stand 10 minutes before slicing.

INDEX

Index

D-E

Index

Index

Microwave Wattage

All microwave recipes were tested in countertop microwave ovens that operate on 625 to 700 watts. Cooking times are approximate because ovens often vary by manufacturer.

Nutrition Analysis

Some nutrient information is given by gram weight per serving. The United States Recommended Daily Allowances (U.S. RDAs) for selected vitamins and minerals are given in the following recipes when the value exceeds 10 percent. The U.S. RDAs tell the amounts of certain nutrients necessary to meet the dietary needs of most healthy people.

To obtain the nutrition analysis of each recipe, the following guidelines were used:
● When ingredient options appear in a recipe, the analysis was calculated using the first ingredient choice.
● Optional ingredients were omitted in the analyses.
● The nutrition analyses for recipes calling for fresh ingredients were calculated using the measurements for raw fruits, vegetables, and meats.
● If a recipe gives optional serving sizes (such as "Makes 6 to 8 servings"), the nutrition analysis was calculated using the first choice.